CW01508634

POWER COUPLES
of the
TUDOR ERA

POWER COUPLES
of the
TUDOR
ERA

Influential Duos that Shaped the History of their Time

JO ROMERO

PEN & SWORD HISTORY

AN IMPRINT OF PEN & SWORD BOOKS LTD.
YORKSHIRE - PHILADELPHIA

First published in Great Britain in 2025 by
PEN AND SWORD HISTORY
An imprint of
Pen & Sword Books Ltd
Yorkshire – Philadelphia

Copyright © Jo Romero, 2025

ISBN 978 1 03610 284 5

The right of Jo Romero to be identified as Author of
this work has been asserted by her in accordance with the Copyright,
Designs and Patents Act 1988.

A CIP catalogue record for this book is available from the British Library.

All rights reserved. No part of this book may be reproduced, transmitted,
downloaded, decompiled or reverse engineered in any form or by any means,
electronic or mechanical including photocopying, recording or by any
information storage and retrieval system, without permission from the Publisher
in writing. No part of this book may be used or reproduced in any manner for the
purpose of training artificial intelligence technologies or systems.

Typeset in Times New Roman 11/14 by
SJmagic DESIGN SERVICES, India.
Printed and bound in the UK by CPI Group (UK) Ltd.

The Publisher's authorised representative in the EU for product safety is
Authorised Rep Compliance Ltd., Ground Floor, 71 Lower Baggot Street,
Dublin D02 P593, Ireland.
www.arccompliance.com

For a complete list of Pen & Sword titles please contact:
PEN & SWORD BOOKS LIMITED
George House, Units 12 & 13, Beevor Street, Off Pontefract Road,
Barnsley, South Yorkshire, S71 1HN, England
E-mail: enquiries@pen-and-sword.co.uk
Website: www.pen-and-sword.co.uk

or

PEN AND SWORD BOOKS
1950 Lawrence Rd, Havertown, PA 19083, USA
E-mail: uspen-and-sword@casematepublishers.com
Website: www.penandswordbooks.com

Contents

Acknowledgements

I AM GRATEFUL to the Pen and Sword team, who have always been incredibly patient and helpful. Special gratitude goes to my editor Kerrin Wilkinson, for pointing me in the direction of exploring couples' contributions to, and their impact on history. It was also fascinating to explore the dynamics of these well-known characters in the context of the partnerships they made. Thank you to staff at The British Library for their advice concerning The Devonshire Manuscript and also to those at Westminster Abbey for answering my questions on the monuments there. Similarly, staff at The Lord Leycester Hospital were also hugely supportive and helpful. Thanks must go to Professor James Clark of the University of Exeter for speaking with me about the Courtenays, and also the staff at West Horsley Place for their help and support. I must also thank Jav, Georgina, Sofia, Viv, Amy and Sue for their continued encouragement and patience as well as Malcolm, Rob, Dave and Mark. Any errors are my own.

Author's Note

I HAVE ENJOYED every second of researching and writing this book, which changed many of my beliefs about how the Tudor age was shaped and developed as we know it today. While reading and examining primary sources took up most of the time, I also visited, where possible, the homes, workplaces and physical legacies of some of these couples. If you would like to walk in their footsteps, many are open to the public.

The Tudor palace of Greenwich where the Courtenays presided over jousts and dancing no longer stands, as well as the palace of Whitehall, in which Edward Seymour conspired to establish his protectorate. But through contemporary drawings and paintings of these buildings we can still gain a sense of the surroundings our couples would have experienced. Hampton Court Palace, where the Seymours, Margaret Douglas and Katherine Willoughby attended the king's wedding to Kateryn Seymour, is open to the public and is well worth a visit for any Tudor history fan. Westminster Abbey is also a must, where the tombs and effigies of so many of our characters can still be seen, and where some were solemnly led to their coronations. Windsor Castle is the resting place of Henry VIII and Jane Seymour and is marked by a plaque on the floor of the quire of St George's Chapel. Charles Brandon was also buried here, the first husband of Katherine Willoughby. Katherine of Aragon's grave can still be seen at Peterborough Cathedral. The location of the burials of the remaining couples have been mentioned throughout the book, including St James' Church in Spilsby and Wimborne Minster in Dorset. Of course, many of them, as well as others they knew personally, rest in the church of St Peter ad Vincula within the Tower of London.

Hardwick Hall and Chatsworth House are also open to the public, although Chatsworth has been visibly altered since Elizabeth Hardwick and George Talbot walked its corridors. Somerset House still stands, although has again been developed since Anne and Edward Seymour's time. West Horsley Place, the home of Gertrude and Henry Courtenay and the site of their meetings with Elizabeth Barton, is open to visitors on certain days of the year. It is worth checking their website for the latest open days and events.

A number of towns and cities are also worth a visit. Southampton's medieval walls that once defended the lucrative port are in good condition and it is possible to gain a sense of the area in which Philip of Spain gallantly downed a cup of local ale in front of its residents. The Red Lion, the Duke of Wellington and St Michael's Church all stood in Philip's time, as did the imposing Bargate, the fortified entrance to the old town. Reading in Berkshire was the site of Philip and Mary's meeting with its mayor shortly after their wedding in the summer of 1554. The exact location of the meeting is thought to have been on the junction of Silver Street and London Street. Its ruined abbey is also open to the public all year round, and is a reminder of the religious fallout of Henry VIII and Katherine of Aragon's annulment.

In Plymouth, you can walk through the cobbled paths of the Barbican and follow in Katherine of Aragon's footsteps as she first landed here in England in 1501. At Plymouth Hoe stands a statue of Sir Francis Drake which commemorates the defeat of the Spanish Armada. Warwick is also worth a visit. St Mary's Church contains the tombs of Robert Dudley, who is buried with his wife Lettice Knollys. His brother Ambrose and his son, 'the Noble Impe', are also buried in the same chapel. A visit to The Lord Leycester Hospital on the High Street really underlines the impact of its foundation on the community, with many parts of the building unchanged from Robert Dudley and Elizabeth's day.

In my other work as an artist, I have also created sketches and paintings of many of the buildings known to our couples, as well as drawings of the couples themselves. It was inspiring to create a portrait of Gertrude and Henry Courtenay, particularly as contemporary depictions of the pair are rare, and in Gertrude's case, have not surfaced. These can be found on my social media Instagram account under the handle @sketcherjoey. Videos of my visits to some of these places can be found on my YouTube channel @lovebritishhistory and my Instagram account at @lovebritishhistorypics. I intend to further research these couples' lives, and any new findings can be found on my blog at www.lovebritishhistory.co.uk.

Thank you for reading this book; I hope you find exploring these couples' lives and walking in their footsteps as interesting and inspiring as I did.

Jo Romero,
June 2024

Historical Timeline

TO FULLY UNDERSTAND the contributions made by these Tudor power couples, it is important to gain a sense of their place in time as well as their personal links with one another. The era was short, lasting just over a century, but was packed with many important events. I have therefore provided the timeline below for reference and context.

1485

22 August	Battle of Bosworth Field in Leicestershire and death of Richard III in combat.
30 October	Henry VII crowned king.
16 December	Katherine of Aragon is born in Spain.

1486

8 January	The wedding of Henry VII and Elizabeth of York at Westminster Abbey.
September	The birth of Prince Arthur at Winchester, first child of the Tudors.

1487

25 November	The coronation of Elizabeth of York.

1489

November	The birth of Princess Margaret Tudor, future Queen of Scotland and mother of Margaret Douglas.

1491

28 June	The birth of Prince Henry, future King Henry VIII.

1492

8 June	The death of Elizabeth Woodville, mother of Elizabeth of York.
July	Princess Elizabeth Tudor is born.

1495

September   The death of Princess Elizabeth Tudor aged three.

1496

March   The birth of Mary Tudor, future Queen of France and
                     Duchess of Suffolk.

c. 1498

                     The birth of Henry Courtenay, future Marquis of Exeter.

1499

February   The birth of Prince Edmund Tudor.

1501

2 October   Katherine of Aragon arrives in England at Plymouth.
14 November   Prince Arthur marries Katherine of Aragon at St Paul's
                     Cathedral.

1502

2 April   The death of Prince Arthur at Ludlow.

1503

February   The birth of Princess Katherine Tudor
11 February   The death of Elizabeth of York.
April   Katherine's mother Isabella requests that she be sent back
                     to Spain.
8 August   The marriage of Margaret Tudor and James IV of Scotland.

1509

21 April   The death of Henry VII and the accession of Henry VIII.
June   The death of Margaret Beaufort, Henry VII's mother.
24 June   The coronation of Henry VIII and Katherine of Aragon.

1511

1 January   The birth of Prince Henry.

1513

June   Henry VIII leaves England, leaving Katherine as regent.
August   The Battle of the Spurs.
September   The Battle of Flodden and the death of James IV of
                     Scotland.

1515
8 October   The birth of Margaret Douglas.

1516
February   The birth of Mary Tudor, future Queen of England.

1519
                  The death of Maximilian I, and the accession of Charles V
                  as Holy Roman Emperor.

c. 1519
                  Marriage of Gertrude Blount and Henry Courtenay.

1519
March   Katherine Willoughby is born.

1520
June   Field of the Cloth of Gold celebrations in Calais.
                  Henry and Gertrude Courtenay are among those present.

c. 1522
                  Henry VIII meets Anne Boleyn.

1525
                  Henry Courtenay is made Marquis of Exeter.

1527
May   Gertrude Courtenay is seen dancing with Princess Mary.
21 May   The birth of Philip, later Philip of Spain and King of
                  England.
                  Hans Holbein the Younger creates his first portraits of
                  Henry's courtiers and designs the pattern for armour
                  garniture at Greenwich.

c. 1527
                  Elizabeth of Hardwick is born.
                  Henry writes love letters to Anne Boleyn.
                  Henry VIII declares his intention to have his marriage to
                  Katherine of Aragon annulled.

c. 1528

George Talbot, future Earl of Shrewsbury, is born.

1530

Margaret Douglas arrives at the court of her uncle, Henry VIII.

1532

24 June   The birth of Robert Dudley, future Earl of Leicester.

1533

Elizabeth Barton makes a series of negative claims about Henry's reign.

23 May   The marriage of Henry VIII and Katherine of Aragon is annulled.

1 June   Anne Boleyn is crowned queen.

June–July   Gertrude Courtenay meets with Elizabeth Barton.

7 September   Princess Elizabeth is born, future Queen of England.

1534

20 April   Elizabeth Barton is hanged at Tyburn.

November   Katherine Willoughby marries Charles Brandon, Duke of Suffolk.

1535

Devonshire Manuscript circulated among courtiers.

Margaret begins a relationship with Lord Thomas Howard.

November   Gertrude Courtenay secretly informs Imperial Ambassador Chapuys on the developments at court.

c. 1535

Anne Stanhope married Edward Seymour.

1536

7 January   Katherine of Aragon dies at Kimbolton Castle.

April   Gertrude Courtenay advises Chapuys on the coaching of Jane Seymour to replace Anne Boleyn.

19 May   Anne Boleyn is executed.

30 May   The marriage of Jane Seymour and Henry VIII.

July   Margaret Douglas and Thomas Howard are imprisoned.

1537

12 October	Prince Edward, future King of England, is born.
October	Margaret Douglas is released.
24 October	The death of Jane Seymour.
31 October	The death of Thomas Howard in the Tower of London.

1538

Henry and Gertrude Courtenay are involved in meetings later referred to as the Exeter Conspiracy.

9 December   Henry Courtenay is beheaded on Tower Hill.

1540

Gertrude Courtenay is released.

28 July   The marriage of Henry VIII and Katheryn Howard.

1541

November   Katheryn Howard is arrested on charges of adultery.

1542

8 December   Mary Stuart, future Mary Queen of Scots, is born.

1543

12 July   Henry VIII marries Kateryn Parr at Hampton Court Palace.

1544

6 July   Margaret Douglas marries Matthew Stewart, 13th Earl of Lennox.

1545

August   death of Charles Brandon Duke of Suffolk, making Katherine Willoughby a widow.

1546

16 July   Anne Askew is executed for heresy.

1547

28 January   The death of Henry VIII at the Palace of Whitehall. Edward VI is now king.

1 February   Edward Seymour is made Duke of Somerset and Protector of the Realm.

1548

September   The death of Kateryn Parr.

1549

        Edward Seymour surrenders his title of Protector.

1551

October   Anne Seymour is heard raising support. She and Edward are imprisoned.

1552

22 January   Edward Seymour is beheaded.

c. 1552

        Katherine Willoughby marries Richard Bertie.

1553

6 July   The death of Edward VI, aged fifteen.
10 July   Lady Jane Grey is proclaimed Queen of England.
19 July   Jane is deposed, and Mary I seizes the crown.
c. July   Anne Seymour is released.

1554

12 February   Jane Grey is executed.
June   Richard Bertie leaves England on the pretext of collecting debts due to his wife.
25 July   Mary I and Philip of Spain marry at Winchester Cathedral.

1555

1 January   Katherine Willoughby secretly leaves England to join her husband.
March   Burnings for heresy begin under Mary's reign.

1557

        England declares war on France; The Battle of St Quentin is fought.

1558

January   Calais is lost.
September   The death of Gertrude Courtenay.
17 November   The death of Mary I. Elizabeth I is proclaimed queen.

1559

                  Katherine Willoughby and Richard Bertie return to England.

1562

October   Elizabeth I urges the council to make Robert Dudley Protector in the event of her death.

1564

                  Robert Dudley is created Earl of Leicester.

April   The birth of William Shakespeare.

c. 1567

                  Elizabeth of Hardwick and George Talbot, Earl of Shrewsbury marry.

1568

May   Mary Queen of Scots flees to England after defeat at the Battle of Langside.

1569

February   Mary Queen of Scots arrives at the Shrewsbury property of Tutbury Castle.

1575

July   Elizabeth I is entertained at Kenilworth Castle by Robert Dudley. Richard Bertie is present.
Arbella Stuart is born.

1580

September   Katherine Willoughby dies.

1582

April   The death of Richard Bertie.

c. 1585

                  Elizabeth Hardwick and George Talbot finally separate.

1587

8 February   Mary Queen of Scots is executed at Fotheringhay Castle.
16 April   The death of Anne Seymour.

1588

May–June   Spanish Armada prepares to sail to England.

August   Elizabeth I gives a speech to troops at Tilbury with Robert
                Dudley, Earl of Leicester, present.

4 September   The death of Robert Dudley, Earl of Leicester.

1590

18 November   George Talbot, Earl of Shrewsbury dies.

1592

                Rumours of a plot to kidnap Arbella Stuart surface.

c. 1595

                William Shakespeare, aged around thirty-one, writes
                A Midsummer Night's Dream.

1603

24 March   The death of Elizabeth I at Richmond Palace. James VI of
                Scotland now also becomes James I of England, marking
                the end of the Tudor era and the beginning of the Stuart
                dynasty.

1608

13 February   Elizabeth Hardwick dies at Hardwick Hall.

Introduction

THE TUDOR ERA was born in the summer of 1485 on a blood-soaked battlefield near Leicester and died with the last breaths of Elizabeth I at Richmond in the spring of 1603. During those 118 years, Tudor communities from all levels of society experienced rapid and irreversible change in almost every aspect of their lives. They lived during the Renaissance, a resurgence of ancient Greek and Roman culture in Europe that reached its peak during the sixteenth century. This, combined with the wider use of the printing press, led to a heightened enthusiasm for learning, debate and the development of old and new skills. The history of the Tudor dynasty runs firmly alongside this cultural awakening. In Italy, the paint was barely dry on Sandro Botticelli's masterpiece *The Birth of Venus* as Henry VII sat enthroned in coronation robes at Westminster Abbey. Around the same time, Leonardo da Vinci was preparing designs for a flying machine and would soon start work on his mural of *The Last Supper* in Milan. Over the next century, scholars in England, inspired by innovations on the continent, grappled with new ideas relating to philosophy, politics, religion and science. Painting and sculpture also transformed from its previously flat, symbolic medieval form to one executed with astonishing realism and individuality.

The Tudor period is also known for its building, with the construction of royal palaces, including Hampton Court, Richmond and Nonsuch. Royal emphasis on architectural projects inspired the aristocracy to follow suit, and luxurious brick homes rose into England's skyline, twinkling for the first time with facades of expensive glass windows. Inside, hosts dazzled guests with displays of wealth and power, putting on banquets and theatrical entertainments. The era marked the beginning of the English theatre, with playwrights such as Christopher Marlowe, Thomas Kyd and William Shakespeare penning the first full-length works that made people laugh, cry, relate to difficult emotions and, sometimes controversially, provoke political discussion. The first permanent theatre in England was established during the reign of Elizabeth I and Tudor literature is still performed, read and studied around the world today. Shakespeare was inspired by tales from Italy, Greece, Scotland and Egypt and the settings of these plays towards the end of the sixteenth century reflect the era's new and greater familiarity with the wider world. Sailors and navigators voyaged to previously unknown lands and established new trading routes, their anchors splashing into waters off the coasts of America, Africa, Russia and the Caribbean. Accordingly, the period drove significant improvements in mapmaking, shipbuilding and the navy.

The period is often remembered as a 'Golden Age', and while there was undeniable progress made to the realm under Tudor rule, the era was also marked by violence, rebellion, uncertainty and reform. The period has uncomfortable associations with human trafficking, carried out by Tudor explorers and privateers. Subjects were tossed from one religion to another, as successive monarchs controlled the faith of the nation, demanding nothing but absolute compliance. England split from the authority of the Pope, returned, and then left again. At the end of the fifteenth century, relics and saintly images were treasured and loaned out to assist in childbirth, pain management and to inspire acts of devotion. By the 1550s, many were lost, burned or abandoned. Images depicting saints were defaced or painted over, while shrines and altars were dismantled and discarded. Abbeys and monasteries that had taken medieval craftsmen hundreds of years to build were suddenly plundered for valuables and building materials, and their foundations left to ruin. All Tudor subjects found themselves affected by these changes and it is not surprising that some expressed frustration through revolts and episodes of social unrest.

Anyone rising up and resisting the authority of the ruling Tudor king or queen risked harsh punishment. Refusal to follow the state religion ('heresy') could result in a public hanging or execution by burning in the offender's town or city. Ringleaders of rebellion were hanged, usually from a prominent place to serve as a warning to others. Subjects spending their days closer to power ran other risks. It was easy to upset a Tudor monarch with a tactless comment, boast of royal lineage, or simply by falling in love. Six queens were either abandoned or murdered at the hands of Tudor monarchs, while many of the era's courtiers, advisors, servants and secretaries met their end on Tower Hill, muttering prayers as an executioner's blade lunged above them.[1] Unquestionably, the Tudors left England and the wider world a vastly different place than they found it.

Not all of these changes can be attributed simply to world events and social factors. It took leaders, patrons and politicians to integrate new concepts and ideas into the lives of Tudor people. Government policy was shaped and enforced by those close to the crown, who conducted ambitious political careers within the dangerous, fickle royal court. The story of the Tudor age is that of its people; the decisions they made, the power they wielded and the changes they introduced. This influence is commonly attributed to individuals, such as Elizabeth I's patronage of the theatre or George Talbot's watch over Mary, Queen of Scots. However, a closer look at the evidence reveals that these well-known figures were in fact creating lasting change from within partnerships, and in many cases the lesser-known partner of the pair has not been fully acknowledged for their contribution. This book addresses that imbalance, and evaluates how far many famous events of the age were in fact the work of couples, rather than individuals, thus highlighting the impact of the less-often recognized member of the duo.

In modern times, we use the term 'power couple' to describe a relationship where partners demonstrate skill in their own right, but achieve new and elevated success when they work together. They can be seen today in business, media, music, film and fashion. But the term can also relate to the Tudor period, where just as in the present day, couples conducted business and actively worked together to protect their combined wealth. Others used their connections with one another to elevate their joint position at court or to deflect harsh criticisms and punishment.

Royal power couples experienced other challenges. Often thrown together for political gain rather than through mutual love or compatibility, they sometimes had to learn to get along as well as contend with imbalances of dynastic or constitutional power. The accessions, and subsequent marriages, of both Henry VII and his granddaughter Mary I saw parliament grapple over the real and perceived differences in their status and that of their spouse.

Many of these high-profile Tudor partners were also influencers, supporting and encouraging new fashions and promoting developments in music, art and the theatre. These couples were early supporters of the theatrical arts and their partnerships inspired and pushed forward this new form of creative expression, influenced too by exotic styles and customs seen in journeys to foreign lands. They also heavily patronized the work of artists and writers and new genres of literary work were published during the era which had an effect on the knowledge and education of the nation. The religious reform which so solidly underlines the period was also triggered, developed and publicized by couples.

An effort has been made to depict these couples as closely as possible to how they would have been seen by their contemporaries. We will visit their homes and the chambers and palaces in which they conducted business. Many of these buildings no longer survive, although some still stand, allowing us to gain a glimpse of what family life must have been like for them. We will also, where possible, examine decorations, clothing and other objects they would have recognized. In many cases, influential ties between these power couples have also been established, and we will discover some of the negotiations they embarked on, important events that they presided over and, of course, their relationships with one another.

All five Tudor courts crackled with suspicion and paranoia under the steady gaze of rival courtiers or a short-tempered sovereign. For a power couple to survive, it was necessary to deploy resilience, tenacity and tact. We will meet couples that faced prolonged criticism from their enemies and embarked on a joint struggle to claim back power. Others endured challenging conditions in exile, forced to flee the realm for their safety and that of their family. Another couple demonstrated a stubborn commitment to one another despite royal displeasure, leaving behind a social and cultural legacy. For one couple, their duties as servants of the state led to doubt, suspicion and serious allegations of misconduct. United by strong bonds, political alliances or romance, our nine Tudor power couples plotted their way out of trouble, resisted verbal and physical attack and attempted to safeguard their future. In doing so, they triggered lasting change and revolution, shaping the course of Tudor history and affecting the lives of millions.

It has been fascinating to explore not only the contributions made by these couples to their time, but also to consider, where possible, the inner dynamics of their relationships. There were some surprises. For example, Elizabeth of York is not often remembered for her contribution as queen, but a closer look at the sources reveals she was not simply a politically-absent figurehead alongside her husband Henry VII. She fulfilled an important public role making state decisions and worked as a diplomat. Similarly, Robert Dudley was not merely Elizabeth I's doting, empty 'favourite', but a strong partner with whom the queen developed the era's learning, culture and administration. Historians too, have generally neglected Philip II's contribution to English history, dismissing his marriage to Mary as a failure characterized by heartbreak, absence and neglect. A new look at the evidence confirms the couple worked together on policy, shared common goals and created long-term change.

Henry VIII famously married six times and choosing the woman to discuss as his 'power wife' took careful consideration. Anne Boleyn's relationship with the king changed the political, religious and social landscape of England forever. But the turbulence in their marriage is well-documented, and a wealth of valuable information has been written on the couple. Jane Seymour was queen for just over a year before her tragic and sudden death in 1537, and Henry was once heard warning her to stay out of state affairs. Anna of Cleves, Henry's fourth wife, was an intelligent and capable queen, but the couple separated just months after their ceremony at Greenwich in 1540. Another brief marriage followed, to the young and captivating Katheryn Howard, who was executed in 1542. Henry's sixth wife, Kateryn Parr, was a strong contender. She was a writer and dedicated reformer of religion, as well as a dignified and dutiful queen. I decided to focus however on a queen that is often overlooked as the older bride Henry settled on for political reasons. As we will see, Katherine of Aragon, Henry's first wife, actively worked with her husband on diplomatic, social, military and religious affairs and fully deserved a reconsideration of her achievements.

While researching, a conscious effort was made to discover power couples from different backgrounds and sexualities. Unfortunately, actions taken by some of the Tudor monarchs affected the way homosexuality was viewed in sixteenth-century society, and altered its historical trace. Sodomy was made illegal in 1533 with The Buggery Act, punishable by loss of lands, goods, the home, occupation and even death.[2] With so much at stake, homosexual couples living in the Tudor age were understandably reluctant to promote their involvement in a same-sex relationship, let alone openly work together for public change. There are examples of homosexual activity during the era, such as the cases of Sir Walter Hungerford in 1540 and Nicholas Uvedale the following year.[3] Modern writers have sometimes interpreted the era's poetic declarations of friendship or affection between people of the same sex as evidence of a homosexual relationship, although in many cases it is difficult, so many centuries later, to prove this beyond doubt. Same-sex relationships between women for the period are less often recorded, but were explored in contemporary poetry by the Scottish writer Marie Maitland and in Italy by Laudomia Forteguerri.

Tudor England also had a level of cultural diversity, and we will meet a number of residents living in the realm that were born overseas. Miranda Kaufmann, in the book *Black Tudors – The Untold Story*, explored Tudors of African descent living in England during the sixteenth century. In many cases, evidence exists of their marriages and relationships with others. However, despite my eagerness to explore their power and impact on society as couples, there was just not enough evidence found to provide a detailed discussion in line with the aims of this book. Historical research into both the sexuality and cultural diversity of the Tudor era is an exciting and growing topic of study, and it is hoped that more of these power couples will emerge from sources in the future. Finally, the couples discussed here are not the only ones of their era that impacted change. Their trace exists in sources and chronicles of the period, and it is hoped that researchers will be inspired to review the Tudor age further in the context of couples' contributions, and their impact on its story.

Chapter 1

Henry VII and Elizabeth of York

IN THE COLLECTION of the Rijksmuseum in Amsterdam there is a black-and-white drawing of a Tudor rose, the arms of England at its centre held up by a lion and dragon. At the top is placed a crown, studded with jewels. Small discs are sprinkled among the petals and leaves, each bearing the name and arms of a subject of the prestigious Order of the Garter honoured under Tudor rule. The solemn faces of their five benefactors, the various Tudor monarchs, stare out at us. The drawing by Flemish engraver Jodocus Hondius, titled *The Union of the Roses of the Families of Lancaster and York*, is dated 1589, which places the creation of the document to the reign of Elizabeth I. But it is not her portrait that appears at the top of the page. Surrounded by a garland of roses, on either side of the crown and facing one another, are the carefully drawn figures of Henry VII and Elizabeth of York.

The relationship between Henry Tudor, Earl of Richmond, and Elizabeth of York set in motion the forging of a dynasty that ruled England for over a century. They were also credited with ending more than three decades of internal conflict, later known as the Wars of the Roses. Thousands of men met their deaths on muddy battlefields throughout the country as aristocrats representing the houses of York and Lancaster wrestled for control of the throne.

The origin of the war can be traced to 1399, when the Lancastrian Henry IV usurped the throne of the Plantagenet Richard II and disrupted the established line of succession. Twenty years later, Henry's grandson, Henry VI, inherited the crown as a nine-month-old baby, unable to govern and naturally reliant on powerful nobles to rule in his name. Dissention broke out, and even as an adult his rule was defined by weakness, rebellion and war. Tens of thousands of men were killed in pitched battles or politically-driven local disputes that played out in towns and villages across the country.

By August of 1485 England and its weary subjects craved peace and consistency. The Lancastrian Henry Tudor, in exile in Brittany, promised that when he defeated Richard III and became king, he would marry the daughter of the Yorkist Edward IV, the nineteen-year-old Elizabeth of York. Uniting the two warring families with marriage and a crown would, a nation hoped, put an end to the conflict.

Early Tudor writers could barely contain their excitement about the royal wedding, expressing hope for a stable future and a new age of peace. *The Most Pleasant Song of Lady Bessy,* believed to have been written by Humphrey Brereton shortly after Henry's accession, spoke of the joining of 'the two bloods of great renown' while the early Tudor historian Polydore Vergil stated that the 'two most pernicious factions should be at once, by conjoining of both the houses, utterly taken away'.[1] Even the Papal Bull confirming the couple's marriage in January 1486 spoke of 'the long and grievous variance, contentions and debates that hath been in this Realm of England between the house of the Duchy of Lancaster on the one party, and the house of the Duchy of York on that other party, willing all such divisions following to be put apart … confirm and establish the matrimony and conjunction made between our sovereign lord King Henry the Seventh … and the noble Princess Elizabeth'.[2]

One hundred years later all those who had established Tudor rule were dead, but the marriage was still being heavily romanticized into legend. Towards the end of the sixteenth century, while penning the final scene of his play *Richard III*, William Shakespeare wrote that Henry Tudor's defeat of Richard III at Bosworth paved the way to 'unite the white rose and the red', calling Henry and Elizabeth 'the true succeeders of each royal house'. He talked of their heirs, who would 'enrich the time to come with smooth-faced peace, with smiling plenty and fair prosperous days'.[3] In around 1580, Raphael Holinshed captured the hope of the age, writing that 'peace was thought to descend out of heaven into England, considering that the lines of Lancaster and York were now brought into one knot'.[4]

The legendary red and white roses of Shakespeare's 'smooth faced peace' were also symbolically hauled out for Elizabeth I's coronation pageant in 1559. Citizens in Gracechurch Street in London prepared a stage adorned with the likenesses of Henry VII and Elizabeth of York, and the new queen's parents Henry VIII and Anne Boleyn. A child stepped forward to explain the pageant's meaning to the queen. Straining to hear above music and 'the press of people', Elizabeth noticed the red and white roses, and 'The Uniting of the Two Houses of York and Lancaster' written on a wreath. The display was centred around her name, Elizabeth. Elizabeth of York was 'the first occasion of concord; so she, another Elizabeth, might maintain the same among her subjects', the citizens explained. Elizabeth thanked the people of Gracechurch Street, promising that 'she would do her whole endeavour for the continual preservation of concord'.[5]

Henry and Elizabeth married within the ancient walls of Westminster Abbey on 18 January 1486. After a day of celebration and feasting, the newlyweds were led in procession to the royal bed. An intricately carved wooden four-poster bed frame believed to have once belonged to the royal couple was discovered in 2010 at a hotel in Cheshire.[6] As she slipped under its heavy ermine-lined blankets, Elizabeth would have looked up at the figures in the woodwork and the shadows they cast in the candlelight. Craftsmen had carefully added fertility symbols including acorns, fruits and flowers into the headboard, along with a representation of Adam and Eve.

For five months Henry VII had overseen parliament and restored order to the realm. But it was all worthless without heirs to continue the Tudor dynasty and safeguard the kingdom after his death. He had learned from the examples of previous kings, such as Henry V, who had been unable to pass his throne to an adult successor. It was this failure that had elevated the power of the nobility, created divisions between them and led to the outbreak of the Wars of the Roses.

By today's standards, the twenty-eight-year-old Henry VII was young. But time was running out in an age where life expectancy was far lower, especially for kings. Henry V died at thirty-five years of age on campaign in France, while Richard III was killed in battle at the age of thirty-two. Edward IV, Elizabeth's father, died at forty, his rich diet and luxurious living said to have been a factor. The fragile Henry VI lived until the age of forty-nine, when he was rumoured to have been murdered by the incoming Yorkist government.

Luckily though, the royal couple wouldn't have to wait long. Just eight months later, in September 1486, Elizabeth gave birth to their first child, a boy. More children quickly followed; a daughter, Margaret, in 1489; and a son named Henry in 1491. Another daughter, Elizabeth, was born in 1492, but died just three years later. Mary was born in 1496 and another son, Edmund, in 1499. Edmund sadly did not survive infancy. Her final pregnancy in 1503 resulted in a daughter named Katherine, but the child died soon after her birth.

In examining these dates, it is possible to see a sense of urgency felt by the couple in strengthening this new Tudor regime. They conceived quickly; their first child born just eight months after their wedding night. In an age when there was no concept of bacterial or viral infections, mortality rates were high among newborns, and Henry and Elizabeth experienced the premature deaths of all but three of their children. Some births appear to have been motivated by the death of a brother or sister: Mary was born in September 1496, exactly twelve months after the young Elizabeth Tudor died; while Katherine was born in February 1503, ten months after the loss of their eldest son. With the average length of a pregnancy at around nine months, these dates suggest the couple conceived soon after the loss of a child, in an effort to maintain a sufficient number of heirs to help secure the future of the dynasty.

A larger family increased the odds of a surviving heir, but gave no guarantees. Elizabeth's parents had borne ten children, and yet not one of them was crowned on the death of Edward IV. Henry knew that the uneasy political climate of the wars could easily return; during his reign he saw off at least three pretenders who claimed the throne for the House of York. It was vital that to preserve peace in the realm, the royal nursery was kept busy with a brood of young, legitimate Tudor royals. The first of these slept, safely swaddled in blankets in his ornately-carved wooden cot in the late September of 1486. His tiny heart beat rhythmically with the blood of both the white rose and the red, ensuring that he would enjoy an unchallenged succession. Bonfires crackled and church bells rang in celebration for the baby that heralded a new start: his name was Arthur.

The choice of the boy's name was no accident, and neither was the location of his birth. Even by 1486 Winchester had historic ties to the ancient legend of King Arthur. Sir Thomas Malory, in *Morte d'Arthur*, a telling of the legendary tale completed in around 1470, identified 'the City of Camelot, that is in English Winchester'.[7] It was the setting for Arthur's meetings with knights and the location of jousts and celebrations. The printer William Caxton, in his introduction to the work, speaks of the Arthurian 'noble acts, feats of arms of chivalry, prowess, hardiness, humanity, love, courtesy, and very gentleness, with many wonderful histories and adventures'. He also noted the 'many remembrances' that survived Arthur's reign, including his seal in red wax at St Edward's Shrine in Westminster, Gawain's skull at Dover Castle and 'at Winchester the Round Table'.[8]

Winchester Cathedral, where the prince was baptized, was built at the end of the eleventh century, although it had a history going back to the Anglo-Saxon period. The resting place of ancient leaders and kings including Egbert, Aethelwulf and Canute, it was a large and impressive building. The site, a religious and political centre during the medieval era, had already experienced a series of renovations since the first stone was laid in 1079. The city surrounding the structure was a huddle of timber-framed homes and shops with smaller medieval churches and a castle, all built inside a defensive stone wall accessed by four strongly-fortified gateways. It was here that Alfred, King of Wessex, in the ninth century, held court and made Winchester the centre of his government.

Where better then, to welcome the first-born prince of the Tudor age into the world than the ancient capital of England and ancestral home of his legendary namesake, where Arthur's Round Table hung inside the city's Great Hall? The boy's name and chosen site of his birth reminded citizens of a time before the conflict that had killed so many of their sons, fathers and husbands. It signalled a new start and evoked a romantic era of fairness, bravery and chivalry. More than that, it implied the transfer of unchallenged, ancient legitimacy.

The names of ancient kings had been used before in a bid to boost a monarch's perceived right to rule. Edward IV commissioned one genealogy to celebrate his coronation in 1461. The manuscript, embellished in vibrant red, blue and gold, features Adam and Eve and claims Edward's descent from royal Britons such as Arthur, Alfred and the Welsh Llywelyn the Great. The impressive bloodline Edward promoted here also therefore applied to his daughter Elizabeth of York.[9] As for Henry, he claimed royal blood from another ancient Welsh hero. Vergil wrote that Henry's grandfather Owen Tudor was a 'gentleman of Wales, adorned with wonderful gifts of body and mind'. He also, writes Vergil, 'derived his pedigree from Cadwalladr, the last king of the Britons'.[10]

Emblems that fluttered on banners alongside Henry as he marched to Bosworth were also significant. Among them was the 'red dragon of Cadwalladr' and the figure of St George.[11] The dragon and the heroic knight were symbols of ancient English and Welsh history and legend, which again evoked Arthur. In one scene in Geoffrey of Monmouth's twelfth-century work, Arthur wears a 'helm of gold graven with the semblance of a dragon' and describes a dream involving a fight between a bear and a dragon. Arthur, writes Monmouth, realized the dragon represented him, and the bear his enemy.[12] Additionally, the dragon was also suggestive of medieval depictions of the sword-wielding, justice-administering Archangel St Michael.

The dragon was a potent and instantly recognisable symbol to the medieval public and appeared again towards the end of Henry's reign in a painting that it is believed he personally ordered to be made. Painted after the death of Elizabeth of York, *The Family of St George and the Dragon* in the Royal Collection Trust shows Henry and his queen, along with all seven of their children, an angel hovering above them. Behind, the figure of St George on horseback prepares to strike a blow at the dragon, who is already impaled with the red-and-white flag of the patron saint.

The name of the child safely tucked away in Winchester was therefore an appropriate choice for the start of a new age of protection, chivalry, bravery and legitimacy. According to the sixteenth-century historian Edward Hall, it worked. He wrote that at the young prince's name, 'Englishmen no more rejoiced [than] outward nations and foreign princes trembled and quaked, so much was that name to all nations terrible and formidable'.[13]

The 1486 Papal Bull confirming the marriage of Henry and Elizabeth declared the king's 'nighest and undoubted title of succession'. All the genealogical posturing and myth-making concealed the fact that Henry's own claim to the throne, in contrast to that of Elizabeth's, was rather flimsy. His mother, Margaret Beaufort, was a descendant of Edward III, as was Elizabeth. However, the Beaufort line had been legally barred from claiming the throne by Henry IV in the early fifteenth century. Henry remained adamant that his own entitlement to the crown came not only by right of conquest, but from 'lawful title of inheritance', as he asserted to parliament in November 1485.[14]

Elizabeth and her siblings had been declared illegitimate on the accession of her uncle, Richard III. Henry repealed this act, reinstating her legitimacy by law. But even though both partners now had the legal right to rule, there was no escaping the fact that Elizabeth's royal status topped Henry's. He addressed this imbalance in two ways: by elevating his own claim to the crown and subtly diminishing Elizabeth's. Lisa Hilton, in *Queens Consort: England's Medieval Queens*, points out that the Papal Declaration of 1486 states that it was Henry's blood, not Elizabeth's, that created legal heirs to the throne. Hilton also refers to the unusual delay in the queen's coronation, which took place over a year after Arthur's birth.[15] This reluctance to acknowledge Elizabeth's royal status from the outset has sometimes been interpreted by readers as arrogance or vanity on Henry's part. But this was much more than an ego-boosting exercise. Ruling purely on the basis of a wife's stronger bloodline was precarious, and would have drawn unwanted attention to Henry's weaker dynastic position. This was particularly dangerous at a time when a husband held the legal power in a common marriage, let alone as a king. In resolutely asserting his own claim to the throne before Elizabeth's, Henry created the basis for a strong legal and royal partnership where, on paper at least, both partners had a hereditary right to their crowns boosted by right of conquest and backed by God. The legal power in the union was his, according to Tudor law, and any imagined conspiracy to seize Elizabeth and rule through her would therefore be rendered ineffective.

Elizabeth may have been sidelined in the early years of Henry's reign, but it would not be long before she was placed centre stage. At her coronation on 25 November 1487, Londoners lining the streets rushed forward to cut off pieces of cloth she had walked on as souvenirs.[16] In 1488 she was present at the St George's Day festival of the Order of the Garter, arriving with her mother-in-law Margaret Beaufort. The reins of her ladies' horses were also conspicuously decorated with white roses, a symbol of her Yorkist heritage. And in May 1500, Elizabeth attended a meeting in Calais between her husband and Archduke Philip of Austria.[17] Holinshed wrote that they enjoyed 'most loving entertainments, banquetings, mirth and pastime', while Rodrigo de Puebla, the Spanish Ambassador, reported that there was a 'long conversation, in which the Queen afterwards joined'.[18] Elizabeth is not always acknowledged for the diplomatic skills she displayed during the reign, but she was soon to prove to Henry and to England that she was far more than a royal trophy with an attractive bloodline.

Elizabeth's role in government is not often discussed, her character summed up as a quiet, submissive woman responsible only for birthing the babies of early Tudor rule. There is strong evidence to the contrary that Elizabeth was a present and active queen who worked for the benefit of the realm alongside her husband. As we will see, she was just as dedicated to embedding the roots of the Tudor dynasty and ensuring its future success as Henry was.

But how did the couple meet? Credit for the idea of their marriage is given to their mothers, Elizabeth Woodville and Margaret Beaufort, who secretly hashed out a plan while Richard III reigned, to see their children married and on the throne. According to Vergil, the two women employed a Welsh physician to negotiate secretly between them, ensuring Henry 'might be sworn to take in marriage Elizabeth ... after he shall have gotten the realm'.[19] Another source though, the fifteenth-century *The Most Pleasant Song of Lady Bessy*, places far more emphasis on the actions of Elizabeth of York. In the ballad, Elizabeth convinces Lord Stanley to support her ambitions to become queen and gather men to help 'bring her love over the sea'. This is done despite the threat of treason hanging over them if the plan should fail, and Elizabeth regularly reminds Stanley of his previous loyalty to her father. She receives and sends communication between the group, their purpose being 'the queen of England for to make thee'. Elizabeth sends Henry a love letter and a gold ring, along with glowing recommendations about her communicated by a servant.[20]

The ballad is thought to have been written by Humphrey Brereton, a Cheshire man who worked for Stanley and had inside knowledge of the period before Bosworth. There is always some caution when relying on a ballad as a historical source and there are some inconsistencies. However, it does correctly name many conspirators and supporters of Henry Tudor, as well as circumstances of the later battle. It is also chillingly accurate on the nature of Richard III's death, its description of injuries sustained by the king consistent with archaeological analysis carried out on Richard's skeleton in 2013 by the University of Leicester.[21]

Is it possible that Elizabeth herself campaigned in the 1480s, as the ballad describes, to become Henry's future wife? There had been rumours (again acknowledged by the ballad's author) that Elizabeth was to marry her uncle, Richard III, although these were publicly denied at the time. Elizabeth certainly had motivation to push for a marriage to Henry, which promised not only a crown, but a new start for England. It is unclear whether Richard ever really seriously considered marrying his niece. In 1485 there were still questions over the disappearance of her brothers, the Princes in the Tower, and also the untimely and recent death of his wife, Anne Neville, in her late twenties. She also had the support of a number of allies, including men who had been loyal to her father and now backed Tudor. The match also benefitted her remaining Woodville relatives, whose influence within the royal circle had waned shortly after Edward's death. It is entirely plausible then, that the young Elizabeth actively fought for her own position as future queen at the same time as Margaret Beaufort's physician was secretly plotting with Elizabeth Woodville.

Elizabeth's mother would have been an invaluable source of support to her daughter at this time. It was also in her interest to encourage her to pursue the marriage. Woodville was an intelligent, ambitious and politically manoeuvrable consort to Edward IV. As queen, she engineered the social advancement of her family members and acted decisively when in danger to protect herself and her children. She did not see the coronation of any of her children on Edward's death, and now had the opportunity to place her daughter as consort to the future King of England. Equally, Edward IV was an able military commander, charming and politically ruthless enough to seize the throne from the Lancastrian Henry VI in 1461. There is no reason to conclude that Elizabeth of York was any less ambitious than her mother, or indeed, her father.

We do have written evidence that Elizabeth of York was known, at times, to express a stronger side. In one letter written while queen, she admonished the Earl of Oxford over a dispute with one Simon Bryant. Elizabeth defends Bryant, reminding the earl that the quarrel was 'not only to his right great hurt and hindrance, but also our marvel; wherefore we desire and pray you right effectuously' to restore Bryant's 'rightful interest and title in the said Manor'. Elizabeth's tone is diplomatic, but assertive, setting out Bryant's legal rights and her opinion that Oxford should restore Bryant to his 'lawful and peaceable possession'.[22] This letter supports the self-confident character of Elizabeth that is hinted at in the ballad far more than the uninvolved, passive queen of historical legend.

So why do accounts contradict one another over Elizabeth's role in the lead up to Bosworth? There is a chance that Brereton later romanticized the ballad to 'fit' well-known events for an optimistic and expectant Tudor audience. He might have overstated Elizabeth's role to give Yorkist supporters a slice of the Tudor legend or, as Stanley's servant, inflated his own and Stanley's involvement in the affair, knitting their destinies with the new queen's. However, this does not explain the author's choice to depict Elizabeth as decisive and conspiratorial, or Stanley's plotting with Elizabeth and not with Henry. As for Vergil, it's possible that he suppressed Elizabeth's and elevated Henry and Margaret's involvement to flatter the lady that was now his patron's mother. On considering the evidence from the ballad and traces left of Elizabeth's personality in sources, it seems likely that Elizabeth did actively promote herself as future queen. The lack of written evidence for her actions, other than the ballad, is to be expected. With Richard still reigning all those involved risked serious charges of treason, and he had shown himself to be a ruthless and effective politician. Letters could easily have been destroyed or conversations carried out privately by spoken word.

Henry was well aware that he needed Elizabeth to secure his new dynasty. As a daughter of the House of York, she was the best placed to help tie the 'knot' that Holinshed later referred to as ending the Wars of the Roses. On learning of her death in February 1503, the Venetian ambassador Alvise Mocenigo remembered her as 'a very handsome woman and of great ability'.[23] She interceded on behalf of wronged subjects, presided at Henry's side at state events and remained gracious and humble to her subjects. Her biggest influence, however, can be found during preparations for the marriage of Arthur Tudor and the Spanish princess, Katherine of Aragon.

Henry and Elizabeth spent the last decade of their reign holding meetings with ambassadors, dictating correspondence and talking money. The result was a marriage that would seal the future of the Tudors; the union of Prince Arthur and the Infanta Katherine, daughter of Ferdinand of Aragon and Isabella of Castile. On 3 December 1497, Elizabeth wrote to Isabella from the Palace of Westminster, expressing the royal couple's 'wish and desire from our heart that we may often and speedily hear of the health and safety of your serenity, and of the health and safety of the aforesaid most illustrious Lady Katherine, whom we think of and esteem as our own daughter'. Calling Katherine our 'common daughter', she urges Isabella to let them know 'if there be anything in our power which would be grateful or pleasant to your majesty … we offer all that we have to you, and wish to have all in common with you'. Elizabeth signs off, adding that 'we should have written you the news of our state, and of that of this kingdom, but the most serene lord the king, our husband, will have written at length of these things to your majesties'.[24]

Here, Elizabeth recorded the nature of the working relationship she had with her husband. His role was in the business of governing, signing off accounts books and communicating essential information about the realm. John Stow wrote that Henry was a 'prince of marvellous wisdom, policy, justice, temperance and gravity'.[25] The Spanish ambassador De Puebla reported in 1498 Henry's practical and blunt aims for the marriage, 'to be entirely secured against troubles in England, so that he may begin war with France'.[26] Elizabeth, in contrast, is respectful, welcoming and familiar. Using a softer tone, she eases the Spanish monarchs towards Henry's policy and provides reassurance for one of Isabella's requests: that once in England, 'the princess should be treated by him and by the Queen as their true daughter'.[27] In the sources and letters scribbled by ambassadors, Elizabeth's active and important role alongside her husband is clear. This dynamic that Elizabeth brought to royal diplomacy has been acknowledged by Thomas Penn who, in *Winter King, The Dawn of Tudor England,* stated that Elizabeth was 'a charismatic counterpart to her increasingly suspicious, controlling husband'.[28] This assessment is fully supported by surviving evidence, and none more so than in the couple's dealings with Spain.

Both Elizabeth and Henry worked hard, in their respective ways, to make the alliance a success. In 1498 the couple attended a four-hour meeting with De Puebla. Afterwards, he reported that they had been eager to receive correspondence from Ferdinand and Isabella, when 'the King had a dispute with the Queen because he wanted to have one of the said letters to have continually about him, but the Queen did not like to part with hers, having sent the other to the Prince of Wales'.[29] Elizabeth leads this 'dispute'. She was either fully aware that De Puebla would report back the couple's attachment to these letters, or she felt confident and settled enough in her role to playfully argue with Henry in front of officials. Either way, it was a valuable exercise in public relations, and De Puebla dutifully reported it to Ferdinand and Isabella. Margaret Beaufort was also present at this meeting. In their dispatches, Spanish ambassadors noted friction between Elizabeth and her mother-in-law, stating that the queen was 'kept in subjection by the mother of the King' and liked by the English people only because she was 'powerless'.[30] In fact, the sources suggest they had a good relationship. They agreed on the welfare of the young Princess Margaret, insisting she should not marry her arranged husband, the Scottish King James IV, until she was older. Henry stated that, as Margaret had 'not yet completed the ninth year of her age … Besides my own doubts, the Queen respecting it, and my mother are very much against this marriage,' adding that 'they fear the King of Scots would not wait, but injure her'.[31]

They also jointly advised Katherine of Aragon to drink wine rather than water to prepare herself for life in England and also to learn French so they could converse with her, neither of them able to speak Katherine's native Spanish. They also shared a joke about De Puebla's continued presence at court when he wasn't needed, suspecting he was coming only to enjoy dishes from the royal kitchens.[32] It's also important to consider the comments of these ambassadors in context. Margaret's active presence at her son's side was perhaps oddly viewed by diplomats used to different protocols and family relationships within a foreign court.

Meanwhile, as Henry negotiated over terms, Elizabeth charmed De Puebla by offering him a 'rich English lady' in marriage and meticulously oversaw the writing of correspondence to both Isabella and Katherine. Elizabeth's Latin secretary complained that she made him rewrite letters three or four times because of 'defects she found in them'.[33] The queen's studious approach paid off, and she maintained a warm, professional relationship with the Spanish rulers. Ferdinand personally informed her of his victory at Baca in Granada on 4 December 1489, writing 'he thinks it is his duty to inform the Queen of England of it'. Elizabeth also sent business to Ferdinand in August 1499, when she backed her husband's recommendation of Henry Stiles, a 'valiant soldier' who wished to serve in Ferdinand's army.[34]

One poignant hint of Elizabeth's importance to the Spanish alliance can be found in Isabella's response to the queen's sudden death. With Katherine now widowed (Arthur had died after an illness in April 1502), the Spanish queen urged Henry to send Katherine back to Spain, 'for, now the Queen of England is dead, in whose society ... the Princess, our daughter, might have honourably remained as with a mother, and the King being the man he is, even though the betrothal were concluded, it would not be right that the Princess should stay in England during the period of mourning for the Prince of Wales'.[35] There were also rumours that Henry planned to marry his former daughter-in-law. Elizabeth had cultivated a welcoming and protective environment for Katherine that calmed Isabella's nerves. Now, without Elizabeth's nurturing presence, Isabella felt that the best place for her daughter was back at home.

The arrangements for the marriage of Arthur and Katherine had taken up years of diplomacy and negotiation and Henry and Elizabeth's combined efforts were vital to its outcome. Drawing on their individual strengths and public roles, Elizabeth's soft, motherly attitude balanced Henry's sterner, more calculating approach. Both met and built professional relationships with ambassadors, corresponded with Spain and helped ease Katherine's transition into a new life as Princess of Wales and future Queen of England. They must have shared a satisfied smile then, as they watched the young bride and groom step onto a stage at St Paul's Cathedral on 14 November 1501 to recite their vows. The smile was well-deserved. In fifteen years, Henry and Elizabeth had ended the Wars of the Roses, produced male and female heirs and secured the future of the new Tudor dynasty, backed with the political and military might of Ferdinand and Isabella's Spain.

Tragically, just five months later there came a sudden blow to the future the couple had worked so hard to build. Prince Arthur, the teenager on whom so much hope rested for the future of the era, died on 2 April 1502 at Ludlow at the age of fifteen. On hearing the news, Henry's first action was to send for Elizabeth, so they could 'take their painful sorrows together'. She comforted the king, with 'full great and constant, and comfortable words', reminding him that he was an only child, 'yet God, by his grace, has ever preserved you, and brought you where you are now'. Looking to what they had built together, she told Henry 'God has left you yet a fair prince and two fair princesses ... and we are both young enough'. When she returned to her chamber, she broke down in grief, and the king in turn, comforted her.[36] Elizabeth's reassurance to Henry that they were both 'young enough' to conceive again, reminds us of the timing of some of her pregnancies, appearing to have been motivated by the loss of a child. They did indeed conceive again, and quickly. A daughter, Katherine, was born in early 1503. Elizabeth died soon afterwards, from childbirth related complications on 11 February, with her death said to have been 'as heavy and dolorous to the king as ever was seen or heard of'.[37]

Henry cautiously dipped his toe into the marriage market again, but never remarried. It does seem as though the grief he felt over the loss of Elizabeth was visible until the end of his reign. The Victorian historian Agnes Strickland believed that after the queen's death, Henry became 'notorious for his rapacity and miserly habits of hoarding money'.[38] He died on 21 April 1509. In his will, he requested 'a foundation of twenty anniversaries to be solemnly holden for [the] King, his Queen, and family'.[39]

We have established some of the public roles Henry and Elizabeth carried out as a couple, but is it possible, 500 years after they lived, to gain some understanding of their personalities and the dynamics of their relationship?

We have discussed the complementary roles the couple played in state business. The queen's soft, maternal style contrasted with her husband's, who once firmly moved an ambassador along by telling him in 1498, 'I do not wish you to trouble yourself about this affair. But if you have power to do so, you may negotiate the other business'.[40]

But there were also similarities. Both were competent administrators, Elizabeth perfecting her letters to Spain and Henry taking an active interest in all aspects of ruling, including personally initialling alongside payments in his accounts book.[41] As individuals they spoke confidently at official meetings, such as the four-hour discussion with De Puebla and the 'long conversation' with Archduke Philip in Calais with both Elizabeth and Henry present. A note in Elizabeth's Privy Purse Accounts of 1502 also records a payment to her groom, John Browne, for 'his costs going from the Tower of London to Richmond to prepare the Queen's lodging there against the coming of the ambassadors of Hungary'.[42] Sources are, however, tantalisingly silent on Elizabeth's involvement in other state matters, including the capture of Perkin Warbeck, who claimed to be her long-lost brother, one of the Princes in the Tower. It is difficult to understand why Henry would not want to know the true identity of the man who may have been his brother-in-law and therefore a threat to his throne, and Elizabeth was the closest and most reliable source to have confirmed or denied this. From what we now know of the working relationship between the couple, it's unlikely that Elizabeth remained completely silent.

The couple also endured adversity, as individuals and through shared experiences once married. As children, both sensed the threat of danger and uncertain circumstances. Henry spent his childhood away from his mother, as the lucrative ward of Yorkist supporter Sir William Herbert, Earl of Pembroke at Raglan Castle. Henry's uncle, Jasper Tudor, later collected him as a young boy and took him to live overseas. Elizabeth fled to sanctuary with her mother and siblings twice; once when her father was briefly deposed in 1470 and again in 1483 on his death. She would have remembered the loss of her brothers and the execution of her uncle Sir Anthony Woodville when she was seventeen years old. Even by then, Elizabeth had already lost significant members of her family to conflict. Another uncle, Sir John Woodville, and her grandfather, Sir Richard Woodville, were beheaded by Lancastrian forces in 1469, when Elizabeth was three years old.

Combined experiences such as these may have shaped the couple's response to emotional hardship and even contributed to the development of a problem-solving instinct. We see Henry very carefully establishing the legitimacy of his rule in 1485 and later in the reign being preoccupied by pretenders and dynastic threats. Elizabeth's reassurance that they could bear more children shows that she, too, understood the risks of starting a royal line from scratch, and was prepared to alter her course to save it. The violence of the Wars of the Roses undoubtedly left a lasting mark on the pair. They had seen England crown a string of monarchs and then witnessed those kings toppled from power. It was not by accident that, despite threats to the succession, the claims of pretenders, personal grief and setbacks, the Tudor dynasty still continued uninterrupted on Henry's death in 1509.

The couple had two experienced advisors to guide them through the challenges of governing, and also of marriage. Henry's mother was a prominent figure during the recent conflict, managing, as a Lancastrian, to remain generally in favour with the Yorkist government. She had carried the train of Anne Neville at her and Richard's coronation, but supported her son's invasion against him just two years later. For advice on queenship, Elizabeth could look to her mother, Elizabeth Woodville, who served as Edward IV's consort for almost nineteen years. Confident and capable, she had lived at a court that was ripe with ambition, paranoia and suspicion. Combined, these women could also provide advice on matrimonial matters, along with insights of royal duty from within the crown as well as outside. Elizabeth Woodville died on 8 June 1492 at Bermondsey Abbey almost seven years after Henry's coronation, while Margaret Beaufort outlived both Henry and Elizabeth of York, dying on 29 June 1509.

While we have established that Elizabeth of York was involved in some aspects of early Tudor rule, her participation in other affairs is uncertain. This does not prove that she was not involved. Sources reveal that Elizabeth was at ease making decisions with her husband and confident enough to add her own terms to agreements, such as that regarding Margaret's marriage. She may have simply been content to leave the majority of ruling to her husband, playing an influential, but supportive role. Strickland addressed this when she wrote in 1854 of Elizabeth that 'when a man governs himself well, it is not often that his wedded partner endeavours to take upon herself that trouble', which is particularly meaningful when we consider the very different relationship dynamics of Henry VI and Margaret of Anjou.[43]

It is difficult to ignore that their marriage was engineered for purely political reasons. For the best chance of peace, Henry needed a wife and heirs that represented the houses of both Lancaster and York. This wasn't necessarily always going to be Elizabeth. Vergil let slip in his *Historie* that on hearing confusing reports of Elizabeth marrying her uncle, Henry became anxious that 'he could not now expect the marriage of any of King Edward's daughters', suggesting it was, at least initially, the bloodline he was marrying, and not the woman.[44]

This typically cool and detached sentiment doesn't seem to have lasted long into their marriage. There are examples of the pair treating one another with respect and ease. They also appear to have had, from what we can see in documents they left behind, a happy marriage. The couple reeled from Arthur's sudden death with tenderness and optimism, and the king was visibly bereft on losing Elizabeth in 1503. Also, despite a reputation as a penny-pinching king, Henry's Privy Purse Accounts show that he doted on Elizabeth and their children, spending vast sums on gifts, entertainment and clothing. In 1492, he paid 6s 8d, the equivalent of around £223, for a bow for the five-year-old Prince Arthur and in 1495, he paid £7 10s (the equivalent today of around £5,000) for 'diverse yards of silk' for Henry and Margaret. The huge sum of £1,314 11s 6d was paid out 'to pay the queen's debts' in 1493.[45] The entry doesn't record what the debts were, but is equivalent today to a staggering £880,000. The couple enjoyed music, too, with a payment of 6s 3d (£223 today) 'to the women that songe before the

King and Quene'.[46] They also gave each other thoughtful and personal gifts. In 1497 Henry paid Elizabeth the sum of £10 (around £6,600 today) for the 'garnishing of a salett', believed to reference the queen's addition of jewels to Henry's helmet. In April 1502, Elizabeth upgraded Henry's Garter robes, her Privy Purse Accounts recording cash paid for 'lace and botons for the Kinges mantel of the Garter'.[47]

Ultimately, their relationship was defined by the ending of a war that killed thousands of subjects and disrupted the established, predictable order of succession. They worked together using individual strengths and drew on one another's support and optimism. Their success was rooted in their shared base principle; to ensure the realm's safety and produce an uncontested heir to inherit the kingdom. It was a hope that Elizabeth, as she turned thirty-seven years of age, died trying to achieve.

It is easy to see why later Tudors romanticized and reinforced the historic union between Henry VII and Elizabeth of York. Henry emerged from a bloody battlefield and Elizabeth from a seething court to establish a dynasty that lasted into the seventeenth century. Their line, ruled by their children and grandchildren, is linked to the British monarchy that wave for cameras and preside over public events today. Without Elizabeth and Henry on their thrones, England would have had no Elizabethan Age of theatre, and no tales of Henry VIII's six wives. Many beloved historic palaces wouldn't exist, or would have a different meaning today. It is also true that the next century was marked by revolution, with the dismantling of once-sacred religious houses, an attempted Spanish invasion and the executions of four queens on English soil.[48]

But Henry and Elizabeth would know none of this. The England they worked towards was one of peace, financial prosperity and unchallenged royal succession. They achieved the first by ensuring any remaining support for the Wars of the Roses was, largely at least, quenched by their marriage and the speedy birth of an heir. Henry left the throne richer than he found it, thanks to the controversial efforts of his wily administrators Richard Empson and Edmund Dudley, who aggressively taxed and fined the aristocracy. Elizabeth's Privy Purse records show that she only occasionally spent larger sums on luxuries, the rest going on food, servants' costs and everyday expenditure such as laundry.

Their reign also marked a new era in exploration, motivated by reports of new trade routes and discoveries of gold. In 1496 Henry gave John Cabot and his sons a patent to 'sail to all parts, regions and coasts of the eastern, western and northern sea, under our banners, flags and ensigns'.

In September of that year, it was reported in a Bristol chronicle that they had landed in America.[49] A number of other payments involving ships can also be found in Henry's Privy Purse Accounts, although often the precise details of these expenses are not given. Elizabeth's thoughts on her husband's maritime projects haven't survived, but judging by her enthusiasm for the Spanish alliance, it is likely that she looked forward to seeing England's place in the wider world. She would have remembered the work of her father who furthered and protected trading opportunities for merchants and in 1462 granted them a charter in the Netherlands 'that ye course of merchandise may be kept in good estate'.[50] As well as Spain, the couple also tied England diplomatically to Scotland. Margaret Tudor was married in 1503 to the Scottish King James IV. Another marriage was promised by Henry after Elizabeth's death, between Mary Tudor and Charles, the future Holy Roman Emperor in 1507. This was later shelved by Henry VIII after his accession to the throne.

Their vision of an England linked via Spain to the wider world had a social effect, too. From the late fifteenth century, we see a greater number of Spanish residents in the country than before. Miranda Kaufmann, in *Black Tudors, The Untold Story*, discussed John Blanke, the first known Tudor resident of African descent, and royal trumpeter to Henry VII. Kaufmann considered the possibility that Blanke came to England as part of Katherine of Aragon's entourage from Spain in 1501.[51] Katherine did bring other members of her Spanish household to settle in England, including Catalina, described as a 'slave of the queen of England'. She is recorded as responsible for making Katherine's bed during her marriage to Arthur and later moved to Malaga and married a crossbow maker named Oviedo. After his death, Catalina and her two daughters settled in Motril, her home town. Doña Maria de Rojas accompanied Katherine to Ludlow and was said to have slept in Katherine's bed following Arthur's death.[52] In 1492 Henry purchased a saddle, bridle and spurs for 'Dego, the Spanish fole', with others performing tricks, playing sports and dancing for the royal family.[53] There were those who settled in England outside the court, too, including the surgeon Pedro Fernandy in 1488, Sebastian de Mosica in 1496 and Francis Dyas in 1497.[54]

As for Elizabeth, her accounts show that she had personal interactions with visitors from around Europe. She paid a Spanish clerk's servant in reward for a gift of oranges, and a Frenchman for apples brought to her at the Tower of London. She also rewarded a Spanish servant that travelled to her from Katherine of Aragon, and settled a bill made out to a goldsmith named John Vandelf, possibly a Dutch surname. In November 1502, while she was pregnant, a Frenchwoman came to Elizabeth at Baynard's Castle 'to have been her nurse'.[55]

Henry and Elizabeth's negotiations with Spain had another outcome that changed the course of Tudor history. Some of the ladies that accompanied Katherine from Spain married men with positions in the early Tudor court. Agnes de Vanegas married William Blount, while Maria de Salinas wed Lord Willoughby. Both women had an influence on two ladies of the next generation who were to make their own powerful mark on the Tudor court, Katherine Willoughby and Gertrude Courtenay. Their stories will be told in more detail in later chapters. As Maria de Salinas was the mother of Katherine Willoughby, had the Spanish match not gone ahead, this confident and significant sixteenth-century woman would not have existed.

The early Tudor court also saw a number of Italian residents, attracted to an increasingly diverse England that welcomed learning and was no longer distracted by civil war. Lewis Einstein, in *The Italian Renaissance in England*, noted Henry's encouragement of scholarship, new ideas and artistic expression at court. Silvestro Gigli served as the king's master of ceremonies and the poet Peter Carmeliano wrote a piece celebrating the birth of Prince Arthur. Henry's reign also saw the first teaching of Greek and Humanities at Oxford University in the 1490s and the patronage of Italian-trained scholars such as Thomas Linacre and William Grocyn.[56] Greek was taught at subsequent Tudor courts, and studied by later monarchs. According to John Hayward, Henry's grandson Edward VI was especially keen to learn the language and would add notes in Greek to some of his writings. Sir Thomas More's daughter, Margaret Roper, was also proficient in the language by the 1530s.[57]

During the couple's reign, works on mathematics, astronomy and science were published. The printing press had been enthusiastically backed by Elizabeth's father, Edward IV, but gained real momentum during the late fifteenth century. Vergil, Henry's own historian, published his *De Rerum Inventoribis*, or in English, *A Pleasant and Compendious History of the First Inventers,* in 1499. These early Tudor readers were interested in how certain mechanical and creative developments had taken place, even if the writer credited many of them to Biblical origins. Another manuscript, named *Arundel MS 66* in the collection of the British Library, dates to 1490 and includes astronomical calculations believed to have been prepared for Henry VII. Henry is depicted in the manuscript as patron receiving the work enthroned with advisors around him.

Elizabeth's role as a patron of literature and learning is less clear and it is more difficult to find works dedicated to her. She is, however, repeatedly mentioned in ballads, as we have seen, and her actions are described in the early written histories of the age. There is no doubt that she was a popular queen, and it may be that scholars preferred to dedicate works to their king, in the hope of attracting his favour, attention and patronage. We cannot entirely rule out that Elizabeth was uninterested in literature and learning; her father and her uncle, Anthony Woodville, were both keen supporters of the early printing industry and the royal court of her childhood was alive with music and culture.

Among these artists, thinkers and mathematicians were humanist scholars, whom Henry particularly supported. As Lewis Einstein wrote, 'Just as in Italy scholars had lived under the patronage of princes ... so humanism, newly introduced into England, was fostered and encouraged by Henry the Seventh, first of a new race of English monarchs'.[58] This also had an impact on the education of future Tudor monarchs as these men took up positions in the royal household as tutors to the young Arthur, Henry, Margaret and Mary. The writer and poet Bernard Andre was tutor to Prince Arthur, while Giles D'Ewes taught young Prince Henry the French language. The poet John Skelton, described by A.F. Pollard as 'the greatest name in English verse from Lydgate down to Surrey', was the young Henry's tutor.[59] This early exposure to the fertile and rapidly-spreading culture of the Renaissance undoubtedly had an effect on the future king, the organisation of his court, and arguably influenced some of the later policies enforced during his reign. He would prove to be a critical thinker and lover of music, composing pieces of his own including the song *Pastime with Good Company*. As for Elizabeth proudly watching her children speaking French, playing musical instruments and questioning what they had learned in their books, she too had the respect of a great thinker. Erasmus thought very highly of the queen, once praising her as capable of good judgement and prudence.[60]

The development of Tudor theatre is usually attributed to the later efforts of Elizabeth I. But we can see the beginning of new, theatrical expression at the court of Henry VII and Elizabeth of York. Their attendance was noted in at least two performances known as 'disguisings'. The early twentieth-century historian Robert Withington acknowledged that these celebrations involving costume, a play and music had been popular at royal courts since the fourteenth century. However, he saw something new emerge under Henry and Elizabeth; the use of increasingly complex backdrops and scenery. In

1494 the couple were present at a Twelfth Night revel featuring St George and a castle, while in 1501 craftsmen produced not only a castle, but a ship and a mountain to set the scene.[61] While theatrical entertainments would become far more exuberant and costly under subsequent Tudor monarchs, Henry and Elizabeth showed they were eager to experiment with and be associated with new styles and methods of artistic expression.

Finally, one of the most enduring legacies left by Elizabeth and Henry was their skill in early public relations. Reinforcing their individual legitimacy through ancient legends and in parliament, they stood together as strong, undisputed rulers. This gave subjects a brave, patriotic ideal to cling to along with nationwide gratitude for ending the Wars of the Roses. Vergil, Holinshed and Shakespeare reimagined and romanticized their achievement, capturing and engaging imaginations for hundreds of years. They planned relentlessly to ensure that the new regime survived after their deaths and demonstrated foresight and an ability to adapt, recovering politically after Arthur's sudden death in 1502. The couple's inscription on their tomb at Westminster Abbey praises Henry's wisdom and wealth, and Elizabeth's beauty and fertility. However, their combined contribution was far more than this. The changes they made together politically, dynastically, socially and financially within the realm must not be underestimated.

Chapter 2

Henry VIII and Katherine of Aragon

ON 11 MAY 1509, Henry VII's body was lowered into his grave at Westminster Abbey to the echoing swell of a choir singing *Libera Me*.[1] Servants of state and the royal household broke their staves and ceremoniously dropped them into the grave after him, signalling the end of their duties to the monarch. As mourners shuffled over the cool, stone slabs towards the abbey's ancient wooden doors, England was a significantly different realm from the one Henry had conquered at Bosworth twenty-four years earlier. Apart from a few quickly subdued uprisings, the nation was at peace and royal chests filled with gold. He and Elizabeth had left the buds of the Tudor dynasty swollen with potential. It was the next royal couple that set them in bloom.

We tend to think of Henry VIII's wedding to Katherine of Aragon as a foregone conclusion and a marriage of convenience. It finalized Henry VII's vision of an England connected with Spain, the negotiations had been completed and Katherine was already living in England as Arthur's widow. And yet the death of the old king seems to have thrown the princess' position into confusion. Her father, Ferdinand, sent a series of frantic letters on the day of Henry VII's funeral, urging officials to help secure his daughter's future. The first ordered his ambassador, Gutier Gomez de Fuensalida, to by 'all the means in his power persuade the new King of England to marry the Princess without any delay', while sharing his concern that the French would now try and stop the marriage. A second letter to Henry VIII offered condolences over the recent loss of his father, referred to Henry as a 'son', and offered military support including men, infantry, ships and weaponry in case his accession had not been peaceful. A third letter, to Katherine, promised that 'the speedy conclusion of her marriage' was concerning him more than 'anything else on earth'.[2]

No doubt Henry listened to Ferdinand's deal-sweetening military offer with interest, but Katherine was an attractive bride in her own right. A royal woman with powerful connections in Europe, she had already been praised by English subjects and displayed tenacity and independence during the seven years she lived as Arthur's widow. A dispensation granted by Pope Julius II cleared the obstacle of her first marriage to Henry's brother, and the couple exchanged vows at Greenwich in June 1509.[3]

For England's citizens, the reign of Henry VIII and Queen Katherine promised an exciting new start. Writers rushed to praise the new king's qualities, with William Blount, Lord Mountjoy referring to him in a letter to the writer Erasmus as a 'hero'. Mountjoy, who would become the queen's Chamberlain, noted 'how wisely he behaves, what a lover he is of justice and goodness, what affection he bears to the learned', as well as calling him 'this new and auspicious star'. Excitedly promising Erasmus that if he could see the king he would struggle to hold back 'tears of joy', he proclaims 'The heavens laugh, the earth exults, all things are full of milk, of honey, of nectar!'.[4] Later, Stow wrote that Henry was a 'young and lusty' king, whose accession marked 'the golden world, such grace reigned then within this realm'.[5]

At the centre of Stow's golden world, surrounded by 'all abundance and riches', sat Henry and Katherine.[6] Their personalities over the centuries have often developed into caricature; Katherine depicted in modern period dramas as unfashionable and generally miserable, contrasting with the younger Henry's fun-loving nature and preoccupation with jousting. Nicholas Sander, in his Elizabethan work *Rise and Growth of the Anglican Schism,* stated that Katherine was devout, waking at midnight to hear matins and believing 'the only time wasted was the time spent in dressing'. The couple had only a five-year age gap, said Sander, but their difference was 'over a thousand years in character'.[7] Sander was born in around 1527 and would have been around nine years of age on Katherine's death. He therefore gathered his information from other sources and hearsay that cannot now be verified. Many of his informants may also have been heavily biased, particularly when we consider how divisive the couple's separation would become in the 1530s. There is no question that Katherine was a highly religious woman, but evidence points to the couple being far more similar in personality, particularly earlier in their marriage, than Sander gave them credit for.

Together, as they processed to their joint coronation on 24 June 1509, Henry and Katherine looked every inch the Renaissance royal power couple. In contrast to today's popular image of the bloated and scowling middle-aged king, the seventeen-year-old Henry was athletic, tall and praised for his physical and intellectual abilities. In a marked contrast to the sombre attire worn by his father, Henry sparkled in colourful fabrics and jewels as he progressed through London accompanied by servants and nobles of the realm. He wore a 'robe of crimson velvet, furred with ermines, his jacket or coat of raised gold, the placard embroidered with diamonds, rubies, emeralds, great pearls, and other rich stones'. Around his neck he wore a collar of balasses, a type of large pink gemstone.[8] This description by Edward Hall sounds strikingly similar to the portrait of the clean-shaven king painted in around 1509, attributed to Meynnart Wewyck and in the Berger Collection of the Denver Art Museum.[9] He appears in a gold and crimson jacket lined with fur, with a collar made up of wide, oval pinkish stones. Painted early in his reign, the portrait may have been commissioned specially for Henry's coronation, although it is of course possible that Hall, writing before 1547, based his description of Henry on the existing painting.

Katherine, too, was richly and fashionably dressed. Seated in a litter pulled by two white horses, she wore white embroidered satin, her long auburn hair hanging loosely around her shoulders and trailing down her back. On her head she wore a coronet 'set with many rich orient stones'.[10] From these descriptions, it's no wonder English subjects identified the couple with a new beginning. They had been used to glimpses of the gaunt, greying Henry VII, shuffling about his palaces, clutching papers under his arm. Now here were two young rulers gleaming in jewels, cloth of gold and white satin. Their appearance promised wealth, combined military resources and unchallenged legitimacy, along with a modern revival of the monarchy.

Portraits of Henry show his love of fashion, jewels and material excess, and his queen was similarly keen to display the latest styles. A portrait of Katherine currently on loan to the National Portrait Gallery and painted in around 1520 shows her as she wanted her subjects to see her. She wears a muted red gown with gold edging at the bust, her gold sleeves embroidered with black. Her wrists are lined with the same white frills Henry can be seen wearing in a portrait painted in around the same year. She also wears a gable headdress, again with accents of gold, her neck draped with strands of pearls. As she posed for the painting, created around the time of the historic meeting of English and French monarchs at the Field of the Cloth of Gold, Katherine had been queen for a decade and was at the height of her influence.

The court of the couple's early reign was full of colour, influenced by reports of outfits worn overseas. One ambassador at the Field of the Cloth of Gold in 1520 commented on Henry and his courtiers wearing 'long gowns in the Milanese fashion'.[11] The king also wore shorter gowns, which left his legs uncovered, accentuating his height. Later, Hans Holbein, in his Whitehall Portrait of 1537, would depict him wearing a short gown with a garter secured tightly under his knee. These styles – complete with elaborately-decorated codpiece – made the king appear more powerful, slimmed his frame and drew the eye upwards.

Katherine isn't often considered a fashion icon, but she quickly became associated with the gable headdress which continued in popularity long after her death. It had shorter sides than the longer versions Elizabeth of York and other ladies at the court had worn in the early 1500s. Katherine also embellished hers with pearls and other precious jewels. The queen was also portrayed wearing rounder headdresses placed further back on the head, showing that she enjoyed a range of styles.

Despite Nicholas Sander's view that Katherine found dressing tedious, reports show that she was excited about fashion and understood the importance it had on public scrutiny, not just of herself, but also her household. In 1520, on hearing that her nephew the Holy Roman Emperor Charles V was to visit England, she and her sister-in-law Mary excitedly laid out 'great cost on the apparel of their ladies and gentlewomen'.[12] During Christmas celebrations in 1515, Henry and members of the court dressed in 'strange apparel' created from cloth of gold and silver, blue velvet and white satin. On their heads they wore 'bonnets of burned gold', which, wrote Holinshed, 'pleased every person, and in especial, the queen'.[13] Another performance at Greenwich in 1519 had women dressed 'after the fashion of Inde, with kerchiefs of pleasance hatched with fine gold and set with letters of Greek in gold of bullion'.[14]

On 1 January 1511 Katherine gave birth to a son, appropriately-named Henry after his father and grandfather. Following her churching ceremony and return to public life the following February, a tournament in the queen's honour was held at Westminster. Seated under hangings of cloth of gold, Katherine watched as her husband strutted on horseback wearing their intertwined initials of H and K, also in gold, his horse trapped in the same design, with a 'K of goldsmith's work' set on the top of each pavilion in the yard. During the celebrations, Henry cast himself as the character of Sir Loyal Heart *(Coeur Loyal)*, appearing to spectators against a backdrop of trees, mountains and flowers made from velvets and silks. The centrepiece was a castle made out of gold. Henry was visible, but the initials throughout the yard and Katherine's prominent seated position reinforced them both as the centre of the crowd's adulation. Giles Tremlett, in *Catherine of Aragon, Henry's Spanish Queen*, has pointed out that Katherine's willingness to act publicly as the recipient of Henry's acts of love meant they were a good fit for one another, and she actively promoted the concept of courtly love that would endure throughout the rest of the century.[15] She also played a role in guiding the 'script' of the tournament. In one performance, Charles Brandon, Henry's close friend, approached her dressed in a disguise 'like a recluse or religious person', and humbly asked for her permission to join in the jousting. As good a sport as ever, she nodded her consent, and Brandon dramatically 'put off his said habit, and was armed at all pieces with rich bases and his horse also richly trapped'.[16] During these tournaments Katherine demonstrated a skill for accepting her place as the centre of attention, but never openly indulging in it. Instead, she reflected admiration onto the actions and exploits of her husband, underlining their joint presence as a couple.

An example can be found in a performance of 1515. A man in the character of Robin Hood commanded 200 men to shoot arrows for the king and queen, each arrow adapted to whistle in the air as it flew, giving a 'strange and great' noise. However, when 'Robin' requested that the king and queen accompany him into the forest, Henry gallantly asked Katherine and her ladies if they were comfortable going into the woods with 'so many outlaws'. Without missing a beat, Katherine turned to her husband and assured him that 'if it pleased him she was content', publicly underlining her trust in him as her loyal and brave protector amid 200 'fugitives'.[17]

From the very beginning of their reign, the couple established the concept of courtly love at court. An ideal inspired by Arthurian legend and early medieval culture, it consisted of romantic declarations of love with underlying themes of chivalry, respect and honour. Expressed in poetry, song and court banter, the practice endured into the reign of Elizabeth I and lingered to some degree into the Stuart era. Prominent court writers active during Henry's early reign included Sir Thomas Wyatt, the 'father of modern English poetry', and his court contemporary Henry Howard, Earl of Surrey. Both are well-known for their romantic verse, although according to Lewis Einstein, their work formed the basis of other literary genres. For example, he considered Wyatt one of the earliest writers of satire in England.[18]

Henry and Katherine were central to the resurgence of courtly love, which defined and shaped the Tudor era. Later writers would continue to be inspired by performances similar to those acted by the couple at the tiltyard and those of writers at court. Would the poetic advances of Shakespeare's Orsino to Olivia in *Twelfth Night*, written in the early seventeenth century, have had the same substance without Wyatt and Surrey's earlier writings of the 1520s? A group of Henry's courtiers in the 1530s shared a book of love poetry, each of them adding and editing verses depending on their writing styles and experiences. This work, which will be discussed in more detail in a later chapter, is considered vital to our understanding of Tudor love poetry today. The concept of courtly love flourished even in the reign of Elizabeth I, with poets writing love sonnets and allegorical dedications to the queen, including Edmund Spenser and Sir Philip Sidney.

Katherine and Henry were both skilled at playing their individual characters; Henry as the brave, hopeless romantic and Katherine the willing and gracious object of his desire – something other Tudor queens were unable to fully emulate. Anne Boleyn was a firm advocate of courtly love, but clumsily overstepped the mark in 1536 during an exchange with Sir Henry Norris, replying that he looked for 'dead men's shoes, for if ought should come to the King but good, you would look to have me'.[19] This flippant and unwise comment brought to mind the king's death, an act of treason since 1351, and played a part in Anne and Norris' executions in May of that year. Anna of Cleves reacted with awkward shock when Henry rode with eight gentlemen to surprise her, unannounced, at Rochester Castle shortly after her arrival in England. Understandably, she reacted 'somewhat astonished' by being caught off guard by this breach of protocol although they left their first meeting, visibly at least, on good terms.[20] This was exactly the kind of performance Henry and Katherine maintained so well early in their marriage. She not only knew what to say and when, but enhanced his public image as her protector and ardent lover, something that no doubt boosted the young king's own status and ego.

As lovers of learning, art and music, Henry and Katherine were only too keen to support talented artists visiting the court from Europe. Katherine was a follower of literature and spoke many languages, including Spanish, Flemish, French and English. Henry was said to have found it 'monstrous for a Prince not to cultivate moral and intellectual excellence', and studied grammar, philosophy and religion. The Venetian Ambassador Lodovico Falier reported that the king also spoke Latin, Spanish, French and Italian and was particularly welcoming 'to men of science, whom he is never weary of obliging'.[21]

This respect for education and learning was quickly embraced by the Tudor court, and the pair were avid supporters and patrons of foreign artists. The bronze effigies of Henry VII and Elizabeth of York in Westminster Abbey were created by the Italian sculptor Pietro Torrigiano, who was known to Michelangelo. Work began on the monument in around 1513 and the expertise with which it was created shows a considerable leap in artistic form, detail and technique from the work of just decades before. Finished in 1519, enhanced realism can be seen in the folds of fabric worn by the royal pair and in the rendering of their solemn facial expressions. Minute details have also been chiselled on the sculpture including veins carefully carved on the backs of their hands. Torrigiano was also commissioned by Henry VIII to create an effigy of his grandmother, Margaret Beaufort, in the same style. When comparing these sculptures with effigies of just twenty years before, it is clear that by 1513 the new skills and learning of the Renaissance had fully arrived in England.[22]

The couple retained a number of European painters, too. The Italian artist Vincent Volpe was paid 100 shillings for a quarter year's wages in 1516 and appears in other payment records into the 1520s.[23] Florentine painters Anthony Toto and Bartholome Penne are also mentioned in 1528 as receiving wages of £25 per year from Henry, while a woman painter, Alice Carmillion, received a payment of 33 shillings 4d.[24] Henry and Katherine sat for some of the first miniature portraits in England, attributed to the Dutch artist Lucas Horenbout in the 1520s. The queen posed at least twice for Horenbout, one portrait depicting her in dark clothing and another in a red gown with her hair visible, both completed using watercolour on vellum.[25] Dudley Heath identified Lucas Horenbout's father Gerard as also employed by Henry, along with a sister, Susannah.[26] Katherine had also inspired Renaissance artwork in her younger years. A portrait in the collection of the Detroit Institute of Arts is believed to depict the princess before she set off on her journey to England to marry Prince Arthur. Created by the Estonian artist Michael Sittow to portray Mary Magdalene, it shows a young woman cradling a golden lidded cup, her eyes cast down, with waves of reddish-blonde hair falling on her shoulders.

Although he would achieve lasting fame later in Henry's reign, it was while Katherine was queen that Hans Holbein the Younger first arrived in England in 1526. The cultural and art-loving royal court welcomed Holbein who flitted to and from London before returning in the 1530s as court painter. On one of these early visits, he painted likenesses of key Tudor figures including Sir Thomas More, William Wareham, Archbishop of Canterbury, and Sir Henry Guildford. All these portraits date to 1527. Another portrait, dated to 1528, shows Henry VIII's astronomer, Nicolas Kratzer, posing at a desk with his tools. There are no known portraits by Holbein of either Henry or Katherine at this time, probably because the artist was circulating among court officials and merchants rather than among the royal family. Later, having demonstrated his considerable skill in creating these astonishingly lifelike portraits, Holbein returned to England and attracted Henry's attention. However, there is evidence of the royals' early employment of Holbein in another task. An armour garniture in the collection of the Metropolitan Museum of Art in New York has been dated to 1527. Created at the royal workshops at Greenwich, which Henry established in 1515, it consists of different attachments allowing it to be adapted to different military situations, for example a joust or tournament. The metal is decorated with a fine and intricate pattern, the design of which has been attributed to Hans Holbein the Younger. It's believed the armour was presented by Henry to the French ambassador on a visit that year. Later, Holbein depicted many Henrician courtiers and members of the royal family in strikingly realistic images.

The court soon became even more cosmopolitan as craftsmen and traders from Europe provided their expertise to royal palaces. Mario Savorgnano, in 1531, met Henry twice and noted that he was 'glad to see foreigners, and especially Italians'.[27] The king's accounts book reflects the presence of different nationalities at court, for example his purchase of jewellery from John Van Utrike and cloth of gold from Charles de Florence in 1509. A French clockmaker was employed in 1529.[28] Katherine retained a number of Spanish servants, including ladies and gentlewomen, as well as a physician, Dr Fernando. He received, in 1518, a payment from Henry to have his wife conveyed over the seas to join him in England. Elizabeth Vergus and Francis Philippo were both members of Katherine's household that were granted denization, the right to settle in England, with many of the privileges of a native citizen. She also employed an Italian surgeon, Balthasar de Guercis.[29]

Another shared love the couple enjoyed was the study of literature. On one occasion the two of them discussed Erasmus' work, *De Libero Arbitrio*, with the writer Juan Luis Vives.[30] Vives, a keen supporter of women's education, was appointed tutor to their daughter Mary, born in 1516. Antonia McLean, in *Humanism and the Rise of Science in Tudor England*, highlighted Katherine's backing of early Tudor education, embarking on a tour of Oxford's colleges in 1518 and supporting poorer students at the universities.[31] Books written and published during the couple's reign included *The Boke of Husbandry*, a manual on gardening, managing livestock and household duties; and *The Boke of Huntynge*, printed in 1530. An early scientific work, the astronomical *The Kalender of Shepeherdes*, was printed in 1528 and provided guidance on cycles of the moon, structure of the months and constellations of stars. These years saw debates on society and education, too. Thomas More explored the concept of the perfect state in *Utopia* in 1516, while Thomas Elyot campaigned for education in *The Boke Named The Gouernour* in 1531. Elyot in particular was known for writing in English rather than the usual, scholarly Latin. When challenged, he was said to have replied, 'If physicians be angry that I have written physicke in English, let them remember that the Greeks wrote in Greek, and Romans in Latin, Avicenna and the other in Arabic'.[32] Erasmus was also active in England during the couple's reign, and his work would later be fundamental to Tudor education and religious instruction in the middle of the century. Overseen by Henry and Katherine and with the widening appeal of the printing press, these authors impacted the educational lives of subjects of the Tudor age and beyond.

There was another cultural innovation developed by this Renaissance-loving couple that is not often acknowledged. Where Henry VII and Elizabeth of York dabbled in theatrical expression, Henry and Katherine made it the centre of their court. In 1510, the king and queen presided over a banquet with Henry dressed 'apparelled after the Turkie fashion', two other courtiers dressed 'after the fashion of Russia'.[33] Hall commented on one performance in 1512, that 'on the day of the Epiphany at night, the king with eleven others were disguised, after the manner of Italy, called a masque, a thing not seen before in England'. Hall further describes the costumes 'wrought all with gold', the maskers coming in after the banquet with 'six gentlemen disguised in silk' carrying torches. He states that both Henry and Katherine were present for the performance.[34] Robert Withington has pointed out that although there is evidence of what we would consider a masque occurring long before 1512, there must have been something new to this performance for Hall to have singled it out in this way.[35]

Henry's love of foreign influences, especially from Italy, may also have shaped future building. Lewis Einstein argued that it was during the reign of the early Tudors that later Elizabethan and Jacobean architects formed their distinctive style. Referring to the seventeenth-century architect Inigo Jones, Einstein commented that his work 'would scarcely have been possible without the work of the Italians in England, in the first half of the sixteenth century, who prepared and smoothed the way, bridging over the transition between the Gothic and the new style of the renaissance'.[36] Inigo Jones was inspired by Italian influences, working on buildings such as The Queen's House in Greenwich commissioned during the reign of James I for his queen, Anne of Denmark. Surviving buildings of the early reign of Henry VIII do show some Italian references, including dome-topped turrets and ornamentation at Sutton Place and Hampton Court Palace. At the latter, developed by Cardinal Wolsey during Henry and Katherine's reign, the faces of terracotta Roman Emperors gaze down at visitors, while cherubs hold up the royal arms.

It was said that during his early years as king, Henry was occupied with 'such pleasant past-times as his youthful years did delight in'.[37] This has sometimes been interpreted as the king's distractedness and general unwillingness to direct matters of state. Henry was, in fact, a proactive king, even if he did enjoy hunting, buying precious jewels and displaying his talents on the tiltyard. He was said to have known the speed, weight and military power of every ship in his navy and set up a system that sent and received messages between him and his advisor Cardinal Wolsey every seven hours.[38]

If chroniclers considered the king in any way distracted from ruling, they do not give the same impression of Katherine. She was willing to host masques, attend revels and wear expensive gowns, but was duty-bound to her role from the outset. Her journey to the throne had been longer than Henry's, and she had had to work hard to achieve it. In the months and years following Arthur's unexpected death, she displayed tenacity and resilience as she clung to her position at just sixteen years of age. While regularly intervening in negotiations with Henry VII and English and Spanish ambassadors, Katherine spent years under a cloud of uncertainty and in 1507, complaining of dwindling finances, sold personal plate to pay off her debts.[39] She must have felt relief when two years later as queen, she oversaw orders for silks, cloth of silver and jewels while Henry paid the wages of her servants and settled outstanding bills.[40] Presiding over a lavish and abundant new court, Katherine did not retreat into a quiet, subordinate role now that she could finally enjoy all the trappings of queenship. She eagerly stepped into a position she had waited decades to fill. Before Katherine could celebrate five years as England's queen, she would prove to the nation that she fully expected to defend her new country with or without her husband by her side.

On 15 June 1513 Katherine accompanied Henry to Dover as he prepared to sail to France. He had already made arrangements for her to rule as 'Regent and Governess of England, Wales and Ireland' in his absence, exempting her servants from travelling to attend him in the wars.[41] As Katherine travelled back to London, she would have felt a heightened sense of responsibility as governess of the kingdom she had waited so long to lead.

Over the summer of 1513 she followed up on state business, authorized defensive works to be carried out at Berwick and requested that Margaret of Savoy send a physician to her husband.[42] As intelligence arrived towards the end of the summer that James IV of Scotland planned to mount an invasion on England, Katherine reacted with speed. Issuing a list of musters (and reprimanding the mayor and sheriffs of Gloucester for not replying quickly enough), she placed Thomas Howard Earl of Surrey in charge of the army.[43] It was soon discovered that James' troops had been 'spoiling and burning' in the north of England, and Surrey wrote to challenge James to a battle at Flodden in Northumberland. On 8 September 1513 Katherine signed a warrant for the Great Wardrobe to deliver 'standards of the lion crowned imperial according to my lord's standard and pattern' along with banners representing England, Spain and St George.[44] These banners, flickering in the autumn wind, were a silent and powerful show of Henry and Katherine's combined political and military might. They also subtly reinforced their strength as a couple: even with the king absent from the realm, his queen represented the country against their enemies.

On the late afternoon of 9 September, the armies clashed. A contemporary account records that around 12,000 Scottish were killed, others escaping into the early evening darkness before the battle had ended. Among the dead was the Scottish king, 'slain within a spear's length of Surrey', his 'throat cut half asunder'.[45] Katherine wrote to inform her husband of the outcome, but not before putting ships in order at Portsmouth. She wrote of the 'great victory', enclosing a piece of James IV's coat, adding that 'I thought to send himself unto you, but our Englishmen's hearts would not suffer it'. She also enclosed a letter found among the Scottish dead that implicated the French in influencing James' attack.[46]

Henry's trip to France with the Emperor Maximilian ended in triumph for him, too. He claimed victory at the encounter which would come to be named the Battle of the Spurs, due to the speed (it was said) that the French soldiers rode away. Writing to Margaret of Savoy the day after the battle, Henry described the many prisoners that had been taken, including the Duke of Longueville.[47] Thérouanne fell days later, and a truce was drawn up for the town to be delivered to Henry, the inhabitants to 'make oath to the King of England'.[48]

As winter fell on the kingdom in 1513, Henry and Katherine would have felt triumphant. They had proven themselves loyal, dedicated and skilled rulers. Messengers galloped across the countryside and towards dockyards, their leather bags stuffed with correspondence reporting the couple's efficiency and bravery. As fingers heavy with jewelled rings unfurled letters in the courts of Europe, Henry and Katherine made a name for themselves, individually and as a couple. Paolo de Laude, writing to the Duke of Milan, reported favourably on Katherine's ability as regent, while the Venetian Antonio Bavarin wrote of the friendship between Henry and Maximilian, adding that 'Indeed, to everyone the King seems a being descended from Heaven'.[49] The campaign at Flodden during Henry's absence gave Katherine an opportunity to show her dedication to England and her readiness to defend it. She remained cool under pressure, responding quickly and efficiently to the threat to the kingdom.

Up until the mid-1520s Henry and Katherine were every inch a united, dedicated and compatible Renaissance royal couple and had been partners for almost two decades. By 1525, however, there were signs of trouble. Katherine conceived repeatedly, birthing at least two princes early in the reign, but sadly, neither survived their first weeks of life. The couple had one daughter, Mary, but in order to safeguard the kingdom after his death, Henry believed he needed a son as his heir. Thinking back to the dispensation specially granted for him in 1509 that allowed him to marry his brother's widow, the king had a change of heart. Worried for 'the state of this realm and the danger that it stood in, for lack of a prince to succeed me', he became convinced that, by marrying Katherine, he had incurred the 'great displeasure of God'.[50]

It wasn't long, wrote Stow, until rumours began to spread in London that Henry would soon divorce Katherine and take another wife. Gossip spread that the Duchess of Alençon, sister of the French King Francis I, would be Henry's wife number two.[51] By 1530 though, the identity of the woman Henry had chosen to replace Katherine became publicly known. Anne Boleyn was soon the talk of the royal court; Hall writing that 'the queen's ladies, gentlewomen and servants largely spake and said that she so enticed the king and brought him in his amours', something the historian dismissed as 'the foolish communication of people'.[52]

With or without Anne's presence, the doubts Henry had over the legitimacy of his marriage were no fault of Katherine's. Legally and spiritually, Katherine's marriage to Henry's brother Arthur had been disposed of and had no consequence. Henry couldn't deny that she had been a dutiful and obedient wife.[53] For twenty years Katherine had defended his realm, actively participated in negotiations and continually propped up his ego with public professions of loyalty and trust. Still, fear over the security of the kingdom continued to agitate the king. Stow reported that

Henry began to look towards his own death, when 'all our doings in our little time are clearly deface, and worthy of no memory, if we leave you in trouble at the time of our death'.[54] Henry didn't want a repeat of the Wars of the Roses, but more explicitly, he didn't want to be remembered as the king that caused it. Katherine was forty-five in 1530 and considered beyond child-bearing age while Anne Boleyn, no older than around thirty, was touted for her 'apparent aptness to procreation of children'.[55] Katherine had been a good wife and queen, agreed Henry, but he insisted that for the good of his realm, he was seeking an annulment of their marriage.

Before Henry's wobble of conscience in the 1520s, everything points to the couple experiencing a long and happy union. They had many interests in common and enjoyed dancing and hosting masques. In 1519, Henry commissioned Torrigiano, the Italian sculptor who created the tomb of his parents and grandmother, to make another for him and Katherine.[56] This is confirmation that, as the 1520s began, Henry had every intention of remaining married to his wife until they were parted by death. Even as he put forward the case for their divorce in 1529, Henry was emphatic that his queen was 'a woman of most gentleness, of most humility and buxomness ... without comparison, and I these twenty years almost have had the true experiment, so that if I were to marry again if the marriage might be good I would surely choose her above all other women'.[57]

The genuine affection Henry had for Katherine can be gathered from his account books, by the thoughtful gifts he purchased during her early months as queen. In October 1509 he paid thirty shillings for 'the Queen's lavender', and the following January, picked up a bill of forty shillings for her minstrels.[58] In January 1511, soon after the christening of their first child, he also paid for prayers to be said 'for the Queen's good deliverance'. The amount of £6 13s and 4d was allocated for this and is equivalent in today's value to around £4,418. It is possible that the elaborate tournament of that year was not only a celebration of the birth of a son, but also a giving of thanks for the survival, following childbirth, of his queen. This is especially touching when we remember that Henry lost his own mother to the dangers of childbirth when he was just eleven years old.

The couple were compatible as partners, but also as rulers. Both had strong personalities and could be decisive and brutal when they considered it necessary. Together, they understood the importance of public image and worked hard to keep England physically and politically secure.

Katherine also quietly tolerated Henry's mistresses. Elizabeth Blount was the mother of Henry's illegitimate son Henry Fitzroy, born in 1519, and

Alison Weir, in *Mary Boleyn, The Great and Infamous Whore*, examines claims that the king was the father of Mary Boleyn's children, Catherine and Henry Carey, born in 1524 and 1526.[59] Katherine later maintained that she never showed any disapproval over his 'delight or dalliance', but that it was mentioned at all at this difficult time suggests that she had been hurt by it. The birth of an illegitimate son sired by her husband must also have increased pressure on Katherine to conceive. The birth of Fitzroy is also likely to have confirmed, in Henry's mind, that it was their union – and not his with any other – that was being punished by God.

Katherine had been only too willing to play along with Henry's *Coeur Loyal* act and gracefully applaud his dancers. But when it came to ruling, she stepped up with tenacity, professionalism and a sense of duty. On hearing that her husband was seeking an annulment of their marriage, she showed the same courage and resolve. At the trial held at a court in Blackfriars in London, Katherine directly approached Henry in front of the assembled dignitaries. She asked him 'how she had offended and displeased him', declaring that 'I have been to you a true and humble wife, ever conformable to your will and pleasure, that never contraried or gainsaid anything thereof, and being always contented with all things wherein you had any delight or dalliance, whether little or much, without grudge or countenance of discontentation or displeasure'. She also argued that both their fathers, and all their councillors had considered the marriage between them 'good and lawful'. With a low curtsey to her husband, she strode out of the trial, accompanied by her servant. Although Sander maintained that Katherine had her husband's permission to leave, her dramatic stand in front of the judges was a show of strength and power and displayed her conviction that there were, in her view, no legal grounds to dissolve their marriage.[60]

Those that celebrated and rejoiced at the beginning of their relationship felt unsteady shockwaves at its end. Stow wrote that it was 'a strange sight and the newest device that ever was read or heard before in any region, story or chronicle'.[61] The Venetian Mario Savorgnano believed in 1531 that the annulment would not go ahead, 'as the peers of the realm, both spiritual and temporal, and the people are opposed to it ... nor during the present Queen's life will they have any other Queen in the kingdom'.[62]

There is evidence that supports Savorgnano's views, and Henry received notable resistance from Katherine's supporters. According to Holinshed, in 1531 there was 'much preaching, one learned man holding against another, namely in the matter of the king's marriage'; while Thomas Abell, Katherine's chaplain, wrote a book publicly insisting that her marriage to the king was entirely lawful.[63] When told to serve Katherine under her new legal title of 'Princess Dowager, widow of Prince Arthur', some of her household refused, saying they 'were sworn to her as queen, and otherwise would not serve'.[64] One midwife from Watlington in Oxfordshire grumbled that she would gladly assist Queen Katherine in childbirth, but not Anne Boleyn, who she considered 'a whore and a harlot of her living'.[65] And as late as 30 July 1540 three men were taken on hurdles to the gallows and hanged, beheaded and quartered for 'denying of the king's supremacy, and affirming that his marriage with the Lady Katherine was good'.[66] There were even reports of a co-ordinated 'mob' descending on Anne Boleyn as she dined in September 1531. An ambassador noted reports of 'seven to eight thousand women of London', who set out to kill 'the sweetheart of the king'. She managed to escape by boat.[67]

Resistance to Katherine's abandonment also came from spiritual communities. Elizabeth Barton, a Canterbury nun, emerged in the 1530s claiming to have received messages inspired by God. She warned that 'God was highly displeased' with the king over the annulment of his marriage. The king was also cautioned that 'in case he desisted not from his proceedings in the said divorce and separation, but pursued the same and married again, that then within one month after such marriage, he should not longer [sic] be king of this realm; and in the reputation of almighty God, should not be a king one day, nor one hour, and that he should die a villain's death'.[68] Elizabeth and her adherents were hanged at Tyburn.

Katherine herself refused to go quietly. Even with Queen Anne on the throne and the new baby Princess Elizabeth being rocked by her nurses, Katherine refused to be known as Dowager Princess of Wales.[69] Despite the threat of the annulment hanging over her and scholars debating the legitimacy of her marriage and status, Savorgnano reported on his 1531 visit that 'she is not so much visited as heretofore, on account of the king', adding however that she 'has always a smile on her countenance'.[70] It is difficult to evaluate the impact Katherine's refusal to accept the annulment had on later events. Henry repeatedly asked her to agree to it, which suggests he believed he could have secured it more easily with her consent. Sander, writing during the reign of Elizabeth I, also believed that 'the divorce once agreed upon by the king and queen, the queen, a saintly woman, desirous of a more austere life, would without difficulty withdraw into a monastery'.[71] If Katherine had agreed to the annulment of her marriage, would Henry have had to break with Rome in such a violent and revolutionary way?

After some deliberation, Pope Clement VII stated that the marriage was lawful, ruling that 'the said Katherine the queen is to be restored to, and reinstated in, her former rank', and Anne Boleyn removed from the king's side.[72] Predictably, this rebuttal from the Pope led to harsher measures from Henry, including England's break with Rome and the later Dissolution of the Monasteries. But even if Katherine had gone quietly to live in a nunnery, religious restructuring in England at some level was likely before the close of the century. The printing press, the availability of religious texts, new ideas spreading from Europe and philosophical questions about political styles had been discussed since at least the 1520s and so it is probable that England, with or without the King's Great Matter, was already hurtling towards change.

The realm also saw the tragic executions of those who denied Henry's supremacy over the Pope during the 1530s, including monks, priors and abbots. Sander believed the divorce to have been the trigger for these events, stating that 'God did not suffer the king to become the head of the Anglican Church by any other means than by first divorcing Catherine, his most saintly wife, and putting in her place, still living, Anne Boleyn'.[73] Again, if Katherine had quietly agreed to the annulment, would these deaths have happened? Debating 'what ifs' in history can be risky, and while we can speculate over the long-term impact of Katherine and Henry's individual actions relating to the annulment, there are too many factors at play to give a realistic and accurate assessment. What is certain is that the event affected those living in England and Europe during this period, who experienced shock, change and revolution triggered by the king and queen's separation.

During their marriage, Henry and Katherine's support of artists and craftspeople provided work and a welcoming, thriving royal court within which they could network with like-minded creatives and share knowledge. This attracted artists such as Holbein, who first arrived in England during their reign. The nation soon experienced a new wave of Renaissance activity, which impacted the rest of the sixteenth century and beyond. Henry's mother and father had also played host to foreign artists and thinkers, but the longer-term impact is thanks more to Henry and Katherine's interest. They bounded with creative energy, leading new styles in fashion that later epitomized the Tudor age and experimented with elaborate costumes inspired by influences from around the world. The theatrical arts reached a new level of luxury and expression, and they posed for some of the earliest miniature paintings created within the realm. Although this art form reached new heights at the court of Elizabeth I, artists like Nicholas Hilliard owed his later success to Lucas Horenbout and other miniaturists of the early 1500s.

An outburst in education and literature was also driven by the pair. Even Sander, who was no fan of Henry, conceded that 'he was not unversed in learning, that he encouraged learned men, and increased the salaries of certain professors'.[74] Katherine, too, supported education and the growth of literature. Antonia McLean, in *Humanism and The Rise of Science in Tudor England* stated that 'it is therefore partly due to Katherine's interest and influence that a whole generation of highly educated women permeated the upper ranks of English society by the middle of the sixteenth century'.[75] The couple were supporters of writers including Erasmus, More and Vives, authors that would go on to have a profound effect on the education of Tudor royals and their subjects during the age.

Curious onlookers from overseas viewed the Tudor regime as one of power, prestige and ability. Henry and Katherine directed commanders and their armies during war, held academic debate with intellectuals, defended their realm from invaders and presided assertively at state events. We also see an increase in the diversity of the realm. As well as Katherine's Spanish entourage and foreign craftspeople at court, between 1509 and 1530 Italian, Dutch, Spanish, French, German, Scottish and Greek natives settled in England.[76] Not all were welcomed warmly. In 1517, 'evil disposed people' rebelled in London's streets against foreign merchants and tradesmen, triggered by the preaching of an Easter sermon and boasts of Italian and French natives being 'in such favour with the king and his council'. The riot was quickly dispersed and placed under control.[77]

One of the predictions made in 1534 by the mystic Elizabeth Barton was that the 'Lady Katherine should prosper and do well, and that her issue the Lady Mary the king's daughter should prosper and reign in this realm and have many friends to sustain and maintain her'.[78] This prophecy was correct as Mary did reign as England's first queen regnant from 1553 to 1558. Her accession created a new role for women at the head of Tudor society, and one for her partner, as consort. The revolutionary concept of a woman ruler in early Tudor England was an outcome Henry refused to fully acknowledge. He took five more wives after Katherine and fathered a daughter (Elizabeth) and son (Edward), but there is no evidence he fathered any children after 1537. As he lay close to death at Whitehall towards the end of January 1547, Henry realized that he had caused a constitutional crisis. He had only one legitimate heir, Edward; the son of Jane Seymour, his third wife. The daughters from his first two marriages, Mary and Elizabeth, had been made illegitimate by Act of Parliament at the end of their mothers' marriages to him. In theory, Henry could have legitimized them in birth order, but instead chose to shoehorn them awkwardly into the succession after their nine-year-old half-brother. At the time of Henry's death, Mary was thirty-one years old.

As Giles Tremlett has pointed out in *Catherine of Aragon Henry's Spanish Queen*, considering Mary's accession an achievement of the couple is ironic, as it is the one outcome Henry was so determined to avoid and triggered his annulment to Katherine.[79] However they both instilled in Mary, as Henry did with all his children, a love of learning and sense of duty and Mary, once queen, would be remembered for working on state business long into the night. She was also committed to Catholicism despite the religious changes imposed by her father and brother and maintained strong relationships with her mother's family and friends. The couple's work in preparing Mary for an active role in government, although they probably imagined it would be as consort to a foreign prince, must not go unnoticed.

Despite its premature end, the relationship between Henry VIII and Katherine of Aragon shaped the lives of their subjects, the state of the realm and the future of the Tudor era. Their subjects celebrated, rebelled and mourned over various phases of their marriage and enjoyed a more diverse, cultural, patriotic and stable realm as a result of it. Katherine died at Kimbolton Castle in Cambridgeshire on 7 January 1536 and was buried in a tomb at Peterborough Cathedral. Henry died on 28 January 1547 at Whitehall in his mid-fifties and was buried with his third wife Jane Seymour at St George's Chapel, Windsor Castle.

Chapter 3

Lady Margaret Douglas and Thomas, Lord Howard

THE WORKING PARTNERSHIP and personal bond between Henry VIII and Katherine of Aragon caused swift and significant change to various aspects of Tudor life. However, one decision made in 1513 set in motion a course of events and an outcome neither of them could have foreseen. Following Katherine's rapid action against James IV at Flodden in September of that year, the dead and mutilated body of the Scottish king lay lifeless on a battlefield in the north of England. His queen, now widowed, was therefore free to marry again. It was a child born to this second marriage that changed the course of Tudor history.

Margaret Tudor, the eldest daughter of Henry VII and Elizabeth of York, married James IV of Scotland on 8 August 1503 at the age of thirteen at Holyrood, glittering in jewels and a gown of white damask embroidered with gold.[1] One portrait of Margaret, created at the time of her wedding, may give us an idea of her appearance. In 1503 James presented a Book of Hours, now in the collection of the Austrian National Library, to his bride as a wedding gift. In one of the illustrations, James kneels at an altar, crowned and enrobed before Christ. In another, Margaret clasps her hands in prayer before the Virgin Mary, her hair tucked underneath a headdress topped with a crown. She is depicted with a full face and round eyes. Margaret and James' first child was born in 1507, but died in infancy.[2] More pregnancies followed, and in April 1512, their son James, the future James V of Scotland was born at Linlithgow Palace near Edinburgh. The following year, James faced Henry and Katherine's army at Flodden and was defeated and killed. James V became King of Scotland at just seventeen months old.

The accession of an infant ruler to a throne was never a desirable outcome, creating opportunities for imbalances of power, political division and even civil war. James had decided that in the event of his early death Margaret would be appointed regent to guide her son, as long as she remained a widow. Unexpectedly however, Margaret married the ambitious and headstrong Archibald Douglas, Earl of Angus the following year. Margaret was quickly relieved of her regency and fled to England. Here, as brisk winds lashed against the stone walls of Harbottle Castle in Northumberland, she gave birth to a daughter, Margaret, on 8 October 1515.

The daughter of the former Queen of Scotland and the Earl of Angus had a difficult start in life. Her parents separated when she was around five or six years old and from the early 1520s she was brought up by her father with little contact with her mother. After one failed attempt by Angus to seize power, the young Margaret and her father went on the run. They travelled south, temporarily lodging with supporters before reaching Berwick, the home of Thomas Strangeways in 1529. Angus departed the castle, leaving his daughter with gentlewomen and a servant to attend on her. In the summer of that year, Strangeways wrote to Cardinal Wolsey to inform him of Margaret's whereabouts conveying fears that, just around two miles from the Scottish border, 'she would be stolen and withdrawn into Scotland'.[3] The fifteen-year-old made her way south and in early 1530 entered the luxurious court of her uncle, Henry VIII.

Henry welcomed Margaret warmly, awarding her £6 13s 4d (the equivalent of around £2,941 today) to 'disport herself this Christmas' and ordered clothes for her in the latest Tudor fashions. One wardrobe record from Margaret's early years at court includes a black velvet gown furred with powdered ermine, sleeves and kirtles in crimson and black and fourteen pairs of shoes.[4] The teenager's eyes would have flickered across an outwardly extravagant and confident royal court that glinted in the candlelight. Entertainments and dinners were arranged methodically and under heavy protocol, as halls and chambers trickled with laughter, music and dancing. Under the surface though, it was vulnerable and irreparably fractured. Behind closed doors, advisors pored over legal books long into the night, looking for evidence that the king and queen's twenty-year marriage had been unlawful. Anne Boleyn's name was regularly scribbled into ambassadors' despatches, one reporting that the king, still very much married, was 'blindly and passionately fond' of her.[5] The court the teenage Margaret Douglas eyed in 1530 sparkled with revolution, suspicion, jealousy and ambition.

Margaret first served in the household of Princess Mary, later joining that of Queen Anne Boleyn. Strickland saw Margaret's appointment to the queen's household as a deliberate move intended to use Margaret's dynastic status to amplify Anne's perceived power and authority. She stated that the 'pride of the new Queen, Anne Boleyn, required the attendance of a lady so nearly allied to the blood-royal as the daughter of the King's eldest sister', adding that Douglas was also soon made first lady of honour to Anne's daughter, Elizabeth.[6] It was while she carried out duties in the tightly-knit corridors of these royal palaces that Margaret laid eyes on another member of court: the queen's young uncle and half-brother of the Duke of Norfolk: Lord Thomas Howard.

Thomas Howard (confusingly, Thomas had the same name as his half-brother and his father) was at that time in his early twenties. Related by blood to Queen Anne, the Howards as well as the Boleyns enjoyed royal favour as a result of Anne's rise. The Howards had a history of service to the crown, Thomas' father serving as Esquire of the Body to Edward IV in the fifteenth century. More recently, he had carried the sceptre and spurs at Henry VIII's coronation in 1509, and led the English victory at Flodden. His eldest son inherited the title on his father's death in 1524, but for Margaret's Thomas, there was no title.[7] He was the old duke's eighth child, the second son born of his second marriage.[8] Nevertheless, although he didn't hold the same dynastic importance as his older half-brother, Thomas still came from a family that in 1530 was politically and socially strong. More importantly, they were linked to Anne, who then held the adoring attention of the king.

Margaret and Thomas fell in love in around 1535.[9] The romance would not last long, but it had huge political, social and even cultural significance on the period, particularly as its end coincided with another serious event: the execution of Henry's once-beloved queen. Anne Boleyn was found guilty of adultery, in what historians now generally believe were invented charges to remove the influence of the Boleyns at court. Anne, kneeling and whispering prayers for her soul, was beheaded by sword on the hazy morning of 19 May 1536, her body tumbled into its grave at the church of St Peter ad Vincula within the Tower of London. Just weeks later, Thomas Howard and Margaret Douglas were being questioned over the nature of their love affair.

For any monarch, leaving behind an irrefutable succession was vital. It was even more important to the Tudors, who led a strong PR campaign from 1485, taking credit for stabilising the realm and ending the Wars of the Roses. The last thing England needed was a resurrection of a violent and bloody civil war, just twenty years after the death of Henry VII.

At the end of May 1536, Henry was flushed with the thrill of a new marriage to Jane Seymour. The future of the Tudor dynasty, though, still hung dangerously in the balance. Henry had ruled for almost twenty-seven years and was forty-four years old. He had two daughters, both of whom he had made illegitimate, reversing any progress he (and his wives) had made to the succession since 1509. His only recognized son, the illegitimate Henry Fitzroy, would die of a short illness just two months later aged seventeen. If Henry VIII should also die suddenly, there was, at the end of July 1536, no undisputed heir to rule in his place. It can't have taken Henry long to realize that the strongest claimant to the throne was the twenty-year-old woman dressed in black velvet, dutifully carrying the train of Queen Jane Seymour's gown: the Lady Margaret Douglas.

During the spring or summer of 1536, in the Palace of Westminster, Thomas Howard took Margaret to one side and quietly proposed to her. The palace, on the site of today's Houses of Parliament, was once a network of chambers and rooms that had been used by royalty since the eleventh century. Nearby were gardens, orchards and a mill, the Thames just a short walk away. Westminster was used primarily as a base for parliament and government business, but had a private entrance for the king that led from the Old Palace to the abbey for state occasions and worship.

It was here in the network of corridors and chambers that Margaret and Howard agreed to marry. Later evidence suggests the couple were ardently in love, and Margaret would have been elated. However, to the sceptical and suspicious Henry, well aware of his advancing age and fragile dynastic position, Howard's act appeared malicious. Could he have been scheming for power, manipulating Margaret in the hope of one day wearing a crown? The Howards had now slipped from favour and no longer had the benefit of Anne Boleyn's reassuring whispers in the king's ear. It must have dawned on Henry that he had unknowingly brought about this crisis through his own earlier actions. As Strickland observed, Henry's 'clumsy and tyrannical legislation, in disinheriting his own children, had advanced his niece Margaret, and her spouse, one of the ambitious Howards, several steps nearer to the throne than her natural place in the succession'.[10]

Henry responded with panic, furiously clapping the pair into the Tower. Parliament was summoned, and Howard charged with treason. The attainder against him affirmed that the 'whole peace, unity, rest and quietness of this realm ... standeth and dependeth upon the certainty and surety of the succession', a fact Henry hardly needed reminding of. Howard was accused of provoking division in the kingdom, and, without 'the knowledge and assent of our most dread Sovereign Lord the King, contemptuously and traitorously contracted himself by crafty, fair and flattering words' to Margaret.[11]

Henry's own paranoia and shock over these events can be felt in the wording of this Act, which also alleged (without evidence) that Henry's sister Margaret Tudor and her now-divorced husband Archibald Douglas were also involved in bringing about the marriage. Howard, the bill stated, had posed a risk not only to the king's honour, but also to the 'great peril and bodily harm' of Henry's 'most royal person', planning to seize the crown should the king 'die without heirs of his body'. Howard had, according to the wording of the act, aspired to the crown 'by her', and spoke traitorous words 'to and with' her.[12] Margaret's mother wrote to Henry on 12 August 1536 in 'sisterly kindness and natural love' on hearing of her daughter's spontaneous betrothal, asking for compassion and offering to have Margaret conveyed back to Scotland.[13] Henry seemed soothed by his sister's words, but decided to keep Margaret safe and secure in England.

Looking at the evidence, it is highly unlikely that Thomas Howard's proposal to Margaret Douglas was motivated by anything other than love. Their own words (which we will come to) demonstrate a strong romantic attachment to one another and there is no record that any convincing evidence proving Howard's guilt in a conspiracy was ever presented. It is also illogical that Howard would choose to mount such a bold bid for the throne at a time when the Boleyns and Howards were treading carefully at court following Anne's fall. Additionally, there is very little information about Thomas in the wider historical record, suggesting that he was not rebellious, overly ambitious or manipulative. If he were, there would certainly be evidence in support of this. Henry's additional claim that his sister Margaret and her estranged husband Douglas were also behind the conspiracy is irrational. The only 'evidence' of their involvement given in the Act is based entirely on rumour. The Act describes this as 'lately bruted [gossiped] and spoken and come to the king's knowledge'. With the absence of any witness testimony or other evidence, the idea that Margaret Tudor would reunite with her divorced husband and attempt to usurp her brother's throne, raising her daughter 'into the favour of the people' is quite a stretch.

Even so, it's hard to believe Margaret and Thomas thought their relationship and subsequent betrothal would be a success. Margaret was destined, as her mother and aunt had been before her, for marriage into a political or social partnership rather than one of true love with a minor member of the aristocracy. Her status too, meant that she was likely to have been noticed by prying eyes at court. An anonymous servant might have managed to conduct a secret love affair with furtive meetings in the intimate brickwork alleys of Hampton Court Palace; the daughter of a Scottish queen and the king's niece would not. The Tudor court was also probably one of the least effective places to conduct a secret liaison with hundreds of servants, courtiers and diplomats hurrying between chambers and corridors while the king was in residence. And yet, it appears that the matter took Henry by surprise, the Act against Howard expressly recording the king's ignorance of the betrothal. For anyone who knew of their relationship, a promise of marriage would have been the next logical step for the couple to take. But according to Henry, at least publicly, the engagement was sudden, motivated by self-interest and threatened his already crumbling plans for the succession.

Regardless of Howard's real motives, he was sentenced to death. He languished in the Tower for over a year before dying of an illness there on 31 October 1537. Margaret, in November 1536, was permitted to move to cleaner, more spacious lodgings at Syon Abbey. Henry probably also believed the company of devout and virtuous women would do his excitable niece some good. However, Syon also prickled with anxiety over the affair. The abbess, Agnes Jordan, nervously wrote to Thomas Cromwell on 6 November 1536 requesting that Margaret's 'lodging and walks' should be approved by 'some person, such as you do trust and think apt'.[14] Even Syon's abbess didn't want to take any chances over the care of her dynastically-valuable charge.

Margaret returned to court life shortly after the birth of Prince Edward. This was no coincidence. Henry now had his long-awaited male heir, born to Jane Seymour on 12 October 1537. Her release also coincided with Howard's death in the Tower. He had been ill for some time and she either returned to court shortly before his death (in which case it was probably obvious to those around him that he would not live much longer) or soon afterwards, as Stow reported.[15]

The Howard-Douglas betrothal doesn't always receive a mention in the history books. But it was of huge importance at the time, impacting later Tudor events. It may even have added some momentum to Henry's attempts to father an heir. If Jane Seymour delivered Edward full-term, the likely date of his conception would have been around late December

1536 or January 1537, four or five months after news of the young couple's betrothal went public. Henry was already impatient over Jane's lack of pregnancy by August 1536, Eustace Chapuys revealing Cromwell told him Henry confided he 'felt himself already growing old, and doubted whether he should have any child by the queen'.[16] The couple were therefore already trying to conceive and had experienced some delay by the summer of 1536. Considering they had been married for just over two months, Henry's exasperation seems, at first, unreasonably excessive. However, when placed in context alongside the discovery of the Howard-Douglas affair just weeks before, we can see Henry's growing irritation at the still-empty space in the royal nursery.

There is even more evidence that Margaret Douglas and Lord Howard were fresh in Henry's mind that month. Chapuys' letter is dated 12 August 1536, the same day Margaret Tudor wrote to urge her brother to show lenience to his niece. As Henry grumbled about Jane's lack of pregnancy, he was weighing up what action to take over his two prisoners. What he needed to do next was ensure that an episode like this could never happen again.

Presiding over parliament, enrobed and crowned, Henry VIII authorized the enacting of a law that forbade 'any man, of what estate or condition so ever he be … to espouse, marry or take to his wife' any of the king's children, sisters or aunts. The bill also extended to the king's illegitimate children and the 'lawful children' of his brothers and sisters. From the moment Henry gave his agreement, any contract of marriage with a member of the Tudor royal family required the king's 'special licence, assent, consent and agreement … in writing under his great seal'. Anyone ignoring this would be legally branded a traitor and suffer accordingly, with punishments including loss of titles, lands, an inability to claim sanctuary and death by execution.[17] By mid-1536 Henry had shown that he could find a legal argument to fulfil any wish, whether it was a divorce, the execution of his queen or the removal of anyone he considered a threat to his person or reign. The axe had already fallen on Henry's wife, his cousins and members of the nobility. Few couples, even the most infatuated, would now take the risk.

With young Edward safe, Margaret brought to heel and Howard breathing his last in the damp and musty confines of the Tower, Henry must have felt in a far stronger position by the middle of October 1537 than he had in the summer of 1536. But the memory of Margaret and Thomas' relationship lingered in the king's mind for years afterwards. In November

1541, his fifth queen, Katheryn Howard, faced accusations of adultery, losing her life on the scaffold months later. Sir Ralph Sadler wrote to Archbishop Cranmer updating him on the queen's investigation. Margaret had, at around this time, entered into another tentative love affair. Sadler stated it was 'His Majesty's pleasure' that Cranmer should 'call apart unto you my lady Margaret Douglas, and first declare unto her how indiscreetly she hath demeaned herself towards the king's majesty; first with the Lord Thomas; and secondly, with the Lord Charles Howard'. He was advised to warn her darkly 'to beware the third time, and wholly apply herself to please the king's majesty'.[18]

What does the evidence reveal about Thomas and Margaret's relationship? Is it possible to determine their real feelings towards one another and the personality traits that were at play? At first this seems an impossible task, the affair being short-lived and conducted mostly in secret. However, there is one document that could cast light on their feelings to one another and the challenges they faced during their separation.

A 500-year-old volume of work exists in the collection of the British Library. The pages are handwritten, inked by at least nineteen different people and bound together in one album. The work is referenced Add MS 17492, but is better known as *The Devonshire Manuscript*, having been discovered among the papers of the Duke of Devonshire at Chatsworth House in the nineteenth century.

Inside, the manuscript contains almost 200 poems and song lyrics reflecting themes of love, honesty, trust and sadness. They were thought to have been written in the 1530s, around the time Margaret Douglas first came to the Tudor court, and include works by Sir Thomas Wyatt, Mary Shelton and Mary Fitzroy (née Howard), all prominent figures within Anne Boleyn's circle. What makes this even more exciting for us is that the manuscript also contains lines reflecting contemporary events believed to have been written by both Thomas Howard and Margaret Douglas.

The use of *The Devonshire Manuscript* as a historical source has been criticized. Debate still surrounds the identity of its contributors and we should remain cautious about assigning biographical meaning to poems within. However, there is compelling evidence for Margaret and Thomas' involvement in the project. The provenance of the manuscript involves Margaret Douglas directly and places it firmly in her possession. Also, the topics and themes explored in the works attributed to the pair closely reflect their biographical timeline, including their separation and imprisonment.

Some of the phrases attributed to them are just too close to known events and circumstances to have been purely coincidental. Alison Weir, in *The Lost Tudor Princess*, called the poems 'deeply personal and minutely relevant' to the couple's struggles and experiences.[19] When placed in their historical context, some of the phrases in the *Devonshire Manuscript* provide a tantalising backdrop to Margaret and Howard's personal life and their feelings towards one another.

In one phrase identified as written by Thomas Howard, there is a reference to imprisonment and a forced separation from a loved one. The original spellings are included here, for accuracy. He writes, 'alas that ever pryson stronge, sholde such too lovers seperate' (f.26r). Margaret Douglas echoes this in her writing, promising 'to love hym best unto my grave' (f.28) and acknowledging the 'great pains he suffereth for my sake, continually, both night and day' (f.28). These lines suggest the couple were, despite Henry's suspicions of a planned political conspiracy, very much in love. The 'pains' suffered by the lover seem to refer to Howard's continual imprisonment after Margaret was moved to Syon and also suggest a sense of guilt. She unleashes bitterness towards Henry and his advisors with a touch of defiance, as she writes 'do what they wyll and do ther warst' (f.59r).

There is also mention of the couple's promise of marriage. Howard writes of his 'suche faythful love to yow I bere' and 'ower harts shal be of one estate', adding that the subject of his affection was 'to whom for ever my hart ys plyte' (f.26r). He also refers to Margaret as 'my lover swete' (f.26r). There is also resilience, reflected in the couple being asked by jailers to give up their love for one another. Howard's is especially moving, considering his later death in the Tower, as he writes of his reluctance to 'deny, whom I wyll love moste hartely, untyll I dye' (ff.28r). Margaret writes that 'I know he wyll not slak hys love, nor never chang hes ffantecy' (f.58r).[20]

Margaret would one day publicly relinquish her love for Howard, although this was likely to have been a calculated decision so that she could return to court and pacify her wounded uncle. She penned a somewhat rehearsed and diplomatically-worded letter to Thomas Cromwell in 1536 stating, 'I beseech you not to think that any fancy doth remain in me touching him [Howard]; but that all my study and care is how to please the king's grace'.[21] There is no record that Howard ever gave up his love for Margaret.

We know that Margaret took great care of *The Devonshire Manuscript*, and continued to remember Howard in her later years. When imprisoned in

1574 by Elizabeth I for her part in another dynastically-sensitive marriage between her son Charles and Elizabeth Cavendish, she was said to have remembered the events of 1536. Strickland quoted a Tudor source that claimed to have recorded Margaret's words 'as I heard her speak it'. It states that Margaret complained, 'Thrice have I been cast into prison, not for matters of treason, but for love matters. First, when Thomas Howard, son to Thomas, first Duke of Norfolk, was in love with myself; then for the love of Henry Darnley, my son, to Queen Mary of Scotland; and lastly, for the love of Charles, my younger son, to Elizabeth Cavendish'.[22] The Howard affair had occurred almost forty years before, but Margaret remembered it as one of 'love matters'.

Raymond Southall, in *The Courtly Maker, An Essay on the Poetry of Wyatt and His Contemporaries*, stated that Margaret had the manuscript in her possession on her marriage to the Earl of Lennox in 1544, having added more of her own writings to the volume in 1540.[23] Alison Weir, in *The Lost Tudor Princess*, gives an even earlier date for Margaret's ownership of the manuscript, considering it likely sometime after 1537.[24] If this is correct, Margaret's possession of the poems dates to her release, and Howard's death in October of that year. It's possible then, considering the timing, that she intended it as a treasured keepsake of their relationship. She certainly kept it for many years. One poem, written in around 1560, was added to the manuscript by her son Henry Stuart, Lord Darnley.[25]

Today, the volume reveals a great deal about the language of courtly love and themes that courtiers of the 1530s were inspired by. It also establishes tentative links between the various authors and poets whose work was featured. Although the manuscript was the collaborative work of a number of writers, the words of Margaret and Thomas are especially intriguing when set against the dramatic unfolding and dismantling of their budding relationship. Even the fact that we are able to read their words today may be down to the couple themselves. As Margaret faced an arranged marriage to Matthew Stewart, Earl of Lennox in 1544, it is entirely possible that she felt compelled to keep the volume in her personal possession in Howard's memory.

Margaret Douglas and Thomas Howard were not a Tudor power couple in the sense that they dictated world events, fought wars or ruled a nation. Their power came from a quieter place of strength and resilience against a king who felt threatened by the dynastic potential of their partnership.

In this case, the greater political strength of the duo belonged to Margaret. She was close in blood to the English throne, her grandparents the founders of the Tudor dynasty. Her mother was a former queen and her half-brother a king. Thomas was the younger half-brother of the Duke of Norfolk and very little about his life and personality is known. The idea that Margaret was naively manipulated by Howard into an ambitious plan to seize the kingdom goes against what we know of her character as a strong and intelligent woman. In this case, Henry grossly underestimated her. Margaret's later life is well documented, and she continued to exert influence throughout the reigns of subsequent Tudor monarchs. It is far more likely from the evidence examined that their attraction was mutual. The Italian Ambassador at the time certainly saw them in more equal terms. He reported, on 17 August 1536, that 'the daughter of the Queen of Scotland, the king's sister, has fallen in love with the Duke of Norfolk's son, and he with her, and they promised marriage'.[26]

Despite the likelihood that Margaret Douglas and Thomas Howard's affair was based on mutual attraction and love, it was also politically reckless and their betrothal would never have been allowed by Henry VIII. She was not the first royal woman to choose a partner of lower social status than herself. Henry VIII's aunt Cecily of York married a Lincolnshire knight named Thomas Kyme and Henry's sister Mary, Dowager Queen of France, married the king's childhood friend, Charles Brandon, Duke of Suffolk. The secrecy with which the pair boldly conducted their meetings strongly suggests that they were fully aware they would attract the king's displeasure, but continued their courtship anyway. Their writing of bitterness and anger at being separated also hints at rebelliousness and defiance. Had the manuscript been discovered while they were imprisoned, the identification of the couple would have been easily ascertained and used as further proof of their insolence. Perhaps the communication was carried out in verse for entirely this reason; that if the manuscript ever fell into hostile hands, it could have been dismissed as a simple collection of poems of courtly love, a theme we know Henry encouraged at court. Their writings and Howard's refusal to yield, even when seriously ill, show quiet protest and persistence, a brave affront to Henry VIII and his power. They also challenged the traditional social customs of the time, particularly the expectation that Margaret, as a woman of royal blood, was too high-born for a life with the man she loved.

The most obvious legacy left by the Douglas-Howard affair is the law created as a result of their betrothal in 1536. This Royal Marriage Act aimed to tighten control over who could marry into the royal family and heavily regulated access to the line of succession. That Margaret could freely contract herself to a minor member of the nobility such as Thomas greatly alarmed Henry, especially when he realized its future dynastic implications and threat to his person. It must have shocked him even more when he grasped that it was his own fumbling decisions that had contributed to its severity.

Secondly, the episode highlighted Margaret's position as a serious claimant to the English throne. As discussed, it may even have provoked Henry to direct new energy into his efforts to sire a son with Jane Seymour. He was certainly impatient for her pregnancy at the time news of the couple's betrothal became known, and the birth of Edward indeed placed Margaret safely further down in the line of succession.

Few members of court defiantly stood up to Henry, who demanded subservience and loyalty from all his subjects. Margaret and Thomas' love affair and betrothal without his knowledge was an insult not only to him as her uncle, but to his royal power. It was also an unwelcome display of boldness, and later, of indignation. Howard's refusal to deny his love for Margaret must have irritated the king further, and it may be for this reason that he remained locked in the Tower and was never released, even after his health noticeably declined. Henry was not used to being challenged, particularly by the younger half-brother of a duke, and this may explain the king's intense reaction towards him. Of course, Howard's links to the Boleyn family and the recently-disgraced queen would not have helped his cause. Today, their story survives as an early example of a young couple standing boldly against the might of Henry VIII, providing a sense of balance to our modern-day perceptions of power in the Tudor court.

The couple left a literary legacy, too. Along with the other contributors to *The Devonshire Manuscript*, they left behind poems and verses that preserve courtly love themes from the 1530s, the period of Anne Boleyn's rule as queen. This is hugely valuable to historians today, considering that Anne's time as consort was just three years in length, between 1533-1536. The historian Carol McGrath, in *Sex and Sexuality in Tudor England*, sees the manuscript as a 'captivating glimpse into the youthful aspect of Henrician courtly society'.[27] We may have Margaret and her relationship with Howard to thank for this. Not only did their relationship inspire some of the verses within its pages, but the document was kept safe throughout the sixteenth century by Margaret herself, in recognition of Thomas Howard, the man who died 'for her sake'.

After Thomas' death in the Tower, Edward Seymour, Earl of Hertford was sent to inform the king. Howard's mother, the Dowager Duchess of Norfolk, had requested to receive his body so that he could be buried by the family. There is no evidence of Henry's reaction, other than he was 'content' to allow her to have the young lord's body, to be buried 'without pomp'.[28] Margaret Douglas lived into the reign of Elizabeth I and died in 1578 in her early sixties. Her elaborate, painted tomb of alabaster and black marble in Westminster Abbey celebrates her life, the children she had with the Earl of Lennox and her royal lineage.

Chapter 4

Henry Courtenay and Gertrude Blount Courtenay, Marquis and Marchioness of Exeter

THE TOWER OF London, where Margaret Douglas and Thomas Howard spent the late summer of 1536, was a strong Norman fortress built by William the Conqueror close to the shore of the Thames. Rising up into the London skyline, it was joined by the spires of the city's many medieval churches. The Tower's central location, tight security and close proximity to other palaces and government buildings in the capital meant that it was a perfect location to lock up anyone who incurred the displeasure of the king.

Margaret Douglas and Thomas Howard would not be the only couple of the Tudor age to be led through its corridors during the increasingly volatile 1530s. Our next power pair moved in conspiratorial circles, holding beliefs and alliances that opposed the crown's own interests while maintaining a shatterproof veneer of obedience and loyalty.

Gertrude Blount was a daughter of William Blount, Baron Mountjoy and his first wife Elizabeth Saye. The Blounts were a prominent family during the Wars of the Roses; the first baron, Walter Blount, created in 1465 by Edward IV. Walter also fought in the Battle of Towton in 1461 in Yorkshire, when the river was said to have run red with the blood of the dead and wounded soldiers.[1]

Walter's descendant, William, was the fourth baron, and served as Master of the Mint during the early reign of Henry VIII, when he excitedly wrote to Erasmus in 1509 promising 'nectar and honey' in England. He would later be appointed Chamberlain to Katherine of Aragon. Erasmus counted Blount among his friends, once referring to him as one of 'the most learned of nobles'.[2] By the time of Katherine and Henry's coronation, William had been widowed by the early death of his first wife, Gertrude's mother, Elizabeth. He remarried, taking as his new bride one of the Spanish ladies that waited on Katherine of Aragon, Agnes de Vanegas. Agnes was listed as present with Katherine at the funeral of Henry VII, and she had therefore served during her uncertain years as Prince Arthur's widow. Working as the queen's Chamberlain, William Blount maintained a good relationship with both Katherine and Princess Mary, and later Gertrude would also enjoy close connections with the two royal women.[3] Loyalty to Katherine of Aragon and her cause, then, was very much a family affair for the Blounts.

In around 1519, in her late teens or early twenties, Gertrude married Henry Courtenay. Courtenay was around twenty-one years old, and had been married before; Gertrude was his second wife. Courtenay's father William was a member of the distinguished aristocracy, but it was through his mother that Courtenay inherited a powerful royal bloodline. She was Katherine Plantagenet, one of the younger daughters of Edward IV and Elizabeth Woodville, making her husband William brother-in-law to Henry VII. Naturally, because of William's close association with the Yorkist royal family, suspicion hovered over him during the reign of Henry VII. Even though he had fought for the king against the Yorkist Pretender Perkin Warbeck in 1487, Henry suspected him of involvement in a rebellion later in the reign. He was deprived of his title, but restored as Earl of Devon following the accession of Henry VIII.[4]

The young Henry VIII and his cousin Henry Courtenay enjoyed a good relationship. They were similar in age and had grown up together in the royal household. Courtenay was trusted by the young king to appear at state events and occupy a coveted position at his court. A keen jouster, he was regularly seen competing at tournaments and was present at the Field of the Cloth of Gold festivities in Calais in 1520.

The Field of the Cloth of Gold marked the historic meeting of two rulers: Henry VIII of England and Francis I of France. The men were accompanied by their wives and other members of their family, their nobility and household servants. Designed as a grand spectacle of peace between the two nations, the kings hugged, enjoyed feasts and dances, and publicly celebrated their intended future relationship as allies. The festivities were typical of early sixteenth-century showmanship, and no expense was spared to show each side as a powerful, wealthy and cultural royal court. There was even an element of the respectful, courtly love theme that Henry and Katherine enjoyed at home, when Francis dined with Katherine and Henry dined with the French queen, Claude. Wine flowed freely, tents were covered with gold fabric and a tiltyard was erected to show off the chosen competitors from each country.

The Courtenay newlyweds each fulfilled individual roles for their king and queen at this significant event. Courtenay was given the opportunity to display his fighting skills at the tiltyard in front of Francis I and his court.[5] Gertrude was probably one of the women described by an onlooker as 'superbly arrayed' as they rode near Katherine of Aragon in wagons and on horseback.[6]

As the sumptuous fabric from gold tents and banners fluttered in the breeze, Courtenay ran in a contest against Francis, where, stated Hall, 'they ran so hard together that their spears brake, and so maintained their courses nobly'.[7] As well as accompanying Henry diplomatically as a senior noble of the realm, Courtenay's careful selection as competitor against the French king helped show off his court as one of chivalry and strength. Courtenay had already proven himself a gifted challenger at home; Henry wouldn't have risked putting an unenthusiastic fighter in front of Francis at this important event.

A painting in the Royal Collection Trust which dates to around 1545 portrays the occasion with frank honesty. Henry VIII rides into the scene from the left clothed in gold, accompanied by an impressive cavalcade weaving through the landscape consisting of guards, nobles, servants and religious advisors. Dogs leap from their owners and horses obediently trot in line with their riders. There are tents decorated with gold cloth, one of them the site of Henry VIII and Francis' meeting. Two fountains in the foreground spout flowing wine, and it is clear that some courtiers have overindulged in the refreshments. Two men nearby can be seen fighting, while another sits at the base of the fountain, hunched over. To the right is the large jousting arena, with wooden boxes erected for spectators. We can just make out competitors on horseback at the central barrier, while ladies and gentlemen look on from the boxes and around the yard.

While Courtenay was lapping up applause at the tiltyard, Gertrude was with Katherine of Aragon and the rest of the queen's ladies. Accounts of the event during that June describe the weather fluctuating between blustery wind, rain and scorching heat. One eyewitness noted that the Englishwomen attending their queen drained large flasks and cups of wine during the tournaments, although this is not perhaps unreasonable, owing to the long hours the ladies spent outside as well as the changeable weather.[8]

Back in England, as the tents and fountains were being dismantled in Calais, the Courtenays resumed positions at their monarchs' sides. Courtenay once again appeared at jousts, including one in front of

Charles V at Greenwich in 1523. In the same year he was sent to receive Christian, King of Denmark and his wife at Dover on behalf of Henry and Katherine.[9] In 1525, Henry rewarded Courtenay with the title of Marquess of Exeter.[10] Gertrude, now a Marchioness, was observed in May 1527 at Greenwich Palace with the ten-year-old Princess Mary walking 'hand in hand', approaching the king 'to the sound of trumpets'. French ambassadors and other spectators were treated to one of the court's typical acts of showmanship as Mary took off her cap, revealing 'a profusion of silver tresses as beautiful as ever seen on human head'. The dancing and feasting continued, observed the Venetian Secretary, as the sun came up.[11]

A painting of the Palace of Greenwich, or 'The Palace of Placentia' as it was also known, shows it as spectators of these festivities would have seen it. Near to the river, it was an ordered collection of red-bricked walls, towers and tall chimneys, from which grey smoke curled up into the sky on colder days. It had a central gatehouse facing the river, flanked by two turrets. In front, rowing boats and small ships sailed past, convenient for speedy travel by barge to other royal houses or those of courtiers. Built in the fifteenth century, like other Tudor palaces it was a complex of interconnected chambers, corridors and halls. Sadly it is one of the 'lost' palaces of the Tudor age, perishing in the seventeenth century when it fell into ruin and was dismantled.

Portraits of Henry and Gertrude Courtenay are difficult to find. However, one contemporary depiction of Courtenay does survive in the *Black Book of the Garter* at Windsor. He is drawn standing in profile with a round face and small nose. He wears a cap and his brown hair falls around his ears. In the drawing, created in 1535, he bears a strong resemblance to portraits of his grandfather Edward IV. It is therefore likely that he somewhat resembled his cousin the king in appearance. As for Gertrude, no authenticated likeness of her has emerged.

As Gertrude danced and processed with Mary at Greenwich in front of the ambassadors, Henry VIII and Katherine of Aragon kept up the public pretence that all was well. They presided over jousts, banquets and dances; the couple's heraldic arms hanging over balconies where musicians played. Henry would have smiled lovingly at his wife as their daughter received the applause of diplomats. Secretly however, his marriage was beyond repair, Henry's passion now fully focused on the queen's young lady-in-waiting Anne Boleyn.

Anne arrived at Henry's court during the early 1520s. It is not certain when the king first became attracted to her, but his love letters (Anne's replies do not survive) are thought to date to 1527, the year Gertrude Courtenay and Princess Mary were seen together at court.[12] Unsurprisingly, because of their close relationship with Katherine and Mary, the Courtenays, and in particular Gertrude, were not supporters of Anne. The genealogist George Cokayne noted that Courtenay signed his name in support of the royal annulment, but it was arguably dangerous for him to refuse even if he had wanted to.[13] The couple's later actions suggest that they remained secretly aligned to Katherine even after Anne Boleyn's coronation. Just months after Anne was crowned, the new royal couple decided to thrust the Courtenays centre-stage.

An account written by Stow describes the christening of the newborn Princess Elizabeth, Anne and Henry's daughter, in September 1533. The church was 'hanged with arras', and a silver font prepared, which 'stood in the midst of the church three steps high', so the ceremony could be seen by onlookers. Among the throng of bishops, dukes and earls who solemnly nodded their respect for the child were the Courtenays. Henry carried a taper of virgin wax and Gertrude was named the princess' godmother.[14] Courtenay's ceremonial role was expected, but there is something surprising about Gertrude's appointment as godmother, especially given her close family ties and relationship with Katherine and Mary. There is, however, a rational explanation. The Boleyn family had aristocratic and even distant royal blood in its line, but Anne was the daughter of a court official and diplomat, and the sister of one of Henry's previous mistresses. She was created Marchioness of Pembroke in a move to boost her social status, but realistically her own credentials as queen were far from regal. It was therefore important for her to gain assent from members of the higher nobility. Just as Strickland saw Anne amplifying her social position by recruiting Lady Margaret Douglas into her own household, the Courtenays also lent much-needed aristocratic support to the birth of Elizabeth. Henry Courtenay was the next male in line to the throne after the king, and a grandson of Edward IV. Gertrude's role as Elizabeth's godmother had another, longer-term benefit to Anne. The role, meant to provide for the religious and moral education of the child, forced an implicit relationship between the marquis, his wife and the new princess. The Courtenays therefore not only provided implied validity and legitimacy to Elizabeth's birth, but also a subtle ceremonial acknowledgement of Anne's status as queen.

After the christening, Stow tells us that once trumpets sounded in celebration guests enjoyed goblets of hippocras along with a selection of wafers and comfits. But as Gertrude drank spiced, sweetened wine and bowed obediently to the king, she would have harboured a dangerous secret. She had been arranging visits, in disguise, with a controversial woman later known as the 'Nun of Kent', Elizabeth Barton.

Barton was a nun from Canterbury who claimed to fall into spiritual trances in which, it was believed, she had 'revelations' and was able to communicate 'inspiration from the Holy Ghost'.[15] As Barton entered these trances, her face contorted and her voice changed. To the God-fearing and superstitious Tudor nation, these trances were treated with curiosity and wonder, Hall reporting that she was 'brought into a marvellous fame, credit and good opinion, of a great multitude of the people of this realm'.[16] The king tolerated her for a while, but when Barton's prophecies began to veer into 'reproach and slander', predicting Henry's own death, he took a sharper interest.[17] In November 1533 Chapuys reported that Barton, who was now imprisoned, insisted that Henry would soon 'lose his kingdom' and was 'damned'. She also declared, precariously, that she had seen the 'seat prepared for him in Hell'. Chapuys added that although the nun had tried repeatedly to see Katherine of Aragon, the former queen wisely never granted her an audience. Katherine, said Chapuys, didn't fear for herself, as she hadn't been involved with Barton, but did have 'fears for the marquis and marchioness of Exeter, and the good bishop of Rochester, who have been very familiar with her'.[18]

In 1538, Gertrude's gentlewoman Constance Bontayn remembered some of this 'familiarity' when questioned on the Courtenays' involvement with Barton. Bontayn told of an old journey Gertrude had undertaken, in disguise, to visit the nun in Canterbury. She maintained that the marchioness never revealed the reason for her visit nor did she disclose any communication the two women shared, except that Barton believed she would one day have 'a very shameful death'. This prophecy was not too far of a stretch, considering the seriousness of her other predictions by this date. On another occasion, the nun came to the Courtenays' home at Horsley, where she 'lay in a trance'. Bontayn initially said she didn't know if Henry Courtenay was at home during Barton's visit, then had a change of heart and said that he was, but she never heard him speak about the nun, 'for whenever he conversed with his wife or any other, this examinate [Bontayn] and others always departed'.[19]

In her own confession given in November 1533, Barton spilled more details of her meetings with the marchioness. She dated the visits to around 'Midsummer last', which placed them in late June or early July 1533. Gertrude had consulted her, said the nun, because she was in the early stages of pregnancy and concerned about the health of her unborn baby. Under interrogation, Barton and her followers also admitted to more scandalous revelations. Barton had shared predictions about the king's reign with both Gertrude and Henry Courtenay, along with Courtenay's chaplain Mr Crispyn and Courtenay's servants.[20]

The site of these meetings, the couple's home at West Horsley Place, is a manor house near the local church of St Mary the Virgin in the village of West Horsley, near Guildford. The couple would have known the twelfth-century church, although they had access to their own private chapel at home.[21] The Courtenays spent much of their time together at West Horsley Place, meeting fellow courtiers and friends in the halls and in their gardens. Today's building has been altered over the centuries, and is now a red-brick mansion with seventeenth- and eighteenth-century renovations.[22]

An inventory of the Courtenays' home in 1538 described Horsley as a sprawling complex of chambers, parlours and other rooms. Gertrude and Henry had their own individual bedchambers, access to a private chapel and kept important papers in an old wooden ship's coffer. In one chamber, the Courtenays kept saddles, harnesses, bows and arrows. Gertrude slept in a nightgown made from black velvet, and owned a number of gowns and jewels. Their servants slept in the house, rising early each morning to work in the buttery, cellar, kitchen, laundry, stable and dining hall. Many of them could play musical instruments, and the rooms and corridors of Horsley would have once rung out with singing as well as the sounds of lutes, harps and virginals. Edward Courtenay, the couple's son, had his own chamber and an Oxford-educated tutor named Robert Taylor. As expected from their position and rank, the couple maintained a large number of servants; Henry had nineteen gentlemen, while Gertrude was waited on by five gentlewomen, one of whom was a Spaniard named Joan Grasgon.[23] The Bishop Richard Fox, in February 1528, had gifted to Henry Courtenay in his will a series of hangings, in nine pieces, called *Le Hercules*, along with a gold salt-cellar with a cover. It is likely that these hangings were unfurled over the walls at West Horsley.[24]

It was against this backdrop that Barton was led inside the Courtenays' sumptuous and extensive Surrey home. Pregnancy and childbirth during the medieval and Tudor periods were dangerous for both mother and child, and Gertrude wouldn't be the first woman to seek spiritual assistance or advice. Barton's claim that the marchioness sought reassurance over an anxious pregnancy may indeed be true. On the other hand, some of the facts don't add up. Bontayn admitted that Gertrude attended at least two long visits with Barton. A simple discussion and request for prayers could have been achieved in one visit of a few hours, and yet there were eyewitness reports that the women dined together and had meetings in a private chamber as well as at Horsley. Gertrude's disguising herself to meet the nun also implies something more conspiratorial. Their first visit, if Barton's timeline is correct, occurred just weeks after Anne Boleyn, visibly pregnant, was crowned queen at Westminster. Could there have been a political motive for Gertrude and Barton's meetings? With her husband so close to the throne, it would have been natural for Gertrude to wonder whether the unborn child of Anne Boleyn was a prince. The discussion of Barton's revelations concerning Henry's reign with not only the couple, but also members of their household, is also suspicious, having nothing to do with requests for prayers or predictions over a pregnancy. In 1538, Courtenay was described by the French ambassador as 'after the King's children, the closest to this crown'.[25] Either of these events; the birth of a prince or Barton's prediction that Henry would fall from power, had the potential to dramatically affect the Courtenays' future. Without further concrete evidence, this is purely speculation, but with so many inconsistencies it is reasonable to wonder whether Gertrude and Henry Courtenay solicited Barton in 1533 to find out if they might one day wear a crown.

Barton had worn out Henry VIII's patience and her supporters were charged with encouraging 'common division and rebellion in this realm to the great peril and danger of our said sovereign lord', and hanged at Tyburn on 20 April 1534.[26] The Courtenays, at least for now, escaped further punishment. Gertrude wrote to the king thanking him for his 'gracious letter' in which he pardoned her for her involvement with the nun. Adeptly swerving from recent events, Gertrude branded Barton 'unworthy, subtle and deceivable' and insisted that she had been 'easily seduced and brought to abusion and light belief'. She also added a note protesting that she never intended 'malice or grudge against the king, the queen or their posterity' and asked him to intercede with her husband Courtenay, 'who is much displeased, to forgive her'.[27]

Gertrude's claim that she never meant 'malice or grudge' to either Henry or Anne was an attempt to pacify the irate king and represent the Courtenays as his loyal servants. And yet there is evidence that within two years of this statement, Gertrude and Henry were actively working towards Anne's destruction.

Alison Weir, in *The Lady in the Tower, The Fall of Anne Boleyn*, identified the Courtenays as among those at court who systematically plotted

Anne Boleyn's fall from power in 1536, along with the Poles, Seymours, Sir Francis Bryan and Sir Nicholas Carew.[28] The couple were certainly very active in state papers during this period. Henry Courtenay was appointed to sit at the queen's trial on 15 May 1536, alongside the Duke of Norfolk, the Earl of Arundel and the Duke of Suffolk.[29] Publicly, Courtenay listened as the queen pleaded innocence of the charges against her. Privately, however, the Courtenays had been jointly conspiring towards Anne's fall for the last six months.

The Imperial Ambassador Eustace Chapuys was no fan of Anne Boleyn. He was, after all, working on behalf of Katherine of Aragon's nephew Charles V, and had no loyalty to the woman who had ousted her. He continued to call Anne 'the concubine' long after she was queen and once wrote of an encounter where he was unable to avoid paying her 'reverence', suggesting that he spent afternoons avoiding the queen in palace corridors.[30] As Charles' representative, it was Chapuys' duty to look out for the interests of Katherine of Aragon and her daughter Mary, and he eagerly listened to news and gossip that had the potential to affect them. The ambassador had one informant in particular who visited him in disguise and whispered valuable information not disclosed during his formal diplomatic meetings with the king: Gertrude Courtenay.

In early November 1535, Gertrude approached Chapuys with a warning. The king, full of typically explosive bluster, announced to 'some of his most confidential councillors' that he wanted to be rid of Katherine and Mary at the next Parliament. Fearing the worst, Gertrude urged Chapuys to inform the women so 'that they might take counsel, and send someone to the Emperor'. She returned to the ambassador again a few weeks later, this time in disguise, revealing that the king was committed to their downfall, and she blamed Anne for her influence in the matter.[31] The following January, Chapuys received more information, this time from both Henry and Gertrude. 'The lady [Gertrude]... and her husband [Courtenay]' revealed that the king had confided to an advisor over suspicions that he was 'seduced by witchcraft' in his relationship with Anne and was already looking to take another wife.[32]

If Henry was already resolved to take a new queen, Anne Boleyn's days were numbered, and further intelligence from Gertrude reveals the couple's involvement in her demise. By 1 April 1536, just six weeks before Anne was beheaded with a sword on Tower Green, Gertrude Courtenay was excitedly informing Chapuys of developments concerning the king's new relationship with Anne's lady-in-waiting

Jane Seymour. She revealed how Jane had kissed a purse of coins from Henry, returned it and declared that she put her honour before any riches. This 'young lady', reported Chapuys, 'has been well taught for the most part by those intimate with the king, who hate the concubine'. Gertrude told Chapuys how Jane was told to push relentlessly for marriage with the king, and was encouraged to bring up his unpopular and now crumbling marriage to Anne. She added that Jane was also to offer the testimony of certain 'titled persons, who will say the same'. That Gertrude knew this strongly suggests that she and her husband were among those 'intimate with the king' who disliked Anne. Courtenay, with his close position of trust and long relationship with Henry, may indeed have been one of the 'titled persons' placed on standby to back up Jane's comments. Chapuys signed off his intelligence by reporting that Jane's rise as queen would be a 'great thing for both the security of the Princess [Mary] and to remedy the heresies here'.[33] Chapuys believed that by removing Anne and installing the more traditional Jane in her place, Henry could be persuaded to slow down or even halt England's new religious policies.

Anne Boleyn's fall was swift and meticulously planned. Gertrude and Henry Courtenay are identified by name as Chapuys' informers in his reports to the Emperor, and Gertrude's statements show she had an awareness of sensitive matters that it was not in her place to know, much less openly discuss. Chapuys is sometimes dismissed as a reliable witness because of his dislike of Anne Boleyn, and this may be true of his descriptions and opinions of the queen. However, we are concerned here with the communication flowing between the Emperor, the Courtenays and Chapuys, for which there is ample evidence. In any case, even idle, unsubstantiated gossip had the potential to damage reputations and deplete power. The intelligence spread by the Courtenays contributed to a wider, anti-Boleyn propaganda movement that reached courtiers, ambassadors, the king (through the lips of his new love Jane) and the foreign rulers of Europe.

Anne was tried and charged with sleeping with her brother and four men of the court; saying that 'the king never had her heart' and that she loved each of these men more than him, and finally, conspiring Henry's death. The charge of witchcraft, alluded to in Chapuys' correspondence, was never brought formally against her during her trial.[34] Nonetheless, the Courtenays' divulging of Henry's private and confidential suspicions did the queen's reputation no good, and Anne's almost certainly false association with witchcraft did indeed endure into later centuries.

After Anne's execution on 19 May 1536, the Courtenays settled back into court life. A sense of calm accompanied a sighting of Gertrude pouring water during a banquet in October 1536 where Jane Seymour, now the queen, the king, Mary and Elizabeth were present. Both partners also attended Prince Edward at his christening on 15 October 1537, Gertrude bearing the three-day-old child, assisted by her husband and Charles Brandon Duke of Suffolk.[35] However if the couple felt any sense of order and tranquillity as 1538 approached, it would soon be shattered.

As 1538 came to a close, the French Ambassador reported that Henry Courtenay, Marquis of Exeter had been sent to the Tower of London along with his friend Lord Montagu. In a hasty, rushed tone, he wrote to the Constable in France relating that the king was 'looking for every opportunity we can think of to ruin and destroy', adding ominously, 'I believe that few lords are secure in this country'.[36] This new plot, named the Exeter Conspiracy after the Courtenays' title, changed the lives of the family and those within their circle forever.

By the August of 1538, Henry's heir, Edward, was almost a year old. The queen, Jane, died shortly after his birth at Hampton Court Palace in October 1537. Henry had already voiced doubts concerning his age and ability to have children. As he inched closer to fifty, his thoughts turned towards ensuring that after his death Edward would enjoy a peaceful succession, as he had done in 1509. Lords, dukes and earls bowed with reverence as Henry strode through palace corridors, but the presence of old, Yorkist blood among them continued to unnerve the increasingly irrational and suspicious king.

Highest on the king's hit list was an Englishman living in Italy, his cousin, Cardinal Reginald Pole. In 1536, Pole had written a book, *De Unitate Ecclesiastica*, in which he criticized the king's actions in breaking with Rome, encouraged Englishmen to take up arms against Henry and hoped once again for an English church under Catholic obedience. Pole's own royal blood added an extra sting to these criticisms. He was the grandson of George Duke of Clarence, brother of Edward IV, and therefore Henry and Pole shared the same great-grandfather, Richard Plantagenet, Duke of York. Pole's writings were both provocative and divisive. Madeleine Dodds, in *The Pilgrimage of Grace and The Exeter Conspiracy*, linked the concepts presented in *De Unitate* as similar to the aims of those in what later became known as the 'White Rose Party', subjects who desired a change of government and the return of

Catholicism to England. Dodds cautioned that the party's goals were ultimately unrealistic, but consisted generally of a plan where 'Charles V should invade England, marry Mary to Reginald Pole, force Henry to acknowledge Katherine, and establish a sort of regency, leaving Henry only the title of King'.[37]

Enraged over the publication of Pole's book, Henry suggested the Cardinal return to England. Pole was not so naïve. The humiliated king and cardinal then embarked on a cat-and-mouse game throughout Europe, with Englishmen even sent abroad to assassinate Pole. As part of the king's investigations into the allegiances of the Pole family and the aftermath of the Pilgrimage of Grace rebellion, Reginald's brother Sir Geoffrey Pole was arrested and questioned. Trembling, the anxious knight promised that he would give the king's interrogators any information they needed.

Over the course of Geoffrey's increasingly unstable examinations, he began to talk about his brothers Reginald and Lord Montagu, but also spoke of the Courtenays and meetings the group held at their home in West Horsley. He testified that they had grumbled about the state of the realm and speculated on Cardinal Pole's whereabouts. On one occasion they discussed the planned assassination of the cardinal and gossiped about who had been sent to carry it out. Montagu had also said the king would soon die, referring to his painful and ulcerated calf. 'His leg will kill him', he had joked unwisely, 'and then we will have jolly stirring'.[38]

These revelations sparked a new round of arrests and interrogations. Witnesses were called and anyone who knew the Courtenays, Poles or other members of the group were rounded up and examined. Mrs Couper, the wife of a London goldsmith, remembered Courtenay's yeoman of the horse telling her at her shop that the marquis would dismiss anyone that read the Bible in English, one of the reforms imposed by the king. Gertrude's gentlewoman Constance said that she had once heard her mistress complain that 'noble men are put out and the king takes in others at his pleasure', possibly a veiled reference to men like Thomas Cromwell, who were not of high birth, but had risen to their elevated positions through hard work and royal service.[39]

Lord Montagu and Henry Courtenay were taken to the Tower on 4 November and Gertrude was also questioned. Her previous involvement with Elizabeth Barton in 1533 was raised along with comments from one of Courtenay's servants back in 1531, who stated that one day Courtenay would be king and they would be lords.[40] The rehashing of these prior events attempted to publicly discredit the Courtenays, building a case against them as disloyal, meddling and ambitious traitors. Sir Edward Neville was also accused of singing songs about the planned assassination of Reginald Pole and expressing the hope that 'lords should reign again one day'.[41] As the net widened, investigators arrested Margaret Pole, the ageing Countess of Salisbury and mother of Reginald, Geoffrey and Montagu. Her house was searched, and she was later quizzed and installed in the Tower. Investigators later accused her of writing letters to Reginald and claimed to have found Catholic symbols in her possession, similar to one used during the Pilgrimage of Grace uprising.

During the trial, Courtenay gestured with 'casting up of eyes and hands as though those things had never been heard of before', in visible disbelief of his charges as well as in frustration. It was observed that 'the Marquis of all the rest stuck hardest ... was stiff at the bar, and stood fast in denial of most things laid to his charge'.[42] It did no good for his cause, and sentence was proclaimed. Gertrude Courtenay was singled out as having 'traitorously, falsely, and maliciously confederated herself to and with the abominable traitor Nicholas Carew, knowing him to be a traitor and a common enemy to his Highness and the realm of England... also hath herself committed and perpetrated divers and sundry detestable and abominable treasons to the fearful peril of his Highness's royal person, and the loss and desolation of this realm of England'. Henry Courtenay was, according to the judgement, 'a false traitor, machinating the death of the king, and to excite his subjects to rebellion ... seeking to maintain the said Cardinal Pole in his intentions'.[43]

Cokayne believed that the Courtenays intentionally plotted against the king, stating that Courtenay 'drifted into a treasonable conspiracy with the Pole family, endeavouring to raise the men of Devon and Cornwall'.[44] However other historians doubt that an 'Exeter Conspiracy' ever actually existed, let alone posed any real risk to the king. Madeleine Dodds, in a detailed study of these events, called the charges 'ridiculous', pointing out that the group were 'less a political party than a group of friends, who loved the old Faith, hated Cromwell, and longed for a change of policy. They met and talked treason and sang political songs in the marquis' garden at Horsley and in the woods at Bockmore'.[45] Bockmore was a residence of the Pole family in Buckinghamshire.

And yet, there was a common theme between them all: every one of them was a descendant or supporter of prominent Yorkist families. Henry

Courtenay was the king's first cousin, sharing Edward IV as their grandfather; Montagu and the other Pole brothers descended from Edward IV's brother George, Duke of Clarence; Margaret Pole was Clarence's daughter. The Courtenays, who had been on the other side of secrets and conspiracy for so many years, should have known the risks of listening to bawdy, political songs in their garden, complaining about the king and loudly hoping for future change. Henry was also rattled by talk of letters shared among his cousins and then burned, presumably to avoid them reaching him or his officials. This, along with the testimonies of witnesses, sparked new doubts over the group's real intentions and their loyalty not only to him, but also to his son.

The French Ambassador wrote in 1538 that 'it was a long time ago that this king [Henry VIII] told me that he wanted to exterminate this House of Montagu, which is still of the White Rose, and the House of Pole of which the Cardinal is'.[46] As historians have acknowledged, there is very little evidence for an organized, serious plot by the Courtenays. The nature of the interrogations, the family ties that existed between them and the jostling of anyone involved into the Tower for questioning points to a rushed political attack on the group rather than any real administration of justice or investigation of a crime. This was picked up by Dr Peter Heylin in the following century, when he wondered why Courtenay and Lord Montagu would have conspired to make Reginald Pole king when they both had stronger claims to the throne than he did.[47] Additionally, the public rehashing of the Courtenays' old, long-forgiven offences during their rushed trial also implies the prosecution lacked convincing new evidence against the pair in relation to the conspiracy. If they had, these older misdeeds would not have been needed.

On 9 December 1538, Henry Courtenay was beheaded, with Lord Montagu and Edward Neville on Tower Hill. Geoffrey Pole remained imprisoned. In the Tower were also Gertrude Courtenay and the couple's twelve-year-old son Edward. Montagu's son was also imprisoned. Margaret Pole faced the axe five months later on the morning of 27 May 1539.

Gertrude was released after almost eighteen months in the Tower, in April 1540. During her captivity in the fortress, she was attended on by two women; a maid and her household servant Constance Bontayn, who had originally related details of her mistress' involvement with Elizabeth Barton in 1533. However, any idea that she lived according to her high status while imprisoned would be inaccurate. Gertrude complained that she had no money with which to pay her maid, and that Constance 'hath no manner of change and that that she hath is sore worn'. Gertrude too, petitioned for a change of clothes, pointing out that she only had that which the king had provided.[48]

Gertrude would have to return home without her husband or her son. Edward Courtenay remained in custody, another sign Henry was anxious over the bloodline of the boy. He was eventually released by Queen Mary following her accession in 1553. Gertrude returned to the court of Mary I and died in 1558. She was buried in a tomb at Wimborne Minster, Dorset.

It is easy to view Gertrude, from the sources alone, as meddling and conniving. She collected secrets from court and spread them to powers that stood to gain the most from them. Meanwhile, she appeared obedient and loyal, playing the dutiful noblewoman in public. But what if Gertrude was motivated by a desire for real change? She was a supporter of Katherine of Aragon and her daughter Mary, and had seen first-hand how the king had treated the two women. She also had previous family ties to them, through her father and stepmother. Chapuys told the Emperor in 1533 that Gertrude was 'the only true comforter and friend the Queen [Katherine] and the Princess [Mary] have'.[49] If Gertrude could use her position and influence to assist them, then this explains her interference from a more sensitive angle.

Henry Courtenay was also involved in his wife's exchanges with Chapuys. He is identified, along with Gertrude, as conveying highly sensitive and damaging allegations of Anne Boleyn's supposed 'witchcraft'. The information did not find itself in the charges against the queen, but was a shocking and valuable piece of propaganda and quickly forwarded to the Emperor. It is also likely, considering Courtenay's position close to the king, that much of Gertrude's information came directly from her husband. Gertrude's sources are identified in cloak-and-dagger descriptions in Chapuys' letters as prominent persons, confidantes or advisors. Courtenay was perfectly placed to overhear or witness these exchanges. Henry VIII was not, as far as we know, aware that Gertrude was feeding information to Chapuys and wouldn't have been concerned at his cousin's presence during private conversations.

There are more questions over the couple's involvement in the Elizabeth Barton affair. In late 1533 Gertrude complained to the king that her husband was 'so displeased with me, to mine extreme sorrow and discomfort'.[50] These words imply a sense of shock that Courtenay had stopped speaking with his wife in punishment for the disapproval she had brought upon the family. Yet, it is unlikely that Courtenay knew nothing of his wife's involvement with the nun. The couple's servants testified that Barton visited West Horsley, with the family at home at the time. They even knew she had been in one of her famous trances there. It is illogical to conclude that Courtenay was oblivious of visits from a well-known and controversial personality, especially as his servants knew so much about them. Testimony from Barton and her supporters also acknowledged that the marquis had been told of revelations concerning the king. Gertrude's agonising plea for matrimonial support from the king then, seems somewhat ingenuine. While this is indeed speculation, it is possible Gertrude used the letter to consciously create distance between her husband and Barton. With Gertrude leading all communication with the nun, she was able to simply plead ignorance and foolishness on being discovered (as she did), while Courtenay's own, more detached, position was protected. If Courtenay had been discovered initiating visits with Barton and welcoming her into his home to discuss the king's future, the outcome would have been decidedly different. Here, Gertrude held her own significant power in the relationship. The sources show that she was intelligent, versatile and articulate, but could innocently plead 'womanly' ignorance when in trouble, and was believed. Unlike her husband, Gertrude posed no threat to Henry, one historian remarking that the reason she was saved from the axe was 'because she had no Blood-Royal in her veins'.[51]

Henry and Gertrude Courtenay are not well-known, household names today, but they impacted the lives of many Tudor figures that are. By warning Chapuys over Henry's deteriorating patience with Katherine of Aragon, trouble could be pre-empted and the Emperor consulted for his advice. During Anne Boleyn's trial, Courtenay watched as she eloquently fought for her life, but privately spread propaganda and conspired to trigger her downfall. We can also find their trace in the rise of Jane Seymour. Gertrude had knowledge of the coaching Jane received from anti-Boleyn courtiers and related it to Chapuys with excitement. Charles V would have read his reports with interest.

Through their gatherings of 1538, the couple may also have affected the future of Reginald Pole. Examinations revealed their friendship group held delicate and potentially explosive knowledge, including Henry's plan to assassinate the Cardinal. They even knew the names of men sent to carry out the murder. Investigations discovered that Lord Montagu and Margaret Pole had been in touch with Reginald by letter, raising the possibility that they were able to warn him of the king's plans. This would have helped influence his whereabouts and contributed to the safeguarding of his life so he could return to England later in the era. The deliberate burning of letters within the group implies that their contents were certainly secret or even treasonous, but we have no way of knowing. Reginald Pole later returned to England at the request of Mary Tudor in 1553, to assist the queen in re-establishing the Catholic faith.

The fallout from the Exeter Conspiracy lingered long after Henry Courtenay's head had been struck from his shoulders. The deaths of Lord Montagu, Edward Neville and Nicholas Carew affected their own families and children. Margaret Pole was implicated towards the end of the investigation of the Courtenays and Poles. The daughter of an attainted royal duke, she had survived the later Wars of the Roses, the accession of Richard III and the disappearance of her cousins, the Princes in the Tower. She had also navigated five decades of Tudor rule, winning the support of Henry VII and Henry VIII. And yet her life ended on the block at 67 years of age, over letters she had sent to her sons and the discovery of an embroidered tunic.

Henry VIII was always conscious of rival claimants to his throne, but as his reign progressed, the king's actions became more temperamental and indicative of paranoia. The Exeter Conspiracy extinguished some of the last few Yorkist relatives that hovered at court, but the affair couldn't have helped his already troubled state of mind, and may have even exacerbated it, leading to increasingly irrational behaviour. In the 1540s, immediately after the Exeter Conspiracy, a trail of those once loved by the king filed solemnly to the block. Among these was Thomas Cromwell, Henry's astute and wily secretary who paved the way for Katherine of Aragon's annulment, Anne Boleyn's fall and co-ordinated the closing of the monasteries. Unfortunately, in 1540 he led the king into an unsatisfactory marriage (and subsequent divorce) with his fourth wife, Anna of Cleves. He met his end at the block in July of that year. Two years later Katheryn Howard, Henry's fifth queen, was beheaded over allegations of adultery and failure to inform the king about her sexual past before their marriage. Kateryn Parr narrowly missed a potentially similar fate over her religious beliefs, but interceded with the king and won his trust. As the end of Henry's reign approached, his sanctioning of the axe seems to have been almost a knee-jerk reaction to any perception of mistrust or humiliation. At the end of his reign, Henry authorized the execution of Henry Howard, Earl of Surrey. The earl had quartered the royal arms with his own, tactlessly advertising the prestige of his distantly-acquired royal blood. He was executed in January 1547, just days before the king himself died.[52]

The Courtenays, through Henry and his mother's royal Yorkist blood, held dynastic power that had the potential to unsettle Henry VIII as he sensed his growing vulnerability. However, the real strength in their combined influence came from their understanding of the currency of knowledge. As active participants at the centre of royal life, they witnessed events and formed close ties with others within the king's circle. At the centre of all they were part of was information: it was sought from Elizabeth Barton, shared with Chapuys and ridiculed during the Exeter Conspiracy. Behind it all seems to have been a genuine incentive to effect change; in religion, court politics and perhaps also in rule. But they were also careless. Aligning themselves with the Poles, who had lived under Henry's fury since 1536, was their big mistake. Mocking the king, joking about his death and listening to songs written about sensitive and damaging state secrets drew the king's attention to the Courtenays and the events that had taken place at Horsley.

Chapter 5

Edward and Anne Seymour, Duke and Duchess of Somerset

ON 20 MAY 1536, as news of Anne Boleyn's death trickled into the taverns and ale houses of England, Henry and Gertrude Courtenay looked forward to a new style of queenship under her successor, Jane Seymour. But two other courtiers watched Jane's rise with keen, personal interest. The fall of Anne Boleyn set in motion a chain of events that, almost a decade later, made the Seymours the most powerful duo in England.

Anne Stanhope was a descendent of Edward III, her lineage proudly inscribed in gold on her tomb in Westminster Abbey. Her parents were Sir Edward Stanhope and Elizabeth, the daughter of Sir Fulke Bourchier, Lord FitzWarin. The monument traces her bloodline through Thomas Woodstock, Duke of Gloucester to Edward III and Queen Eleanor and refers to her as a 'Princesse descended of noble lineage'.[1]

By the mid-1530s, Anne married Edward Seymour, then about thirty years of age.[2] She was his second wife, his first Catherine Fillol, daughter of the Essex knight Sir William Fillol. Edward's marriage with Catherine produced two sons, John and Edward, who were later disinherited in favour of his children with Anne, who has often been blamed for pressuring her husband to write the boys out of their inheritance. However, there are also rumours that Catherine was unfaithful. Neither accusation against these women has ever, as far as can be ascertained, been proven.

Like the Stanhopes, the sixteenth-century Seymours were also of royal descent, claimed through Edward and Jane's mother Margaret Wentworth to Lionel, Duke of Clarence son of Edward III. Henry VIII certainly considered the Seymours' bloodline of significance, obtaining a dispensation for his marriage to Edward's sister Jane, in May of that year.

The Seymours enjoyed a speedy rise to power through their service to the crown, although this was obviously boosted by Jane's new status as queen. Edward was created Viscount Beauchamp just over two weeks after the wedding and raised to Earl of Hertford a few days after the birth of Prince Edward. Edward and Anne both served in the royal household. Edward is prominent in Henry's Privy Council records and entertained French ambassadors at his home in January 1546. Anne met Anna of Cleves on a visit to Hampton Court Palace in 1541 and conducted her to her apartments, accompanied by the Duchess of Suffolk and other ladies. Both Anne and Edward were also present at the wedding of the king and his sixth wife Kateryn Parr at the palace in 1543.[3]

There is some evidence that together the couple eased the way for Jane Seymour's rise as queen in 1536. Gertrude Courtenay told Chapuys that Cromwell was ordered to vacate his chamber so the king could visit Jane in secret, lodging there in his place 'the eldest brother of the said lady [Jane] with his wife, in order to bring thither the same young lady'.[4] This links the Seymours with another power couple, the Courtenays, both enabling Jane's rise during Anne Boleyn's last months as queen.

Tragically, it was probably the circumstances of his sister's early death that protected Seymour's long-term friendship with the king. Jane died in October 1537 following the birth of Prince Edward, having been married to Henry for just over a year. She had produced the king's longed-for male heir, and her unexpected death at the height of her power left no cloud or scandal over their relationship. She was painted, in a wall mural at Whitehall Palace, standing with her husband and the Tudor founders Henry VII and Elizabeth of York, taking her place in the dynasty. Holbein completed the work in 1537, the year of her death.[5] It is also with Jane that Henry requested to be buried, and they share a tomb in the quire of St George's Chapel in Windsor Castle. With Jane's lasting legacy and Henry's enduring fondness towards her, Edward was able to exercise influence over Henry for the remainder of the reign, unlike the relatives of disgraced queens Anne Boleyn and Katheryn Howard. Henry clearly trusted Seymour and after his sister's death was trusted with duties including negotiations with France in the 1540s and serving as Great Chamberlain of England and Lieutenant General of the North.[6] An ever-present companion and servant of the king, he was there until the very end of the old king's reign. At the close of January 1547, as Henry sucked in his last, laboured breaths inside the vast Palace of Whitehall, Edward Seymour was made an executor of his royal brother-in-law's will. As Edward VI later wrote in his journal, it was also his uncle Seymour who rode to personally inform him of his father's death.[7]

Surprisingly, Seymour's assumption of the role of Lord Protector to oversee the nine-year-old Edward VI during his minority rule was not something Henry had ever arranged. Keen to establish a peaceful succession for his son, the king instead planned for a group of sixteen carefully selected councillors to guide and steer the young king in his duties until he was old enough to rule alone.

But as Henry lay dying, Seymour and Henry's Chief Secretary William Paget whispered to one another their plans for a protectorate government with Seymour at its head. A private letter from Paget to Seymour, dated 7 July 1549 and written when he was firmly in place as Protector, is thick with intrigue. 'Remember what you promised me in the gallery at Westminster before the breath was out of the body of the king that dead is', wrote Paget. 'Remember what you promised immediately after, devising with me concerning the place which you now occupy ... And that was to follow mine advice in all your proceedings, more than any other man's'.[8] This arrangement, beneficial to both men, changed the course of history.

In the hours after Henry's death, Seymour sprang into action. He first rode to collect Edward, who was at Hertford, and brought him to London. He had the support of Paget, but Seymour also needed the backing of other members of the king's council. Susannah Lipscomb, in *The King is Dead, The Last Will and Testament of Henry VIII*, points out that Seymour even canvassed the support of Sir Anthony Browne, Master of the King's Horse, while on their journey to retrieve Edward.[9] When the council finally met, Henry VIII's vision of a sixteen-man regency council was shelved in favour of Seymour's protectorate. Edward VI later wrote in his journal that the men agreed because Seymour 'was the king's uncle on his mother's side'.[10] This was a heavily simplified version of events. The protectorate was in fact formed by conspiracy, negotiation and campaigning and not the simple presence of family ties. As part of the deal, Seymour was elevated to the title of Duke of Somerset and, the day after Edward was proclaimed king, he was named Lord Protector and Governor of the King's Person on 1 February 1547. It had taken Seymour just four days to take control of the kingdom.

Sir John Hayward, writing during the Elizabethan period, considered Edward Seymour a man who never had 'haughtiness in himself, or in contempt of others, but remained courteous and affable ... never aspiring higher than to be the second person in state'.[11] And yet Seymour's desire for power appears so strong that he would disregard the terms of his brother-in-law's will to achieve it. On the other hand, having worked so closely with Henry, he would have known that the ageing king's biggest fear was to leave the kingdom at risk of civil war. It is possible that this is what drove Seymour to seize control, knowing that the previous shared regency between the brothers of Henry V in 1422 had resulted in just that.

Seymour's activity in the weeks immediately before and after Edward VI's accession is well-documented. There is little written evidence, however, for Anne Seymour's involvement in his swift elevation to power. For a woman who would become so notorious for her prominent role advising her husband, this might seem strange. For an explanation, we can look to Paget's letter, highlighting in its secrecy the very real risk of speaking of the king's death. Bearing this in mind, the married couple would have had plenty of opportunity at home to discuss plans verbally and privately, particularly if they were of a politically sensitive nature. We should not conclude that the absence of written evidence of Anne's involvement in her husband's rise demonstrates that she had no part in it. Her own actions and character, as we will see, in fact make it very likely that she was involved in the events of January 1547, although her impact can be seen far more clearly once her husband was established as Protector; as his supporter, promoter and advisor.

Despite being the wife of the most powerful man in the kingdom in 1547, Anne Seymour is rarely credited for any specific influence she had with her husband over mid-Tudor events. Hayward stated that the duchess had a 'monstrous pride', and was 'both subtle and violent in accomplishing her ends'. He quoted a speech he stated was made by Richard Rich, Lord Chancellor, which accused the duke of being 'so peevishly [opinionated] and proud, that he would neither ask, nor hear the advice of any, but was absolutely ruled by that obstinate and imperious woman his wife, whose ambitions and mischievous will so guided him in the most weighty affairs of the realm'.[12] It is not clear whether Rich actually spoke these words or if they were added by Hayward as imagined context, but the inference is clear: Anne had gained a reputation for her heavy involvement in state affairs.

Early historians are unforgiving when it comes to their assessments of Anne, but they were confined by contemporary views and driven by gender and societal expectations of their time. Anne would not be the first or last woman in history to be verbally attacked for having confidence, outspokenness and ambition; the Empress Matilda, Margaret of Anjou and Anne Boleyn are other women of power who experienced similar treatment from writers of their time. Hayward summed up feelings that were acceptable during the Tudor age, but shocking to modern readers when he wrote that 'a woman was first given to man for a comforter but not for a councillor, much less a controller and director'.[13]

Portraits of the couple created in their lifetimes reveal how they would have appeared to their contemporaries. Edward is usually portrayed in sombre robes, complete with a cap and sporting a long reddish beard. His expression is serious, his eyes either gazing off in the distance to one side or glancing out at us, slightly guarded. There are fewer authenticated likenesses of Anne, but one created in the eighteenth century is said to have been copied from an original by the sixteenth century artist Antonis Mor. She is portrayed with a small, pursed smile, round eyes and curls of light-coloured hair peeking out from under her headdress. She wears an elaborate high-necked gown of the period with a small ruff under her chin. Her sleeves are long, and the fabric ruched. In her hands she holds a pair of gloves and a miniature painting depicting the face of a man, most likely her husband.

As a woman of power, Anne could be blunt and proud, and was known to display arrogance and stubbornness. In 1547 Thomas Seymour, Edward Seymour's younger brother, secretly married Henry VIII's former queen, Kateryn Parr. Somerset showed visible anger on hearing of the marriage, the king later writing in his journal that 'the Lord Protector was much offended'.[14] Anne too, resented the match and both Somersets dealt coldly with their new in-law. One of Thomas Seymour's servants acknowledged the particular and deliberate animosity Anne displayed towards Kateryn. After Parr's death he stated that 'if any grudge were born towards him [Thomas Seymour] by my Lady of Somerset [Anne], it was as most men guess for the queen's cause', adding that now the queen is dead, 'she will bear him as good heart as ever she did in her life'.[15] It is not clear whether Anne was jealous of the queen's attention within the family or if the couple were angry at Thomas for marrying her covertly, and so soon after the king's death. Later, Thomas Seymour would show himself to be highly driven by status and power, taking enormous risks to try and achieve it. Surely Anne and Edward would have encouraged Kateryn into the fold, welcoming the Dowager Queen's knowledge, experience and social connections as well as her dedication to religious reform.

Instead, the Somersets made their dislike of the marriage obvious, even to Kateryn. In one letter the former queen wrote to her husband telling him that the Protector had made her so angry 'I should have bitten him', and 'what cause have they to fear having such a wife?'.[16] The matter was brought into the public arena when, on a visit to court,

Kateryn requested Anne carry her train. She refused, on grounds that 'it was unsuitable for her to submit to perform that service for the wife of her husband's younger brother'.[17] Kateryn might have been Dowager Queen, but Anne was wife to the man now in charge of the country. There is another view, however. It is possible that the exasperated Kateryn, known to have had a 'pregnant wittiness', engineered the awkward situation, flexing her social superiority in an attempt to put the proud, haughty Anne publicly in her place.[18]

The family feud had spilled out into court circles. Next it would affect state business. In his will, Henry VIII had raised the possibility of Kateryn becoming regent on his death, a duty that was now denied to her. Thomas also wondered why Somerset was Protector *and* Governor of the King's Person when these roles had been shared between uncles in previous minority governments. This request also fell on deaf ears. Somerset then withheld Kateryn's jewels, Thomas still frantically seeking possession of them in December 1548 after her death.[19]

It was around this time that building work began on the couple's family home, Somerset House. In 1538, Henry VIII granted Seymour a house called Chester Place, located outside Temple Bar in London near the river. After Edward assumed the role of Protector, the Seymours' income increased and funds were diverted to creating a building that not only served as a luxurious home for the family, but was also large enough to run government affairs from it. Its construction caused some controversy, with reports that 'a church near Strand Bridge and two Bishops' houses' were demolished by Somerset's builders, and 'in digging the foundations whereof the bones of many who had been buried there were dug up and carried into the fields'.[20] Situated close to the Thames, it was accessible by barge and perfectly placed for visiting other London palaces and the homes of influential courtiers. St Paul's, London Bridge and Westminster were all close by. The house was sadly left unfinished during the Protector's lifetime, although Seymour's presence there was recorded on state business between 1547 and 1550, marking it as his personal and political headquarters.[21]

As builders lumbered Somerset's stone and timber at the edge of the Thames, Londoners were grumbling about the duke's 'monstrous' wife. It wasn't long before she was blamed for events leading to Thomas Seymour's execution in 1549. Hayward believed she steered the duke to the 'destruction' of his brother, while the sixteenth-century writer Nicholas Sander wrote that 'as the rivalry grew from day to day, and as the Protector's wife gave her husband no rest, matters came at last to this: the Protector, who, though he ruled the king, was yet ruled by his wife, must put his brother to death that he might satisfy his ambition without let or hindrance'.[22]

The relationship between Anne Seymour and her brother-in-law Thomas was a difficult one. In 1551, Sir William Sharington remembered that 'The Lord Admiral [Thomas Seymour] doth not love my Lord Protector because of my Lady of Somerset ... and therefore my Lord Protector loved him the worse'.[23] Thomas Seymour was ruthlessly ambitious, but made poor decisions and acted spontaneously. He was arrested in 1549 for numerous offences including plotting against the government, planning to abduct the king and for making overtures to marry the Lady Elizabeth without consent of the council. Edward Seymour signed the warrant for his brother's execution on 17 March and he was beheaded three days later.[24] Hayward described Thomas as 'fierce in courage, courtly in fashion, in personage stately, in voice magnificent, but somewhat empty in matter', an assessment somewhat supported by his actions.[25] The Lady Elizabeth later wrote to her sister Mary, remembering what she had heard from the Protector after Thomas' fall. 'I heard my lord of Somerset say, that if his brother had been suffered to speak with him he had never have suffered, but persuasions were made to him so great that he was brought in belief that he could not live safely if the admiral [Lord Thomas Seymour] lived, and that made him give consent to his death'.[26]

Elizabeth's words confirm that there was much more at play in Thomas' downfall than a tense relationship with his sister-in-law. While it's possible that the 'persuasions' she mentions came from Anne, it's more likely her husband's decision to execute his brother was made following advice from the council on the basis of damning evidence collected from correspondence, eyewitness reports and confessions, which all survive today. There was no love lost between Anne and Thomas Seymour, but there is nothing concrete to suggest that she was the cause of his downfall. Somerset's admission that the matter could have been dealt with if Thomas had approached him privately implies that he was not as ruled by Anne, or malicious gossip, as earlier commentators argued. Ultimately, Thomas Seymour was to blame for his actions, without which no amount of Anne's muttering in her husband's ear would have led him to the axe.

Throughout the late 1540s the duchess was busy working quietly to support her husband in his public role. As early as April 1547, the Lady Mary wrote to Anne to recommend two men, one of whom wished to be installed as one of the Knights of Windsor.[27] In December, Dorothy Wyngfield wrote to ask her to 'move the Lord Protector' over the sale of lands in Suffolk.[28] Katherine Willoughby, Duchess of Suffolk had taken in Kateryn Parr's baby daughter, and it was to Anne that she wrote, requesting 'some pension alotted unto her' to help pay for the child's care.[29] These appeals, written by important and prominent members of Tudor society show that even early in the protectorate, Anne's influence on her husband was recognized and regularly made use of within aristocratic circles. The duchess' presence in royal business was further recorded in 1549, when it was noted that silks, plate and jewels had been conveyed out of the king's 'secret houses' by the 'Duke and Duchess of Somerset and others'.[30]

Anne's influence is also visible in more notorious events of the protectorate. In 1548, Thomas Parry, a member of Lady Elizabeth's household, was examined in connection with Thomas Seymour's behaviour around the princess. Kat Ashley, Elizabeth's governess, told Parry that she had been angrily confronted by the Duchess of Somerset who 'had found great faults with her, for my Lady Elizabeth's going in a night upon a barge upon [the] Thames, and for other light parts, whereupon she should say to the said Mrs Astley [sic] then, she was not worthy to have the governance of a King's daughter, and many other things'.[31] Ashley received another rebuke from the duchess when, during a meeting with the Protector, she was told that 'another should have her place, fearing that she bare too much affection to my Lord Admiral'.[32] This comment also confirms Anne's presence at meetings between her husband and royal staff. One further mention of the duchess is especially interesting. During a conversation about whether Elizabeth would marry Thomas Seymour if he asked her, Parry told Elizabeth that if she was to 'sue out the Letters Patent' she would need to 'go to my Lady Somerset at your coming and by that mean to make suit to my Lord's Grace ... and to entertain her Grace for your furtherance'.[33] Elizabeth was the daughter of Henry VIII, but she still needed her plans for marriage rubber-stamped by the Protector's duchess, who would put in a word for her with Seymour.

The couple were in an enviable position at the head of the realm and it wasn't long before enemies began to circle. In 1549, rebellion, religious protest and disorder spread throughout the kingdom and the Protector was imprisoned and accused of mismanaging the country. The young king noted the reasons in his diary, which included 'ambition, vainglory, entering into rash wars in mine youth ... enriching of himself of my treasure, following his own opinion and doing all by his own authority'.[34] Paget, who had been so instrumental in Somerset's rise to power, blamed the duchess. In a conversation with the Imperial Ambassador Van der Delft in August 1549 on the state of the country, he grumbled, by way of explanation, 'he has a bad wife'.[35]

Somerset was released, but surrendered his title of Protector. His disgrace was short-lived, however, and he was soon back in government as one of the king's council members. By early 1551, Edward VI's journal entries record his uncle acting as a key advisor, attending state meetings and hosting ambassadors. Encouraged by this seemingly warm welcome back into government, Somerset began to seek supporters for his comeback. In February, the king was made aware of Richard Whalley, who was interrogated 'for persuading divers nobles of the realm to make the Duke of Somerset Protector at the next parliament'.[36]

The duke wasn't the only one smoothing the way for a Seymour return to power. In October 1551 it was reported that Anne, overheard by a Spanish ambassador, expressed hope that 'the world might soon change, and that her husband, who was now very low and in debt, might some day be in a position to do something for those who wished him well'.[37] This was a clear and unsubtle solicitation for Seymour's supporters to once again back the duke in return for later reward. Somerset had used this tactic before, in 1547, confirmed by Paget's letter. Anne's involvement here raises the possibility that she could have been behind the similar events of January 1547, dangling the promise of future influence in return for present backing. Sadly this time, if Anne's loud appeals were meant to increase support for her husband, she failed. According to the observer who reported them, her comments only motivated the Duke of Northumberland to finish Somerset's career once and for all.

In 1551 Somerset was arrested and sent to the Tower, charged with plotting to imprison and kill the king's advisors, raise the residents of London in rebellion and seize power for himself.[38] Anne and a number of their servants were also imprisoned on grounds of being involved in the plot, including Somerset's supporters Sir Ralph Vane and Sir Thomas Arundel. The duke's servant Francis Newdigate and Anne's half-brother Sir Michael Stanhope were also imprisoned.

While Anne lingered in the Tower on 1 December, her husband defended himself at his trial. On hearing that he had been found guilty of the crimes of which he was accused, Somerset 'made suit for his life, wife and children, servants and debts'.[39] Sir Thomas Wyatt had written in 1536, after the fall of the Boleyns, *Circa Regna Tonat* (loosely translated as 'Thunder Rolls Around the Throne'). He was referring to Henry VIII, although the sentiment could easily apply to the reigns of any of the Tudor monarchs. In an inventory of Anne's belongings made towards the end of her life in 1587 there is a record of 'two pieces of unicorn's horn in a red taffeta purse'.[40] During the medieval and Tudor periods, unicorn's horn was believed to either detect or protect against poison when placed in a drink. This was not only a sign that Anne was fully aware of the risks a prominent role in government posed, but that she believed someone might have wanted her – or her husband – out of the way.

Anne's imprisonment in the Tower is significant. If she had been uninvolved in state business there would have been no need to detain her. But her imprisonment served another purpose. Locking up the wife of the former Protector gave credibility to the prosecution's claims that the plot had been carried out at their home, Somerset House. Anne was well-known at the time for her influence over her husband and, in some cases, her favour was valued as much as his. She was present at key events and angrily reprimanded those in positions of responsibility, as we have seen. Her active involvement was therefore flipped to add credibility to her supposed guilt over involvement in Somerset's plot. It also justified her long incarceration after his death which kept Anne secured and unable to raise support.

The duke was beheaded on 22 January 1552.[41] The king recorded the event in his journal with a sense of detachment: 'The duke of Somerset had his head cut off upon Tower Hill between eight and nine a 'clock in the morning', he wrote, choosing not to acknowledge his aunt.[42] Later, it was said that whenever Edward remembered his uncle he would shed tears, complaining that the circumstances of his death came about more 'from his wife than from himself'.[43]

The duchess had entered the Tower a day after her husband on 17 October 1551. She was released on Mary's accession in July 1553. As late as March of that year, there were rumours that she still might be sentenced to life imprisonment.[44] Records indicate she was kept in some comfort while in the Tower; she had an allowance of mutton, beef, veal, chicken and rabbit along with beer, wine and bread; and she was attended by two gentlewomen, three of the king's servants and received a visit from the Protestant Bishop Hooper during the Easter of 1553.[45]

On her release, Anne remarried. Her second husband was Francis Newdigate, Somerset's former servant who had been seized at the time of the duke's fall. We know relatively little about Francis, but Anne's defiance and some hint of unruliness can still be seen in later documents. In 1570 the couple found themselves the subject of legal action, having not paid rent on their home in Chelsea for a staggering ten years.[46] The following year she was questioned about the marriage of her son, Edward Seymour, Earl of Hertford, with Lady Katherine Grey, sister of the nine-day queen, Lady Jane Grey. Although Elizabeth I, now queen, was unnerved by news of the marriage because of Grey's royal blood, Anne brushed the matter away. She denied any knowledge of the arrangement and blamed the 'wilfulness of her unruly child', hoping still to be in the queen's favour.[47] And in February 1567 she was in talks with Robert Dudley Earl of Leicester about plans for the succession, something that also involved her son.[48] Anne supported her second husband as she had supported her first. In 1574 she wrote to William Cecil, Lord Treasurer in strong terms, requesting his intervention in a dispute between Newdigate and the Lord Chamberlain Henry Hunsdon.[49]

One of Anne's final acts demonstrates she was not solely the 'monstrous' woman portrayed by writers such as Hayward and Sander. During his lifetime Newdigate had taken Elizabeth Saunders, his orphaned niece, into his custody and care. After his death there was a miscommunication, the Lord Mayor understanding that Anne wished to be 'disburdened' of the child. Anne replied with 'surprise', and requested that as she had cared for Elizabeth since she was an infant, she would continue to do so. The Mayor 'heartily consented', and thanked her for 'her great consideration of the child's welfare' in a letter dated 1 April 1582. Anne was, she insisted, upholding the wishes Francis had made in his will.[50]

Anne died on 16 April 1587. She was unwell when she made her will on 14 July 1586, bequeathing diamonds, pearls, vast amounts of cash and a mansion house in Westminster. She detailed some of her possessions, although other items found among her belongings were also recorded in an inventory. She owned a pair of spectacles and a number of items adorned with true-love-knots, a design that can also be seen on her tomb. One piece of jewellery may relate to her first marriage with Edward Seymour. 'A fayer pendant of mother of pearle, flourished with gold, like an S', although this may also represent their shared title of Somerset, or even her maiden name of Stanhope. It is not clear whether she owned any of these items during her marriage to Seymour or after his death, but they do provide an intimate glimpse into Anne's treasured possessions.[51]

There is plenty of evidence that the couple worked in some capacity together during Seymour's protectorate government. However, evaluations of Somerset's leadership are mixed. Under his watch, the nation swayed deeper into Protestantism and saw aspects of traditional service reformed or removed completely, building on the milder policies that followed Henry VIII's break with Rome. This led to resistance from those who felt forced into a policy that did not fit with their beliefs. Kett's Rebellion resulted in thousands of deaths and rioting in Norfolk, a response to the Tudor practice of enclosure, where sheep competed with tenants for land on account of the lucrative wool trade. England was also engaged in an expensive and ultimately futile war with Scotland, driven by Henry VIII's vision of a 'united kingdom' with one monarchy ruling both nations. The country also later suffered from debasement of the coinage and a virulent sweating sickness, claiming lives and further depleting energy and morale for the reign.[52]

But can we see any impact that Edward and Anne had together on mid-Tudor society? There is one area where they certainly enforced change, and this was in the matter of the kingdom's spiritual administration.

The reign of Edward VI is associated with vast and swift religious change. Under Somerset, the Crown's approach to worship retained some aspects of traditional Catholic service, but abolished others, including some religious processions, images and the use of holy bread and holy water.[53] The clergy was told to hold services in English and study an English-language version of Erasmus' *Paraphrase of the Gospels*, a copy made available in every parish church.[54]

The king's half-sister Mary, despite these new proclamations, was still hearing Catholic mass in her household. Edward VI and his councillors repeatedly requested she desist, but she refused. Eventually, Somerset conceded and granted her a private licence to continue.[55] While this would have angered those in the council who wished to see a more cohesive approach, it also had the benefit of keeping Mary onside. Mary would prove a supporter of Somerset while he was in office, but we can also see Anne's influence in this decision. Mary addressed letters to the duchess with the greeting 'My good Nan', and maintained a good relationship with her.[56] Anne could have advised her husband of the need to appease Mary, who was, for the moment, next in line after Edward VI to be queen. Notably, Mary released the duchess from the Tower almost immediately on her accession.

Seymour also encouraged the public debate of religion, by repealing Acts which formerly banned the printing of religious books in English.

Pollard, in *England Under Protector Somerset*, wrote: 'It would have been enough to entitle Somerset to a claim on the gratitude of posterity had he done nothing but remove the restrictions on printing the Bible in English, but the above clause did much more than that. It relieved not merely the men of his own religion from the penalties of the Six Articles, but the adherents of the Roman Faith'.[57] By making religious texts and services freely available in English, new sections of society now felt that they could discuss and fully understand religious debates. Henry VIII had already introduced the English language Bible into churches, but later removed it. By creating opportunities for the printing of more diverse works, Tudor citizens were able to research and question doctrine for themselves. Naturally, not everyone was excited about this prospect. Sander grudgingly complained that there was 'discussion of faith in every workshop, tavern, and alehouse ... everyone took up the sacred books, pulled them to pieces, taught them to others before they had been taught them themselves'.[58]

The Protector also privately inspired his royal nephew to ponder religious arguments and develop his writing skills. The young king, aged about twelve, wrote *A Small Treatise Against The Primacy of the Pope* in 1549, dedicating it to 'his most dear and well-beloved uncle, Edward Duke of Somerset, Governor of his Person and Protector of his Kingdoms, Countries and Subjects'. Because of the duke's 'life and actions', the king wrote, and 'that you have a great affection to the Divine word, and the sincere religion, I dedicate this present work to you'.[59]

Anne, too, was a dedicated reformer, her monument at Westminster referring to her 'firm faith in Christ'. Jehan Scheyfve, the Imperial ambassador, believed Somerset and Anne had swept in the new religious reforms together. He wrote on 21 October 1551 to share news of their imprisonment, noting dryly that 'It seems that God wishes to punish him and his wife, as they were the instruments of the introduction of the new religion into England'.[60]

Anne's association with reform was not a new one. She had been named during the examination of Lincolnshire woman Anne Askew in 1546. Askew was charged with heresy late in the reign of Henry VIII, having denied the concept of transubstantiation (that bread and wine transformed into the body and blood of Christ after consecration). She was questioned by Henry's advisors on her religious views and ordered to reveal her supporters. When she replied she had none, the councillors offered up the names of those they suspected of funding her. 'Then they asked me of my lady of Suffolk, my lady of Sussex, my lady of Hertford, my lady Denny, and my lady Fitzwilliams', Askew wrote. 'I said, if I should pronounce anything against them, that I were not able to prove it'. They pressed Askew further, and she admitted that 'there was a man in a blue coat which delivered me ten shillings, and said that my lady of Hertford sent it me ...'. Askew insisted it could not however be proven that the money came from Anne (then Countess of Hertford), and her interrogators strapped her to the rack, 'because I confessed no ladies or gentlewomen to be of my opinion'.[61]

Askew's tentative identification of Anne during her examination is significant. There is no reason the man in blue would be a servant of anyone else, and ten shillings was a substantial gift, with an equivalent worth of around £200 today. Anne would become well known for her later support of reformist writers, so could Askew have been an early beneficiary? If so, and it is likely, Askew's claim means that Anne was not only aiding early religious reform, but also furthering the status of women in religion. As an interrogator told Askew in 1545, 'For St. Paul ... forbade women to speak, or to talk of the word of God'. Anne was 'rebuked' by the men and told she was 'much to blame for uttering the scriptures'.[62] With Anne Seymour's financial and moral support, Askew was able to study texts, form debates and then share these within Tudor communities, a revolutionary concept in Tudor England.

Both Anne and Edward were patrons of Protestant authors and a number of works were dedicated to them. Thomas Becon dedicated *The Flower of Godly Prayer* to Anne, a 'worthy patron both of the godly and of godliness, both of the learned and of learning'. He pre-empts her sharing the book of prayers with others, suggesting the duchess not only inspired and supported the writing of religious works, but distributed them within her circle, putting them 'into the hands of many'.[63] Bernardino Ochino in *The Tragedy*, written in 1549, dedicated his work to King Edward VI, but praised 'your most dearest uncle, the Lord Protector, and of other your trusty and faithful councillors', complimenting them for the religious reforms in the country.[64] John N. King, in *English Reformation Literature*, pointed out the large number of Seymour dedications in other religious works and highlighted writers personally linked to the couple, including William Samuel, Thomas Becon and the future Bishop of Gloucester and Worcester, John Hooper, who had visited Anne in the Tower in 1553.[65]

Anne and Edward Seymour were individually ambitious and powerful, but it was through their combined strength that they reached the height of their influence between 1547-1549. And, from what we can gather, they seem to have had a generally successful partnership. We can see similarities in their key values, driven by a heightened sense of purpose and religious duty. They also embraced political, religious and cultural change. Estimates of when they were born hover at around 1497-1500 for Anne and 1500-1506 for Edward, and so they were also relatively similar in age.

Anne's abrasive personality is well documented. However, her character was certainly more three-dimensional than commentators such as Sander and Hayward would have us believe. It is interesting that Paget, who would have known her personally, dismissed her as a 'bad wife', as documentary evidence indicates exactly the opposite. She loyally supported both husbands during their troubles and continued to care for her second husband's orphaned niece after his death. With Somerset, she advised him, reprimanded those who failed in their duty and acted as intermediary. The works commissioned by and dedicated to the couple had the effect of reinforcing Somerset's policy in religion, while Anne distributed these new books among her wealthy and influential friends. If Anne had lived today, we would probably consider her a natural businesswoman: confident, assertive, outspoken and loyal. In this respect, Anne was an asset to Somerset during his career, both publicly and in private. It is no wonder members of the council resented her interference. She had access to her husband day and night and held his trust. She would also have had the opportunity to speak openly to him in private about his fellow councillors and whether she believed they were serving his best interests.

Edward Seymour was equally ambitious. He was antagonistic, as we learn from Kateryn Parr's confession that she could have 'bitten him', but seems to have been less publicly outspoken and volatile than Anne. He showed ruthlessness in a number of ways, including overriding Henry VIII's will to establish himself as Protector, and having his own brother executed. And yet despite a long political career, he displayed a lack of awareness. His enemies had the opportunity to instigate his fall twice – first in 1549, when he lost his protectorate and again in 1551, for which he would lose his life. The early-twentieth century writer St Maur evaluated Somerset's failings, stating that 'he did not use his enormous power to crush his foes when he might have done so, and in consequence they took advantage of this weakness to crush him'.[66] We get the feeling Anne could not be described in this way. She was prone to displaying superiority and even jealousy, but was firm, diplomatic and politically agile, continuing her influence in the reigns of subsequent monarchs.

Somerset's role of Protector was not an easy one. Anne and Edward were distantly descended from royalty, but neither had any sustained experience of ruling a country. The pressure from members of the council, a foreign war and rebelling subjects could easily have marked the end of their relationship. And yet the couple displayed resilience and loyalty until the end. Somerset considered his wife's opinions despite complaints from his councillors and begged for her safety at his trial. Anne attempted to secure her husband's return to power and suffered imprisonment at the duke's arrest. The Somerset household would not have been without arguments between these two strong, and in some cases very different personalities, but they endured difficulties together. They enjoyed the flush of power as Seymour rose from the 1530s, but maintained defiance, strength and support at his fall.

Arguably the biggest impact of Edward and Anne's relationship was England's religious reform, a cause to which they were dedicated and actively promoted. Although the swerve towards Protestantism under Seymour was milder than later reforms under Northumberland, it was still a significant change for the people. Subjects listened to sermons in English, read the Bible and other religious works and freely debated its doctrine in inns and marketplaces around the country. Chris Skidmore, in *Edward VI The Lost King of England*, stated that for the Tudor people the changes made under the Seymours 'transformed their entire visual structure of belief'.[67] This was not always felt positively, and vehement resistance was displayed by rioters demanding the reversal of these new policies. Askew's tentative acknowledgement in 1545 of Anne as an early patron underlines her role not only as a religious influencer, but as a revolutionary backer of women's roles in religion.

On the accession of Mary Tudor, England was restored to Catholicism. But the Protector's efforts were not lost. When Elizabeth I gained control of the realm just five years later, the country again swerved into a more Protestant-based faith. And working closely with the new queen during this period was one man who had sharpened his quill under the watchful eye of the Somersets.

The couple's support of the early career of Sir William Cecil (later Lord Burghley) is hugely significant to Tudor history. Cecil was employed by the duke soon after he established his protectorate. He was tasked with completing paperwork, issuing requests and rubbing shoulders with key figures of the court. It was soon noticed that he had a gift for politics and administration and it could be argued that Cecil's early work with Seymour prepared him for his later role as chief advisor to Elizabeth I. The impact that William Cecil had on history is vast. He later played a central role in the imprisonment and trial of Mary, Queen of Scots and co-ordinated England's defence against the Spanish Armada. Cecil and his family were known to Anne Seymour, too. Stephen Alford, in *Burghley: William Cecil at the Court of Elizabeth I*, pointed out relationships Anne had with Mildred, Cecil's wife, and other women of the Cecil family.[68] Later, the secretary gave his son Robert some advice on how to conduct business relationships in the Tudor court: 'Be sure to keep some great man thy friend, but trouble him not for trifles, compliment him often with many and small gifts, and if thou hast cause to bestow any great gratuity, let it be something which may be daily in sight, otherwise, in this ambitious age, thou shalt remain like a hop without a pole, live in obscurity, and be made a foot-ball for every insulting companion to spurn at'.[69] Indeed, this may also provide a glimpse into how Cecil treated Edward Seymour, 'some great man' who noticed his talents early in his career.

Elizabeth first corresponded with Cecil during her brother's reign. On 22 September 1550, her servant Thomas Parry wrote to him, advising that 'Her grace hath been long troubled with rheums, but now, thanks be to the Lord, is nearly well again, and shortly ye shall hear from her grace again'.[70] Elizabeth and Cecil then, were known to one another long before she created him Secretary of State on her accession in 1558. If Cecil had not worked for Somerset, and afterwards Northumberland, Elizabeth's England without him and the training he received in government may have been very different.

The couple also encouraged Jane Seymour's rise as queen. By occupying a chamber that allowed the king to meet her away from the sharp eyes of the rest of the court as well as those of Queen Anne, the attraction between them could grow. We know that Edward and Anne were socially and politically ambitious and would have been well aware of the rewards they could receive as the new queen's family. It is also possible that the Seymours were among those who, according to Chapuys, were 'intimate with the king', ready to confirm Jane's criticisms of his current wife, Anne Boleyn.

The building of Somerset House is also significant as, without the Somersets and their rise to power, it would not have existed. An eighteenth-century observer of the original mansion noted that it represented the 'first dawning of taste in England'. Early twentieth-century writers Raymond Needham and Alexander Webster called it 'one of the earliest examples of Renaissance architecture in England; and it undoubtably played an important part in the change of taste which continued during the reign of Elizabeth'.[71] After Seymour's death, the building played a stately role. The Lady Elizabeth appeared here in procession in 1553 before meeting her sister, Queen Mary, for her triumphal march into London. Elizabethan council meetings were held at Somerset House in 1589, 1593 and 1595 and it was also used to lodge foreign dignitaries while they were on business at court. The original building that Anne and Edward would have known is not visible today, having undergone renovations and rebuilding in later centuries. The new building was used as a college, and in the nineteenth and twentieth centuries, it was the site of the General Register Office.[72]

Another significant impact on the state was of course Seymour's creation of the protectorate. The extent of Anne's involvement in the events leading up to her husband's title is highly likely, but has not been fully established with evidence. It was a bold and risky move. As Paget and Seymour conspired, they would have been aware of the dismal success rate of previous regency governments in history. The most recent, led by Richard III, involved the assumption of power by the king's uncle, the later disappearance of Edward V himself and the Protector proclaimed king in his place. To the Tudors, Richard III – the uncle and Protector of a young king – was recast as a 'villain'. The similarity of circumstances, even down to the last crackled breaths of an overweight, bejewelled king, would not have been lost on the two advisors and the council.

There could not be a greater difference between the burials of Anne and Edward Seymour. Anne's life is dedicated at length on her large and elaborate memorial in Westminster Abbey. Her effigy lies painted in full colour, with robes of red lined with ermine unfurling from her frame. She wears a coronet painted with gold and gazes steadfastly upwards, her hands joined in prayer. Edward's resting place is within the Tower of London, marked by a brass plaque on the wall of the church of St Peter ad Vincula engraved with a list of those buried within. His name sits among famous 'traitors' of Tudor governments, among them Anne and George Boleyn, Thomas Cromwell and Katheryn Howard. Men he knew and worked with are also listed, including John Dudley, Earl of Northumberland who supplanted him; Ralph Vane, who supported him; and his brother Thomas

Seymour, Lord Sudeley. If thunder ever rolled around a throne, it was Edward VI's.

And yet Seymour is remembered, lettered in gold, on his wife's tomb. The inscription celebrates her role as 'dear spouse unto the renowned prince Edward Duke of Somerset, Earl of Hertford, Viscount Beauchamp and Baron Seymour, Companion of the most famous knightly Order of the Garter; uncle to King Edward the Sixth, Governor of his Royal Person and most worthy Protector of all his realms, dominions and subjects'.

Chapter 6

Mary I and Philip of Spain

MARY I AND PHILIP of Spain ruled England together for four years between 1554-1558. History has not been kind to them, with Mary remembered as the 'bloody' tyrant and a dowdy, unfashionable wife helplessly infatuated with her husband. Philip has been depicted as cold, unkind and dismissive, taking every opportunity to leave the kingdom to escape his irritating queen. These descriptions far from support the idea that Philip and Mary were a combined, dedicated power couple, but they are also hugely one-sided and completely ignore any positive developments the rulers made during their reign. Contrary to popular belief, the couple did in fact make lasting changes to England's militia, culture and politics and worked closely together on government affairs and policy. However, they certainly had their problems, their struggle to conceive an heir as well as their unpopular religious reform defines their reign even today. Despite this, Philip and Mary were a mid-Tudor power couple that united two legendary medieval dynasties and faced the new and growing world as a combined political force.

Prince Philip of Spain, the twenty-seven-year-old son of the Habsburg Emperor Charles V, stepped onto English soil at Southampton in July 1554.[1] Tall and slim with closely-cropped hair and a trimmed beard, he rested at the busy port behind its defensive stone walls before riding to Winchester Cathedral to marry his bride, England's Queen Mary I. The match had been negotiated by Philip's father with very little involvement from the prince and to all concerned, it was a union driven entirely by politics. Mary might have gazed longingly at Philip's portrait, but later insisted her only motive in marrying him was for 'the good of her kingdom'. Philip's close advisor Ruy Gomez de Silva continued in a similar vein, writing that 'the King fully realizes that the marriage was concluded for no fleshly consideration, but in order to remedy the disorders of this kingdom and preserve the Low Countries'.[2] For the Habsburgs, control over England's seas was crucial to the security of their empire and eased travel and communication between territories such as the Netherlands and Spain. The French were less excited about the match, King Henry II revealing to the ambassador Dr Wotton in December 1553, that the thought of Mary marrying his 'chief enemy' was 'a grief unto me to consider what advantage mine enemies will think to have thereby upon me'.[3]

England also stood to gain from the alliance, and Mary's council was able to negotiate an advantageous marriage treaty that gave England a yearly income along with a clause that confirmed the couple's heir would rule over not only England, but also the Low Countries and Spain.[4] There were also economic and security interests. The Bishop of Winchester, Stephen Gardiner, publicly cited 'the wealth and enriching of the realm' among other 'weighty considerations' in favour of the marriage, while Mary herself told the Commons that, 'on the word of a queen', her marriage 'shall be for the high benefit and commodity of the whole realm'.[5]

But Henry II wasn't the only one grumbling about the new power of the bride and groom to be. There were fears in England that Philip would exert control over his wife, and therefore the crown, and lead both into a purely Habsburg agenda. This was a reasonable worry in Tudor England, when the husband was the legally dominant partner in a marriage. How would this work in Mary's case? Never before had a sole queen been crowned in England, let alone one expected to marry a foreign prince, and this was one of the first hurdles Mary and Philip needed to overcome.

Resistance to the marriage and general Spanish influence was evident among Mary's subjects. The year before Philip's arrival, Wyatt's Rebellion had been raised against 'proude Spanyardes' and aimed to 'abolish them out of this realm'. Londoners also complained of Spaniards outnumbering Englishmen in the City four to one and there were other rumours that Philip had 12,000 soldiers waiting to mount a full invasion to take the crown by force.[6] Name and birth-place evidence from state records does support claims that there was an increase in Spanish-born residents living in England, but not at the levels suggested by the Londoners above. In any case, many had probably settled since the early 1500s, as associates of Katherine of Aragon. Salacious gossip surrounding Philip's extramarital love life was also used to spread bitterness and negativity about England's new king. As late as 1557, John Capstocke printed a paper that stated Philip would love the queen 'better if she give him the crown' with chaste living 'contrary to his nature', having the choice of three or four women in one night 'not of ladys [sic] and gentlewomen but of bakers daughters and such other poore whores'.[7]

These reports were spread by a nervous population anxious at the thought of uncontrollable Spanish dominance in England. It wasn't just Mary and Philip that had to deal with the queen's new role, but also the people. Steps were therefore taken to quell this unease, and clauses were added to the marriage treaty severely limiting Spanish influence at court. Philip's role was to be 'rather as a subject than otherwise' with Mary the central figure. Spaniards were not permitted in the council, to hold offices in the 'queen's house' or to own castles or forts.[8] Despite these limitations, Philip remained the chivalric, respectful consort, at least in public. The Venetian Ambassador Giacomo Soranzo quipped that even if Philip had wanted to invade England by force, he lacked the spare manpower to do so as they were busy elsewhere defending the empire. He guessed that Philip would choose to 'rule in peace and quiet', which he seems, largely, to have done.[9] There was the odd scuffle and sign of unrest during the period, but Mary and her husband would never be toppled. As Anna Whitelock in *Mary Tudor: England's First Queen* points out, Mary's own rebellion against Lady Jane Grey in 1553 was the only successful one to have unseated a sixteenth-century English government.[10]

The royal wedding that fused England to the might of the Habsburg Empire was a carefully stage-managed piece of theatre, heavy with prestige and symbolism. The ceremony took place on a raised stage so spectators could see the couple dressed in their luxurious outfits. The queen also sent her bridegroom a diamond and pearl-encrusted robe of cloth of gold embroidered with pomegranates and roses, but Philip later remembered he chose not to wear it as it was 'ornate'.[11] Pomegranates were the emblem of her mother Katherine of Aragon and roses one of the symbols of the Tudor dynasty. Katherine had been a popular queen, and Mary might have calculated that the sight of the Spanish prince wearing pomegranates and roses may have appeased her subjects, reminding them of her faithful and loyal Spanish mother.

Immediately after their marriage, Mary and Philip listened to their joint titles proclaimed. The couple were now 'King and Queen of England, France, Naples, Jerusalem and Ireland, Defenders of the Faith, Princes of Spain and Sicily, Archdukes of Austria, Dukes of Milan, Burgundy and Brabant, Counts of Habsburg, Flanders and Tyrol'.[12] If Mary's aim was indeed to safeguard England and connect it politically and economically to one of Europe's most powerful dynasties, then she must have felt a sense of achievement on hearing these words echo around Winchester's stone walls. The Tudor and Habsburg dynasties were now combined.

A bronze medal in the collection of the Metropolitan Museum of Art in New York is thought to have been commissioned by Philip in 1554 to commemorate this marriage. Created by Jacopo Nizolla da Trezzo, it shows Mary in detailed profile, her chin raised confidently. She wears an extravagant gown and jewels. On the reverse is the allegorical figure of Peace who, amid a storm, sets fire to a stash of weapons and provides the people with calm and safety. The museum states that Peace was intended to signify Mary's aptitude for good government, her success in defeating rebellion and the restoration of the Catholic faith in England. If this was indeed minted at the time of their wedding, it reveals the objectives Philip and Mary hoped to achieve in government. Mary had already seized the throne from Lady Jane Grey and defeated Wyatt's Rebellion. By referring to Mary's success in these events on the coin, Philip was expressing confidence in his new wife as commander of her country. A silver medal created by Da Trezzo the following year depicts Mary in the same pose, but with a profile of Philip on the other side. Fully armoured, he stares intensely, conveying strength, courage and boldness. Historians often talk about the use of imagery to convey power in Henry VIII, Edward VI and Elizabeth's reigns, but Mary and Philip employed 'power couple propaganda' throughout their reign, too.

After the ceremony, the newlyweds had a bumpy ride getting used to their new roles. However Philip's conduct in public was impeccable from the minute he reached England's shores. The French ambassador Antoine de Noailles noted how Philip deliberately showed respect to the English, telling his Spanish lords at Southampton that they must 'henceforth forget all the customs of Spain, and live in every way like the English', downing a cup of local ale in front of curious residents.[13] Philip, however, must have been inwardly frustrated at the council's micromanagement of Spanish influence at court. They also pointedly refused to grant him an English coronation.

Tied by protocol and the cautious murmurings of her council, Mary publicly acknowledged Philip's value in other ways. Shortly after the wedding she ordered writs to be sent across England, Wales, Ireland and elsewhere to advertise their new titles. Orders including warrants were issued in their joint names.[14] A new set of coins were minted, showing the couple in profile, staring intensely at one another with a single crown floating between them. Mary made a public show of Philip's role as her consort at Reading in Berkshire just days after the marriage ceremony. When the town's mayor Robert Bowyer handed the ornamental mace to Mary, she acknowledged it, handed it back, and asked the mayor to also present it to her husband as a mark of his authority.[15] Mary ensured Philip was acknowledged culturally, too, in entertainments at court that her mother would have once enjoyed. Mary's palaces bustled with Spanish games, songs and dancing, with John Elder commenting that 'to behold the dukes and noblemen of Spain dance with the fair ladies and the most beautiful nymphs of England, it should seem to him that never see such, to be another world'.[16]

Philip continued to carry out his public duties with ease. 'Merrily smiling', observed Elder at the wedding, Philip was also seen processing publicly to mass, competing at the tiltyard and presiding over St George's Day events in April 1555, while Mary watched from a window. In July 1557 he dutifully appeared as godfather at the christening of the Duke of Norfolk's son.[17] De Silva remarked on the couple's happiness shortly after their wedding, observing that Philip 'strives to give her every possible proof of it in order to omit no part of his duty'.[18] Robert Dudley recorded the king's kindness to him following his family's fall on Mary's accession, later remembering that it was to Philip that 'he owed his life'. In October 1554, three months after the king's arrival in England, Dudley was released and pardoned.[19]

The couple spent Christmas together at Hampton Court Palace, a red-bricked, turreted mansion built by Cardinal Wolsey in the reign of Henry VIII. According to Stow, he 'bestowed great cost of building upon it, converting the mansion-house into so stately a palace, that it is said to have excited much envy'. In 1526 the palace was transferred to the king, who built a deer park there in his later years because of his 'sickness, age and corpulency of body', meaning that he was unable (or unwilling) by the late 1530s to travel and hunt elsewhere. The building experienced some alterations during the Georgian era, but thankfully a good part of the Tudor palace survives. Philip and Mary would have known the many chambers within the palace, its corridors and the now well-worn stone steps we tread today.

The year of the celebrations hosted by the couple is the subject of some debate, but the account reveals its luxurious setting. The great hall, with its intricate hammerbeam ceiling was lit with '1,000 lamps curiously disposed', so the faces of the diners flickered in the shadows. Mary's half-sister Elizabeth was seated at the same table as Mary and Philip. After the meal the king and queen were entertained by revels, maskings and disguisings. On 29 December Philip, Mary and Elizabeth presided over a joust, where half of the combatants were attired 'in the Spanish fashion'. It was an enthusiastic contest, resulting in the breaking of 200 spears.[20] The nature of these celebrations dispel the idea that Philip and Mary were a miserable, disengaged couple and instead reinforces their enjoyment of music, dancing and the joust as much as any of the other Tudor monarchs.

There is also a hint that Philip developed a personal fondness of his time in England. On Mary's death in 1558 he requested certain items of his to be returned to him, including gifts he had been given by the queen. Included on the list were five jewelled pieces with the likeness of St George (England's patron saint), as well as robes and ornaments he had worn on state occasions. He also asked for the return of the wedding outfit Mary had chosen for him and the robe embroidered with pomegranates and roses.[21]

Philip is rarely portrayed as an active or enthusiastic English ruler, but state documents from the couple's reign reveal he took a keen interest in England's development and safety. The Privy Council regularly sent queries to Philip and his replies survive, scrawled in Latin in the margins of the briefings. During one question on taxation, he referred the matter to 'a Council of eight selected Councillors', but stated that 'his Majesty, for his earnest love to the Kingdom of England ... desires also that nothing should be proposed in parliament without its having been first communicated to his Majesty, in order that he may signify his opinion'. In another, Philip showed concern for the power of the English navy, which he considered crucial against any threat from a foreign power. 'England's chief defence depends upon its navy being always in good order to serve for the defence of the kingdom against all invasion', Philip noted, adding, 'it is right the ships should not only be fit for sea, but instantly available'. To achieve this, he advised they should be moored at Portsmouth rather than on the Thames. Portsmouth, near the centre of the south coast, offered quick and easy access to the Solent and the open seas. Today, ferries depart from Portsmouth to France, Spain, the Isle of Wight and the Channel Islands. He also authorized the repair of ships recently damaged by bad weather and mentioned a future opportunity for English ships to accompany his father on a journey to Spain.[22] These notes reveal Philip's attentiveness to government and his concern for England's security. It also demonstrates his pride in English ships, happy to offer them as part of a joint English-Imperial convoy. His wider-world experience as a Habsburg leader and son of the Emperor gave him valuable insight on how to troubleshoot

England's weaknesses, particularly concerning the royal fleet. Linda Porter in *Mary Tudor: The First Queen* has pointed out that by 1557, toward the end of the couple's reign, the Tudor navy with its twenty-four royal ships and thirteen others ready to sail had reached a record not seen during the reigns of either Henry VIII or Edward VI.[23]

There are also traces of official collaboration between the couple. Mary issued a public declaration of war on France on 7 June 1557, citing Henry II's unreasonable conduct and invasion of Flanders 'which we are under obligation to defend'. On 21 June the Bishop of Arras wrote to Philip, remarking slyly that 'the English declaration (of war) is in the very best vein. It looks as if your Majesty had a hand in it'.[24]

Shaping the wording of England's declaration of war was not the only military involvement Philip led in his new country. He also enlisted English soldiers to fight with Imperial forces at the Battle of St Quentin in August 1557. After gaining the victory, Philip commissioned an impressive stained-glass window in the Sint Janskerk in Gouda in the Netherlands, depicting both himself and Mary, a sign that he valued his role in England and was grateful for Mary's support. Unfortunately, as Philip basked in celebration, the French were already planning their revenge. On 2 January 1558 Philip received 'sure information' that France was preparing to occupy the English territory of Calais. He wrote immediately to John Wentworth, Calais' deputy, urging him to 'report by special messenger to the Queen, our consort, informing her of everything that you require from that kingdom', adding that the security of the Pale required their 'best efforts'.[25] Philip's delegation of Calais' defence to Mary further confirms that he was confident she would act quickly and decisively. Sure enough, Henry Machyn writes that the queen learned of the threat the day after Philip wrote his letter, and soldiers set sail the following day. By the time they had arrived, Calais had fallen.[26]

Mary's courage had already surfaced during the Wyatt Rebellion, when she refused to leave to a place of safety, instead bravely rallying Londoners to support her. One eyewitness remarked of the queen that 'many thought she would have been in the field in person'.[27] That both monarchs were hardworking is beyond doubt. Mary put vast amounts of focus and energy into managing her realm. The Venetian Ambassador Giancomo Soranzo stated she woke early and took breakfast at around 1pm, adding that she 'transacts business incessantly, until after midnight'. His description reveals a resolved and attentive ruler, listening to 'every detail of public business' from her Privy Council and anyone else requesting an audience with her.[28] Philip was active, too, although he also bore responsibilities for wider Habsburg territories and travelled often. Sixteenth-century travel was risky, took time and used valuable resources. In an age before telephones, the internet or even a secure postal system, all business was carried out either by letter, in person or through a trusted representative. Philip's repeated absences from England were likely to have been more about dealing with Habsburg business rather than plainly trying to avoid his wife, as some writers have suggested in the past. That Philip intentionally went about avoiding his queen during their marriage is not a likely or logical assumption. The birth of an heir was in his interests as much as it was in hers. Philip would have realized with every departure from the kingdom that time spent away from Mary jeopardized the long-term effects of the work the couple had begun.

In 1555 the couple established a new relationship with an ally that, it was hoped, would boost trade. Shortly before his death, Edward VI had sent three ships headed by Richard Chancelor 'to open a way and passage to our men for travail to new and unknown kingdoms'. The young king died soon after the sailors departed England in 1553, but by the time ships limped toward Russia it was 1555 and Mary and Philip were on the throne. Negotiations began, and the pair wrote jointly to the Emperor Ivan Vasilivich on 1 April introducing themselves, assuring their friendship and requesting him to appoint an ambassador to deal with them at court. Subsequent voyages followed, with one appropriately-chosen ship deployed to Russia named *The Philip and Marie*. Vasilivich graciously called Mary his 'cousin' while the queen and Philip wrote of the hope of 'profitable adventure'.[29] They would later use this relationship to provide sailor Anthony Jenkinson with passage from Moscow to the Caspian Sea and Persia in April 1558.[30]

In March 1557 Osep Napea, England's first Russian ambassador, arrived in London, 'most honourably brought to the king and queen's majesties' court at Westminster'. Greeted by the Mayor, aldermen, merchants and servants, he was taken to Mary and Philip in a 'chamber most richly decked and furnished'. On 23 April, St George's Day, Napea met with the royal couple again and attended service with them in the chapel. His visit included banqueting, discussions with members of the English council and a tour of London, which included St Paul's Cathedral, the Tower and the Guildhall. Vasilivich had sent Napea to England with gifts for Philip and Mary including sables, skins and a white falcon. They returned the gesture with offerings of their own including expensive fabrics and a piece of body armour covered with crimson material and studded with gold nails. It is tempting to read a subtle assertion of dynamic power in another of the gifts sent to the Russian leader. Along with the sumptuous fabrics allocated for Vasilivich, they sent Napea back to Russia with two lions, one male and one female.[31] This gift may have been chosen for a number of reasons. The animal was anciently associated with England and had been featured in its royal arms since the twelfth century, but also has connotations of dominance. There is an implied symmetry in the male and female lions snarling and roaring on their way to a new trade ally and how Philip and Mary may have perceived their own growing influence around the globe.

Philip was far from the absent ruler he is often depicted as, and appeared often with his wife on public occasions. With her, he shaped and guided English policies concerning war, economics and domestic security. Where his influence is less clear is in the religious policy enforced on the nation in the mid-1550s. Certainly, both monarchs were pious and devoted Catholics and together they engineered England's return to the religion in late 1554. They were also seen together at a mass held at Westminster accompanied by 'all the bishops and the lords in their parliament robes' with a company of trumpeters and heralds.[32] But was Philip involved privately in the brutal burnings of Protestants that Mary would become so well-known for? John Edwards, in *Mary I: England's Catholic Queen*, sees potential traces of Philip's collaboration in some of the similarities between England's policy and the Spanish Inquisition, as well as the involvement of his religious advisor Bartolomé Carranza.[33] Mary herself credited Philip for his work in restoring some of the religious houses that had been dissolved by her father, when she wrote in 1558 'which said houses are lately by my said dear Lord and husband and by me revived and newly erected according to their several ancient foundations'.[34]

Mary will always be remembered for the hundreds of deaths ordered in the name of religion during her reign, the horror of which can be felt through to our own times. Anna Whitelock, in *Mary Tudor: England's First Queen*, suggested that Mary never intended for so many of her subjects to be burned at the stake, hoping they would more readily comply with her religious policy when threatened with harsher punishment.[35] If this is true, Mary deeply underestimated the spiritual resolve of the English people. Although there was some initial success in reintroducing elements of Catholicism to the nation, the policy ultimately failed. The relentless deaths of heretics only produced hundreds of Protestant martyrs, their stories written into legend in *Foxe's Book of Martyrs*. It also failed for another reason: there was no Catholic heir to continue Mary and Philip's work.

Philip, Mary and Charles V all understood the urgency of producing an heir that would succeed Mary and Philip. Just four months after the wedding, Charles asked an ambassador 'how does my daughter's belly forward?' and spoke eagerly of 'so much good hanging thereupon'. Letters were even prepared and signed by both Philip and Mary in advance, in 1555, to inform European leaders of the queen's safe delivery of a child.[36] A healthy baby would solve all their problems: it would neutralize Elizabeth's threat to the succession, ensure the continuation of the Catholic faith in England and establish Habsburg interests for generations to come. It would also provide an English monarch that would one day rule not only England, but also the Netherlands and Spain. But no matter how many times Mary and Philip lay together in their marital bed, the much-awaited child never came.

Mary's false pregnancies have been widely discussed, and there were two that we know of. The first was soon after the wedding, when the ambassador Simon Renard eyed Mary's widening frame and tighter clothes, and wrote to Charles V with 'no doubt' that she was pregnant.[37] Mary entered the traditional confinement to await the birth, but no baby came. Even worse, Londoners mistakenly celebrated the birth of a prince with a 'great ringing through London' which would have done nothing to alleviate the humiliation and confusion that must have been felt by the queen.[38] Mary quietly returned to state business. She believed herself pregnant again on 30 March 1558 when she wrote her will. No baby arrived.

Historians have debated the cause of these symptoms, some suggesting that a tumour, cancer, other long-term illness or depression was to blame. Some believe Mary suffered from false pregnancy, or pseudocyesis, which presents symptoms including a swollen belly, milk produced from the breasts and a lack of menstruation. A 2017 review study by M. Azizi and F. Elyasi found that psychological factors influencing the onset of pseudocyesis included the desire for a child, the mother's own childhood trauma and deprivation, and a poor network of family support. They also cited cultural and social factors such as pressure to become pregnant and an unstable relationship.[39] Mary strongly desired an heir, and there was significant pressure on her to conceive, especially as ambassadors and courtiers mumbled to one another about her advancing years. Philip was also frequently away from her, which further narrowed the possibilities of a pregnancy. Mary's past may also have been a factor. She had endured rejection and shock in childhood at her parents' separation and further suffered the death of her mother and a rocky relationship with her father. In the end, the couple's failure to produce an heir meant that any progress they made in England ended after Mary's death. The state returned to Protestant rule under Elizabeth, and the Anglo-Habsburg alliance abruptly ended.

From the moment the royal couple exchanged vows in Winchester Cathedral in the summer of 1554, England was politically tied to a vast area of the continent, and links were established with Habsburg territories in the New World. Philip believed England's influence would secure the seas between Habsburg states, while Mary was convinced her husband could provide security to the realm.

They ushered in cultural and commercial changes, too. Machyn wrote of Spaniards singing and dancing in London and carrying out their own customs at state occasions. In 1555 Gomes de Navarete was granted a licence by Mary to produce Spanish leather for the first time in England and in May 1558 she commissioned a translation of the tale *Aeneidos of Vergill* for 'the erudition of youth and honest recreation of the readers'.[40] This story had cultural significance for the couple, describing the foundation and development of the Roman empire despite setbacks and difficulties. Philip and Mary indeed embarked on a new foundation of England, with reform in military, religious and political aspects of the reign.

A vibrant community of Spanish settlers had reached England with Mary's mother, Katherine of Aragon, but during the 1550s there is evidence for a wider and more visible Spanish presence. They were represented at court, in Tudor neighbourhoods and their entertainments and customs were adopted. Some Spanish citizens living in England at this time were of African origin. The book *Pleasant and Compendious History of the First Inventers* mentions a black craftsman who lived in Cheapside, London during Mary and Philip's reign. This Spaniard was the first to make 'Fine Spanish Needles' in England, but, understandably protective over his craft, was reluctant to show the Englishmen how to make them.[41] The merchant and explorer William Towerson reported four men from Guinea living in England between 1554 and 1555. They had journeyed here to learn the language so that when back in Guinea, they could act as interpreters for English sailors.[42] As a result of Philip and Mary's union and their integration of Spanish and English cultures and crafts, Tudor subjects in 1556 walked through cities wearing Spanish leather. Songs sung in the language floated across the air, as shillings cast with the likenesses of the king and queen jangled in purses.

Henry VIII and Elizabeth I are often referred to as pioneers of the English navy, but as we have seen, Mary and Philip boosted the size, location and effectiveness of the fleet. The queen often stated that she believed England to be safer with Philip's influence. His experience and wider relationships with other territories likely instigated this change. It might not be too much of a stretch to consider that Philip's initial reform of the navy in 1554 might have set the ball rolling for its later upkeep and modification, affecting the success of his own naval attack on England in 1588. In any case, Elizabethan documents mention fleets being prepared at Portsmouth for overseas voyages. Philip's recommendations then, were most likely listened to and implemented.

There are other ways the Elizabethan Age might not have evolved as it did, had it not been for Philip and Mary. For example, D.M. Loades in *Mary Tudor* sees Elizabeth's choice in adopting a feminine approach to queenship as a very deliberate contrast to her sister's sober, masculine strategy.[43] Elizabeth's image of the 'Virgin Queen'; powerful, chaste and at the same time vulnerable under a mass of red curls and lace, may have been led by what she learned watching Mary navigate queenship for the first time. Laura Brennan, in *Elizabeth I: The Making of a Queen,* considers that Mary's 'long-distance' relationship with Philip deterred Elizabeth from marrying a foreign prince.[44] This has wider implications, as, if watching their union turned Elizabeth against entering into a marriage of her own, it could have been the reason she died childless in 1603, marking the end of the Tudor dynasty.

Elizabeth I is often considered an innovator of sixteenth-century public relations. But there is at least one more hint that she took a cue from her half-sister's reign. In 1588, Elizabeth cast a medal celebrating her navy's defeat of the Spanish Armada, now in the collection of the Yale University Art Gallery. It depicts lightning, a standing tree and general themes of overcoming adversity and establishing calm. These are, by inference, attributed to the actions of the queen, who is gorgeously dressed in a gown and jewels on the other side. While this coin may have been based on a standard allegorical design, the iconography and message have close similarities to Mary's 'Peace' medal of 1554, believed to have been commissioned by Philip to celebrate their marriage.

It is fair to say that Philip and Mary's relationship was not bound by mutual love, but as Prince of Spain and Queen of England, neither of them would have expected it to be. They shared a need for security, influence and power and this is what brought them together. They were also united in an unshakeable belief that their royal duty lay in the progression of their kingdoms and the advancement of the Catholic faith.

Posturing confidently and assertively in European politics, they put pressure on France and, despite England's reluctance, ventured into a war together. Propaganda on coins, portraits and medals sent a clear and united message that inspired their supporters and intimidated their enemies. Both were equally hardworking and evidence shows they collaborated on state business and policy. Attempting to soothe anxieties over Spanish involvement in England, they also untangled fresh and complicated issues surrounding the new expectations of a queen regnant and her consort king. Their reign was short, but it was marked by political, religious and military reform. Throughout all of this, they also maintained a professional and mutual respect. This continued until Mary's death, when she made her will in the spring of 1558. As well as requesting prayers be said for her 'most dearest lord and husband' she added a codicil the following October asking Philip to continue as a 'father' to England. She wrote, 'for the ancient amity sake that hath always been between our most noble progenitors and between this my realm and the Low Countries ... that it may please his Majesty to show himself as a Father in his care, as a brother or member of this realm in his love and favour, and as a most assured and undoubted friend in his power and strength'.[45] Even as she knew she was dying, Mary longed for England to retain the state relationship created by her marriage to Philip.

Theirs was not a love match. Their marriage was forged in each partner's duty to their respective realms. There are, however, signs that they respected one another's contributions and were confident in their spouse's abilities freely delegating, cooperating and appearing together as a strong union. There is a veiled and subtle reference to Philip's thoughts about his wife in a letter written to the king by De Feria in 1558, after Elizabeth I's accession. Comparing the new queen with Mary and discussing a future marriage proposal to Elizabeth on behalf of Philip, De Feria wrote that Elizabeth may be more fertile, but otherwise 'she compares most unfavourably with her'.[46] De Feria would have known his master's opinions of his queen, and this description supports the idea that Philip considered Mary a capable and authoritative ruler in every other regard, the only downside having been the failure of the couple to conceive an heir.

Of course, even power couples sometimes fall short of expectations. The reign will always be associated with 'Bloody Mary's' persecution of Protestants and the loss of Calais was felt heavily by the English people. It was Philip's own De Feria who told him that in England 'the people are wagging their tongues a good deal' about how much Philip was to blame for money being spent out of the kingdom, the loss of Calais, and that 'through your not coming to see the Queen our lady, she died of sorrow'.[47] Fulke Greville, Lord Brooke later wrote that the reign of Philip and Mary was 'yet so fresh in memory', with the couple's victory in St Quentin blemished by the loss of Calais. He wrote of 'the carrying away of our money to foreign ends ... and their short reign here felt to be a kind of exhausting tax upon the whole Nation'.[48] Sander, supportive of Mary and Philip's advancement of Catholicism, blamed their failure on the high expectations of her short reign, stating that 'the sins and the sacrilege of Henry VIII, and the wickedness of the people, were such that they could not be thus lightly expiated'.[49] Their marriage was by no means 'perfect'. The couple spent long periods of time away from one another and the English refusal to give Philip equal control over the realm and a coronation of his own must have created private tension between them. Whatever the citizens gossiped about their king and queen, it cannot be denied that the couple's ultimate failure was their inability to ensure the progression of their work in the longer term.

Today, in the church of Sint Janskerk in Gouda, just to the north-east of Rotterdam, a twenty-metre-high stained-glass window celebrates Philip and Mary's 1557 victory at St Quentin, in Northern France. Amid religious imagery, Philip and Mary kneel together in the lower part of the window. Their hands are pressed together in prayer, Mary kneeling directly behind her husband, her eyes cast upward. She wears a George and Dragon brooch clasped to her chest, while Philip wears golden armour, complementing the same shades on Mary's gown. Both are crowned. There was a reason Philip chose to commemorate his wife and consort in this way, and to sixteenth-century churchgoers it defined their outward marital relationship as one of power and strength. On hearing news of Mary's death on 17 November 1558, he wrote to his sister Joanna, telling her that he felt a 'reasonable regret' for her passing, adding 'I shall miss her'.[50]

Philip lived on and took two more wives after Mary. He died in 1598 at the monastery of San Lorenzo de El Escorial in Spain, at the age of seventy-one.

Chapter 7

Katherine Willoughby, Duchess of Suffolk and Richard Bertie

MARY AND PHILIP'S combined efforts to reinstate Catholicism in England would have a marked effect on another power couple of the period. As news of forced recantations and the burning of Protestant 'heretics' trickled into Lincolnshire, Katherine Willoughby and Richard Bertie took immediate and decisive action.

Katherine Willoughby was the daughter of William Baron Willoughby and Maria de Salinas, a Spanish lady-in-waiting to Katherine of Aragon. Maria had been a faithful servant to Katherine right until the end of her life, when she was said to have found her way into Kimbolton Castle, comforting the former queen at her bedside until her last breath. Born on 22 March 1519, Katherine was the only child of the marriage and therefore a wealthy heiress to the Willoughby titles and lands. Following the deaths of her parents, she entered the household of Charles Brandon, Duke of Suffolk in February 1529, where he lived with his wife, Mary Tudor.[1]

Brandon was one of Henry VIII's keenest supporters and a close personal ally of the king. His father William served as Henry Tudor's standard bearer at the Battle of Bosworth, and so the families' connections to one another began from the foundation of the dynasty.[2] Both Henry and Charles established a firm friendship from a young age. They were said to resemble one another in looks and contemporary portraits show Brandon had similar tastes in dress, along with a brown trimmed beard, which began to streak with grey as he reached his forties. The duke readily displayed his abilities on the battlefield, but was also regularly seen at the tiltyard and entertainments at court, embracing the showmanship of the period.

Brandon fell temporarily out of favour with Henry when he secretly married the king's sister Mary, Dowager Queen of France, in 1515. Mary had married Louis XII of France the year before, but following his death soon afterwards she returned to her brother's court in England.

Her subsequent wedding to Brandon meant that any opportunity to use Mary as a diplomatic tool in marriage was now lost and Henry was enraged. However, after imposing a hefty fine for their recklessness, the king welcomed the couple back into the fold, attending a second wedding ceremony celebrating the couple's union in May of that year. The couple went on to have four children, but Mary died on 26 June 1533. Looking for another wife, the eyes of the forty-nine-year-old Charles fell on the teenage ward in his household, Katherine Willoughby. On her marriage to the duke in around November 1534, the fifteen-year-old Katherine became Duchess of Suffolk, presiding over state and public occasions with her husband.[3] One of these was the arrival of Anna of Cleves, Henry VIII's fourth wife, who came to England in 1539. Holinshed reported that when Anna arrived at Deal in Kent, 'she tarried there a certain space in a castle newly built, and thither came the duke of Suffolk, and the duchess of Suffolk … with a great number of knights and esquires'.[4] Katherine would have been around twenty years old when she greeted the queen, a fitting role for a young woman that would one day make her own mark on the era.

Katherine settled into marital life and oversaw her husband complete diplomatic and personal missions for the king. In 1536, Brandon was sent to quell rebellion in Lincolnshire and in 1544 served as Captain General of the English army at Boulogne. They were married for just over a decade when Charles died in August 1545.[5] He was buried by the king at St George's Chapel in Windsor Castle. The couple had two sons, appropriately named Henry and Charles, who were educated at Cambridge under the eye of Martin Bucer, then professor of theology and known also to Anne and Edward Seymour. However, tragedy struck in July 1551, when the boys died of the sweating sickness, a virulent infection which presented with symptoms of lethargy and a high fever followed by sudden death. Katherine rushed to them, but only arrived to spend Charles' last hours with him before he too was consumed by the fever.[6]

After 1545 Katherine immersed herself in widowhood, managing her estates and maintaining alliances with key figures of Tudor government. A sketch made of the duchess by Holbein during her marriage to Brandon shows her with a solemn expression as she gazes off in the distance to her right. At the time of the drawing, Katherine was one of the wealthiest women in the realm, and Holbein took care to add details including pearls around her headdress and a laced-up collar under her chin.[7] It has been said that Henry developed an attraction for Katherine, and by February 1546 there were rumours she was the new focus of his adoration. The Imperial Ambassador Francois van der Delft reported in February of that year that 'there are rumours here of a new Queen', and that 'Madame Suffolk is much talked about, and is in great favour'.[8] Katherine was a lady-in-waiting and close friend of Kateryn Parr, Henry's sixth queen, and would not be the first of his wives' ladies to attract his roving eye.

In 1552 or early 1553, during the reign of Edward VI, Katherine remarried. But her second husband was not a king, a duke or a man of wealth or status. As they exchanged vows in Lincolnshire, the man looking back at her was the gentleman usher of her household, Richard Bertie.

In contrast to the portly, larger-than-life character of Charles Brandon, Bertie was slim with a pointed beard, long sharp nose and hooded eyes. He was an attentive administrator and proficient in languages including Latin, French and Italian.[9] Bertie's official role in Katherine's household was based on hierarchy and protocol, but they had evidently grown close while working together on the management of Katherine's estates and personal business. He was two years older than his bride, and their marriage was almost certainly based on mutual love and affection. Katherine was wealthy in her own right, and did not need to take a husband for financial reasons. Bertie is mentioned in a letter from Katherine to William Cecil written in 1548, so their working relationship at least had begun by this date.[10] The nineteenth-century writer Georgina Bertie also referenced a letter written by the duchess in 1552 as evidence for the date of the couple's intention to marry. In his will of 1545 Charles requested Katherine remain a widow after his death, a clause not unusual for the time, which aimed to prevent the family wealth being transferred to a new husband.[11] Katherine sent Bertie to deal with the business, writing that 'Master Bertie is in London, to conclude, if he can, with the heirs; for I would gladly discharge the trust wherein my Lord [Brandon] did leave me, before I did, for any man's pleasure, anything else'.[12]

The couple would have had the benefit of getting to know one another over a number of years before embarking on a romantic relationship. Pearl Hogrefe, in *Women of Action in Tudor England: Nine Biographical Sketches*, acknowledged that this initially professional relationship would have benefitted the couple in their later married life, stating that the partnership 'had been tested in depth before the marriage'.[13] This was something many Tudor men and women destined for arranged marriages were unable to experience. We know that Katherine was strongly outspoken against the 'wickedness' of these unions. She later wrote to Cecil regarding a proposed match for her son, stating that 'I cannot tell what more unkindness one of us might show the other, or wherein we might work more wickedly, than to bring our children into so miserable a state, not to choose by their own liking such as they must profess so strait a bond, and so great a love to, for ever'.[14] This statement therefore adds further weight to the Bertie marriage being a love match.

The couple had a home, Barbican, in London, but could also be found at their base in Grimsthorpe in Lincolnshire. The traveller and writer John Leland, who visited the village in the mid-sixteenth century, noted the nearby 'stone bridge under which ran a pretty river', a landmark Katherine and Richard would have known from their journeys around the local area. He described the house as recently rebuilt with 'an old work of stone, and the gatehouse was fair and strong, and the walls of each [side of] it embattled'. He also wrote of a 'great ditch' around the house.[15] Today, the castle sits within manicured grounds and, like many Tudor homes, has been reshaped over the centuries.

The house the couple would have known descended to Katherine from her father, who was granted it by Henry VIII. The oldest part of the building is believed to date from around the end of the twelfth century, but traces of Tudor architecture can be seen in the embattlements and mullioned windows. A visitor to Grimsthorpe in 1903 noted the sixteenth-century banqueting hall and tapestries on display that were once owned by Brandon, acquired through his marriage to Mary Tudor.[16] These tapestries then, may have hung and warmed the rooms of Grimsthorpe while Katherine and Bertie lived there. Grimsthorpe was the scene of so many of the events in Katherine's – and later, Richard Bertie's – lives. It was here that Hugh Latimer, the Protestant minister, preached at the duchess' invitation. In June 1552, Katherine accompanied her groundskeeper on a hunt for a deer in the park late at night. She had wanted to gift venison to Latimer's wife at her churching. The deer could not be caught, leaving Katherine to complain to Cecil in a letter that 'wild things be not ready at commandment'. She wrote the letter at six o'clock in the morning, 'like a sluggard in my bed'.[17]

Even before her marriage to Bertie, Katherine was well-known for her religious beliefs, particularly her opposition to Catholicism. There was hearsay that she had ridiculed Stephen Gardiner by dressing a dog in a white vestment and naming him after the bishop. During a meal hosted by herself and Brandon, the ladies were asked to choose the man they liked best and accompany him to dinner. Seeing as she could not choose her husband, she announced to the assembled party that she would choose the man she liked least, leading Gardiner to the table. On another occasion she shouted insults to him in public as he greeted her politely through an open window.

After Brandon's death, Katherine was, with Anne Seymour and three other ladies, identified as a potential suspect in the support of Anne Askew. Katherine and Anne were also thought to have 'instigated' the queen, Kateryn Parr, to 'heresy'.[18] Despite rumours that her royal husband's eye had once wandered towards Katherine, the queen and the duchess remained close, and Katherine urged Parr to write her book *Lamentation of a Sinner*, published in 1548. The title of the work acknowledges that it was 'Set forth and put in print at the instant desire of the right gracious lady, Catherine, duchess of Suffolk, and the earnest request of the right honourable lord William Parr, marquess of Northampton'.[19] A well-known and visible figure of Protestant reform, the duchess was also known to fellow reformers Anne and Edward Seymour. She had been present with them at the wedding of the king and Kateryn Parr, and served at court alongside Anne. Katherine was also a friend of the Protestant bishop Hugh Latimer. Bertie, too, was a devoted reformer, but was more diplomatic and less abrasive than his wife, a skill learned through years of dealing with requests from craftsmen, tenants and secretaries from all walks of life. While Katherine's response to matters of faith was sharp, direct and blunt, Bertie handled confrontation with a calm and dissimulating attitude. At the beginning of Mary's reign, he would need to deploy these skills when his wife's earlier boldness came back to haunt them.

The martyrologist John Foxe wrote that Gardiner, the man Katherine had so roundly humiliated as a young and powerful duchess, intended 'a holy practice of revenge' on her. Gardiner, at the time, tolerated Katherine's insults; she was one of the premier nobles of the realm, her husband on the closest of terms with the king. But now, the balance of power had swung and Gardiner was one of the most powerful men in the country, having been appointed Lord Chancellor by Queen Mary.

Gardiner's first move was to summon Katherine's husband. After accusing Bertie of shirking the payment of some debts, which he disputed, the conversation turned quickly to religion and Bertie was asked to answer for his wife's actions. Foxe depicts the bishop in a state of rage as he asked him of Katherine, 'is she now as ready to set up the mass, as she was lately to pull it down, when she caused in her progress, a dog in a rochet to be carried, and called by my name? Or doth she think her lambs now safe enough, which said to me, when I veiled my bonnet to her out of my chamber-window in the Tower, that it was merry with the lambs, now the wolf was shut up?'. He remembered, too, the time Charles Brandon had 'invited me, and divers ladies to dinner, desired every lady to choose him whom she loved best, and so place themselves. My lady your wife … said that forasmuch as she could not sit down with my lord [Brandon] whom she loved best, she had chosen him [Gardiner] whom she loved worst'.

No doubt used to backpedalling from the harsh and spontaneous words of the duchess, Bertie tried to ease the situation. He maintained that 'she was neither the author, nor the allower' of the episode with the dog and maintained her religious beliefs 'not only by strong persuasions of divers excellent learned men', but also in fear that she would 'show herself a false Christian'. Bertie left the meeting reassuring Gardiner that it was indeed likely that his wife would one day revert to the old faith, and then headed home.[20]

As high-profile Protestant reformers living during a state-enforced return to Catholicism, the couple must have sensed the hot glare of their enemies. According to Foxe, they received word 'that the bishop meant to call her to an account of her faith, whereby extremity might follow'.[21] This 'extremity' had already claimed the lives of some of their friends and others known to them. Lady Jane Grey, chosen by Edward VI before his death to continue the Protestant religion in England, was executed by Mary on 12 February 1554, along with her husband Guildford Dudley. Jane's father-in-law, the Duke of Northumberland, who had instigated so many of the late king's religious reforms, was beheaded the year before. Katherine's own words reveal that she knew the court was a dangerous and fickle place. Remembering the treatment of Edward Seymour, Lord Protector, she referred to him as 'that good Duke', who had 'lost all that he sought to keep, with his head to boot; and his counsellors slipped their collars, turned their coats, and have served since to play their parts in many other matters'.[22] Status and money were no guarantees of safety in the volatile Tudor court. It was time for Katherine and Richard to leave the realm.

According to Foxe, Bertie applied to Queen Mary for permission to travel overseas to gather debts owed during Katherine's marriage to Charles Brandon. One of the debtors, he claimed, was the Emperor Charles V and he had more chance of obtaining payment, he said, before the queen's marriage to Prince Philip, 'for when the marriage is consummate, the Emperor hath his desire'. Mary agreed.

Bertie made arrangements for his passage and left in June 1554. On 1 January 1555, Katherine left their home in London to follow her husband. Foxe states that it was 'very early in the morning' between four and five o'clock that Katherine and a handful of servants shuffled out of the house, with their infant daughter Susan in her arms. So that no one raised the alarm, she was after all leaving the realm without permission, Katherine was dressed 'like a mean [poor] merchant's wife' and boarded a boat to the Netherlands in such heavy fog that they had to urge the boatsman to embark.[23]

Katherine and Richard found exile a difficult and uneasy experience. Foxe states that they travelled from town to town through darkness, in disguise and on foot, to avoid attracting attention. Despite this, 'at the town of Santon was a muttering that the duchess and her husband were greater personages than they gave themselves forth' which caused some anxiety that they might be discovered and sent back to England. The couple continued towards Wesel in the Duchy of Cleves, with Katherine now heavily pregnant. Their second child, Peregrine, was born there in October 1555.

A coloured drawing of Wesel created in 1572 survives, and shows a city the Berties would have known. It is shown hemmed in by a defensive wall, punctuated by towers and gates. Church spires rise into the sky, while houses with red rooftops huddle between them. Outside the wall flows the Rhine, a wooden bridge connecting the land either side of the river. With a toddler and a newborn and nowhere to stay, Bertie considered taking shelter with his family in a church porch, but overheard two residents speaking Latin. He asked them to take him to the home of Francis Perusell, a Protestant sympathizer he knew. Here, they were welcomed, changed into clean, fresh clothes and fed. But the couple encountered more problems. Talk of English plots to discover their whereabouts reached them, and on their way to Poland, the couple and their children were set upon by armed men in an argument over a dog and false accusations of murder. Bertie ran up a ladder to an upper storey of a building and fended off the attackers using a dagger and his rapier. Eventually, they reached their destination, where they 'continued both in great quietness and honour, till the death of Queen Mary' with the support of the Polish king, Sigismund II.[24]

While it is true that Foxe was writing a sensationalist account of these events, and that we should allow for some element of dramatism, his version of the couple's experiences do tally with documentary evidence. Katherine and Bertie were indeed in exile between 1555-1559 and a document relating to Peregrine's naturalisation in Elizabeth I's reign confirms he was born at Wesel.[25] Another document, written on 17 September 1555 and 'in the King and Queen's Majesty's name', records that the pair 'contemptuously without licence … departed the realm'.[26] The decision to enter into an uncertain and risky voyage into Europe knowing that they had left behind all their goods, friends and business contacts in England emphasizes the real danger they considered themselves to have been in at home. Neither believed in false recantations, Bertie holding the opinion that 'To force a confession of religion by mouth, contrary to that in the heart, worketh damnation, where salvation is pretended'.[27]

Interestingly, although Foxe titles his chapter as dealing with Katherine, Bertie is given much of the credit in the narrative for his proactive approach during their exile. He had written ahead to warn contacts of their arrival, interceded with locals in Latin and engineered the entire opportunity for their sailing. A ballad, named *The Most Rare and Excellent History of the Dutchess of Suffolk and her Husband Richard Bertie's Calamity*, was published during Elizabeth I's reign and seems heavily based on Foxe's account. However, the ballad gives extra acknowledgement of Bertie's efforts, crediting him also with collecting coal and making a fire, carrying the baby when Katherine was tired and sourcing food. Later, it states that 'Master Bertie, Brave and Bold', made a speech hoping that locals would treat the exhausted couple with kindness.[28]

The couple's years in exile would have been challenging and a stark contrast to their previously comfortable life at Grimsthorpe with servants to bake bread, brew ale and take care of daily household duties. Katherine clearly trusted her husband, who demonstrated loyalty, diplomacy and determination.

In 1559, with Elizabeth now on the throne, the couple returned to England and the queen restored them to their lands and possessions.[29] They turned their efforts to other matters, including the adult lives of their children, and asked Elizabeth to consider raising Richard to the peerage of Willoughby, in right of his wife. Bertie, in typical feigned modesty, downplayed these ambitions in a letter to Cecil as 'vain bubbles', but he, as much as Katherine, was active in promoting them. Katherine wrote in 1570, anxious that their petition was not being listened to, while Bertie promised he could provide paperwork proving his claim. In April 1572, a stack of papers thudded onto Cecil's desk, but Elizabeth did not approve Bertie to the title.[30]

The couple remained active in royal business, although Bertie politely declined a public position Cecil offered him in 1563. Katherine, referred to by a Spanish source as 'one of the worst heretics in England', was called on to attend the imprisoned Mary Queen of Scots at Pontefract in Yorkshire in September 1574.[31] Richard accompanied Elizabeth on a visit to Cambridge in 1564 and was also present at the queen's visit to the Earl of Leicester at Kenilworth Castle in 1575.[32]

Towards the end of their lives, Thomas Twyne added a dedication to Richard Bertie in his English translation of Petrarch's *Phisicke Against Fortune* in 1579. Twyne described Bertie as 'no mean personage of this realm of England', who 'gained surpassing preferments at the hands of Fortune'. Twyne went on to praise Bertie's 'valour of Mind, Virtue, Godliness, Wisdom, Gravity and Learning generally in all Faculties, Good letters and Tongues, as few or none the like far and wide to be found in this our age'.[33] Richard Bertie is not often considered for his qualities and what he brought to his marriage with the duchess. However, like Katherine, he was an important figure and regarded as such by his contemporaries.

The couple's monument in St James' Church in Spilsby, Lincolnshire shows Katherine and Richard as they would have appeared in older age. Katherine is depicted at around the age of sixty, with a round face, small button nose and a tight smile. Richard, whose effigy bust stands alongside his wife's, is carved wearing the fashion of the day: elaborately-embroidered doublet, small ruff at the neck and full but neatly-trimmed beard. Their likenesses, which are detailed and lifelike, are further supported by other confirmed portraits of the couple created during their lifetimes.

Seventeenth-century writer Thomas Fuller described Katherine as 'a lady of a sharp wit, and sure hand to thrust it home and make it pierce when she pleased'.[34] What she may have considered provocative, playful banter in her past attracted the revenge of her enemies in the future. Gardiner remembered the duchess' harsh treatment of him after rising to power under Mary in 1553. Richard Bertie was also sure of his Protestant views, but executed his opinions with humility, a dissembling wit and diplomacy. He calmly handled difficult conversations including Gardiner's confrontation and refused a job offer from Cecil with warmth, respect and a scattering of ease. He had worked on Katherine's business for years, and was an able administrator of her estates.

Perhaps it was his reassuring and pragmatic approach that drew Katherine to Richard in the early years of their relationship. Their romance dates from at least 1552, but they had known one another in a business sense for longer. Georgina Bertie emphasized that Richard was 'not only the sharer of her bright days of courtly favour and earthly prosperity, but her courageous and well-tried companion in the hours of affliction, suffering and danger'.[35]

Surviving evidence surrounding their marriage shows a strong element of support given and received by both partners. Katherine interceded on Richard's behalf over his claim to her title, while Richard defended his wife against Gardiner's accusations and later fended off attackers during exile. During their years overseas they provided one another with moral and practical support as they endured various adverse events. Although Katherine was used to living in financial comfort and luxurious surroundings, a striking sense of soberness and logic can be found both in her personal letters and in her behaviour during exile. With Bertie, she travelled by foot through towns and cities, ate what they could find and was prepared to sleep with her family in a church porch for the night. Neither of them flinched and returned to the comfort of Grimsthorpe, but instead jointly established new connections, learned from experiences and remained steadfast in their religious beliefs. Katherine was outspoken and opinionated, but Bertie could also be stubborn and wilful. During one family dispute over Peregrine's chosen bride Mary de Vere, Katherine decided to keep the matter secret from Richard, telling Cecil that her husband 'will give little more than his good will, if he give that'.[36] The couple were therefore well-matched in resolve and temperament.

Did Katherine and Richard marry for love? There is very little else that would have motivated their marriage. Katherine was wealthy and could have remained a widow for the rest of her life. In addition, she was strongly against the concept of arranged marriages. It is clear from the sources that the couple shared a strong bond, trust and respect for almost thirty years of marriage. Katherine and Richard's relationship was based not only on the complementary skills they each brought to the partnership, but also formed out of mutual fondness and love.

The biggest impact Katherine and Richard had on the lives of sixteenth-century Tudor citizens was engineering their survival after 1555. Just weeks after Katherine glanced back at the freezing Kent coast in January of that year, public executions in the name of religion began. Anyone from bishops to barbers were burned alive for refusing to follow Mary and Philip's policy on the Catholic faith. Bishop Ferrar of St David's in Wales was burned on 30 March 1555, bravely tolerating the flames until a spectator named John Gravell 'dashed him upon the head' to hasten his death. The following month, a monk named William Flower was burned in Westminster, protesting that 'this is my faith, which I beseech all men here to bear witness of'. In May, upholsterers John Cardmaker and John Warne died in the flames at Smithfield.[37] John Hooper, Edward VI's Bishop of Gloucester and Worcester, received the same treatment at Gloucester, also in 1555. Sentence was carried out on citizens, whether high or lower-born. Gentlemen, linen drapers, poulterers, clergymen and a tallow-chandler's apprentice, among others, were all burned in 1555 alone, along with Katherine's friend Hugh Latimer. As well as Gardiner's own private score to settle, a prominent and reformist duchess with a sharp and defiant tongue would have been a public and valuable example to unruly Protestants throughout the realm. Katherine's comments on Seymour's own fall indicates that she was well aware supporters could quickly turn to deserters if it suited them. It is clear from their stealth and suddenness in leaving the country that the couple felt they were no longer safe in Mary's Catholic England.

Their safe return in 1559 not only allowed them to take part in some of the political events of the day, but also gave their children the opportunity to exercise influence of their own. Peregrine, Lord Willoughby, served Elizabeth I on a number of occasions and became a respected politician and soldier, having trained under his parents' friend, William Cecil. He was sent by the queen to negotiate with the King of Denmark, and in 1586, secured military support for England. Peregrine also fought bravely with Robert Dudley, Earl of Leicester in the Netherlands and succeeded him in his post on Dudley's return to England in 1587. He later played a decisive role against the invasion of the Spanish Armada, capturing a large Spanish vessel between Ostend and Sluys.[38]

The couple's journey into exile also directly breathed new life into the Protestant cause during Mary's counter-reformation. Katherine and Richard were treated as near-martyrs, their account immortalized by Foxe as well as in the ballad that circulated in the 1580s. Romantic legend surrounded Peregrine's birth, with some accounts maintaining it had taken place in the porch of a Wesel church, an apt and symbolic image for a family so connected with and dedicated to religion. It was perhaps understandable that Mary would seek to track down the couple in Europe, if Foxe's claims are correct. Resolved in their religious beliefs and with good personal connections, the couple displayed boldness, determination and organisation in their maintenance and spread of the Protestant cause. Now public figureheads of resistance to the queen's reforms, they, according to ecclesiastical historian John Strype, established a community of like-minded reformists overseas where they could share news, exchange and debate opinions and worship without fear. This gathering extended to 100 people, maintained Strype, made up of both men and women. He named as part of their community the Bishop of Chichester, Thomas Young the future Archbishop of York and John Rough, who was later martyred.[39]

Strype goes further to state that this gathering of fellow reformists evolved because of Katherine and Richard's presence. The company, he writes, was 'occasioned chiefly by the coming thither of Mr. Berty, and the Duchess of Suffolk his wife, both serious professors of religion: which coming of theirs being heard of, many others flocked thither'. Strype names a Mrs Grantham and Anthony Meres, among others who sought out the couple 'beyond the seas' in 1556.[40] Furthermore, Strype states that when Katherine and Richard left the area, 'this congregation soon brake up ... some followed them, others went to Basil; Coverdale to Geneva, and others to other places'.[41] The Berties then, were responsible for the maintenance and spread of English Protestantism in Wesel and beyond during the late 1550s. Those who worshipped and learned with them later scattered throughout Europe with their reinforced morale and beliefs.

Katherine's suspected support of Anne Askew pre-dates her marriage to Bertie, as does her involvement in Kateryn Parr's writing of *Lamentation of a Sinner*. These examples however demonstrate that Katherine's passion for reform and the Protestant faith simply continued from her first into her second marriage. Miles Coverdale, in particular, was a central character in the Berties' life from 1555. Coverdale translated the Bible into English during Henry VIII's reign and preached to their group of reformers in Wesel. David Baldwin in *Henry VIII's Last Love* has also explored evidence in the Berties' accounts that place Coverdale in their household on returning to England.[42] In a letter, Coverdale refers to Katherine as 'the most illustrious duchess of Suffolk', and relates a conversation he had with Richard Bertie over her debts.[43] In his seventies, he continued to preach at Paul's Cross and resumed religious study at Cambridge.[44]

The couple also left a lasting legacy in the spirit and determination they displayed during their lifetime. This was not just exercised through their approach to religion. Mary clearly considered the couple enough of a threat to send scouts into Europe to track them down. Part of this power came from their strong and unified stance, something they came to be known by. Together, the Berties were a force to be reckoned with; popular, charismatic and relentless in their support of one another. They were also intelligent, forward-planning and were willing to go to great lengths to survive. It is no wonder Mary wanted them found and publicly punished for what she would have perceived as their insolence.

Katherine died on 19 September 1580. Richard Bertie died almost two years later, at Bourne in Lincolnshire, on 9 April 1582.

Chapter 8

Elizabeth I and Robert Dudley, Earl of Leicester

THE RELATIONSHIP BETWEEN Elizabeth I and her court favourite Robert Dudley, Earl of Leicester has divided writers' opinions for centuries. Some were convinced they enjoyed a passionate and secret sexual relationship, while others maintained it was a close, platonic bond. In truth, it is just not possible almost five centuries later to definitively conclude the exact nature of their affair. For the purposes of evaluating their joint contribution to the Tudor age as a duo, however, it is not necessary. Robert Dudley is not always given credit for the impact he made on history and was far more than a handsome courtier willing to receive Elizabeth's flirtations, titles and expensive gifts. Historical evidence proves without doubt that Elizabeth and Dudley formed a close working partnership that dominated state business for thirty years. Through letters, official documents and eyewitness accounts of those who knew them, we can gain a deeper understanding of their joint aims, disputes and the dynamics of their relationship as they shaped the course of future events.

That the pair were close has never been questioned. In fact, the familiarity they showed one another in private sometimes trickled out into public, attracting raised eyebrows from onlookers. In 1564, Sir James Melville watched as Elizabeth created Robert Dudley, Earl of Leicester and Baron Denbigh, remembering that the queen put 'her hand in his neck, smilingly tickling him' under his collar, despite the earl kneeling before her with 'great gravity'.[1] Dudley too, expressed daring familiarity with the queen during a tennis match, when he famously snatched a handkerchief from the monarch's hand to dab the sweat from his face in front of shocked onlookers. Their closeness was noted from the very beginning of Elizabeth's reign. As early as April 1559 the Count of Feria wrote that 'Lord Robert has come so much into favour that he does whatever he likes with affairs and it is even said that her Majesty visits him in his chamber day and night', noting rumours that the two were in love and might marry.[2]

Dudley's favour and seemingly effortless rise to power naturally provoked disapproval from suspicious and jealous courtiers. Even Sir William Cecil, now the queen's advisor, was said to have told the Spanish bishop and ambassador, Alvaro de Quadra, that he 'clearly foresaw the ruin of the realm through Robert's intimacy with the queen'.[3] Gossip was also fuelled by the historic 'treachery' they saw in Dudley's bloodline – his father and grandfather had both been executed by previous Tudor monarchs for treason. Talk of the pair's love life was also rampant, one tale doing the rounds in November 1560 insisting they had secretly married, while a later rumour of 1570 asserted the couple had borne two children.[4]

Although there is no evidence to support either of these rumours, Dudley's brother-in-law Henry Sidney did reveal to Quadra in January 1561 that the couple had a 'love affair', but 'there was nothing illicit about it or such as could be set right by your Majesty's [Philip's] authority'.[5] This aligns with Elizabeth's own words, uttered when she believed herself dying of smallpox in 1562, that she 'loved Robert dearly … but nothing improper had ever taken place between them'. Understandably, her spontaneous annuity of £50 bestowed on Tamworth, Dudley's groom, attracted suspicion, considering the rumours spreading about the pair at the time.[6] However, the queen was intensely aware of the political importance of her virginity, and may have simply wanted to reward Tamworth for his service to Dudley. It is highly unlikely that she would have lied, believing herself so close to death and divine judgement. Elizabeth and Robert Dudley were certainly close friends, and probably 'lovers' in a romantic, 'courtly love' sense. But it is fair to speculate that their relationship most likely stopped short of a full sexual liaison.

This is just as well, because while rumours of Elizabeth and Robert Dudley's flirtatious love affair and illegitimate children spread through the court, Dudley's wife Amy was managing their household and arranging the sale of wool. Scandalous accusations about his marriage began to be hurled at the favourite by his enemies. Quadra reported in September 1560 that Dudley was planning to murder his wife to free him to marry Elizabeth, a charge that would take a deeply sinister turn when Amy was later found at the bottom of a flight of stairs with a broken neck.[7] As many writers have acknowledged, this was the end of any real chance Robert had of one day marrying Elizabeth, the image-conscious queen unlikely to agree to marry a man accused of killing his wife to wed her. Robert, too, would find the accusations followed him during his career. He remained single until the early 1570s, when he embarked on a relationship (and possible marriage) with Lady Sheffield, who bore him a son. He later married Elizabeth's cousin Lettice Knollys, the Countess of Essex.[8]

Elizabeth and Dudley's romantic connection has inspired the creation of books, art and theatrical drama. But it is not this that makes them one of Tudor England's most influential power couples. They supported one another while working for the good of the realm. Dudley's faith and loyalty towards Elizabeth never wavered, and despite arguments between them, she always welcomed him back into favour. During their thirty-year public relationship, they demonstrated resilience, a close bond and a strong sense of duty towards their country. And as patrons of learning and the arts, they also boosted England's continued involvement and contribution to the Renaissance.

As we have seen, all Tudor monarchs supported the visual arts. In an age before modern media, a leader's power and strength was conveyed in portraits and pressed into coins. But during Elizabeth's reign, the arts received a vital and forceful boost. During a visit to the University of Cambridge in 1564, she told assembled students with Dudley looking on that 'there is no way, either for weariness more short, or for certainty more strait, towards either the bettering of your fortunes, or obtaining favour from your prince, than that you employ your best endeavours in achieving arts' perfection; for which cause, as you had semblance to begin, so that you would still persevere, I do not only entreat, but beseech you also'.[9]

The queen was well known for her love of art and literature and, building on the work of other Tudor leaders, writers during her reign published texts on a wide range of subjects including botany, astronomy, travel and mathematics. Elizabeth herself published her own *Precationes Privatae* in 1563.[10] She was also a proficient translator, a skill she had developed in childhood. Henry VIII and Katherine of Aragon had experimented with new expressions of theatrical display in the 1510s and 1520s, but the art's progress stalled during the middle of the century as the country distractedly tussled with religious division. From Elizabeth's accession, however, a new age of theatre began. Dramatists including William Shakespeare, Thomas Kyd and Christopher Marlowe produced work that was, for the first time, performed publicly to audiences in permanent venues. There were also new methods of scientific investigation and the discovery of territories around the world. As a result of this new enthusiasm for learning and the arts, Tudor citizens in the late sixteenth century could enjoy innovative experiences, such as watching a play at the theatre, growing sweetcorn in their garden or marvelling at a map of the solar system.[11]

Without Elizabeth and Dudley's joint influence and patronage, many of these advances might not have happened. Derek Wilson, in *The Uncrowned Kings of England: The Black Legend of the Dudleys*, discussed the earl's involvement in voyages made by sea captains such as John Hawkins, Martin Frobisher and Francis Drake, journeys that the queen also backed.[12] The Spanish ambassador Bernardino de Mendoza additionally noted in 1580 that Leicester was 'behind Drake' in his circumnavigation of the globe and had 'a ship ready to sail on a voyage for plunder on route to the Indies', but also to assist Drake in his mission if they found him.[13] There is also a letter from Sir Walter Raleigh explaining one of Drake's new ventures. 'I doubt not all shall be recupered', he wrote to Leicester, 'I hope your Excellency will assist what you may'.[14] Dudley not only dipped into his purse to support these voyages, but also assisted the queen in an administrative respect. In April 1582 she ordered that Edward Fenton, who was to sail from Southampton to the East Indies, should provide an inventory of goods on board his ships before and after his voyage. These were to be sent to Dudley, along with a report detailing any losses.[15] On 5 July 1585 Elizabeth granted certain noblemen and other subjects some privileges for trade in Barbary (North Africa), placing Leicester and his brother Ambrose at the top of the list, and ordering Dudley 'to make and establish good and necessary order and ordnance' for the arrangements.[16]

Elizabeth and Dudley's financial and administrative support of new voyages increased Tudor subjects' knowledge of foreign lands. Drake's circumnavigation of the globe, which was supported by the couple, revealed new discoveries to Tudor citizens including fruits 'as big … as a man's head', which were broken open to reveal sweet liquid and hard, white flesh. Drake also noted with curiosity the presence of 'fiery wormes flying in the air'.[17] Today, we are used to the sight of coconuts and fireflies, but to the sixteenth-century seafarer these were exotic and magical. Stories of these discoveries along with Elizabeth's famous knighting of Drake on his return triggered a new enthusiasm for mapmaking and navigation, as explorers were inspired to plan daring and lucrative voyages of their own.

As Elizabethan ships limped around the globe with their owners incentivized by glory and cash, a new hobby among the Tudors developed. Thomas Platter, on a visit to London in 1599, observed the many costumes, weapons and relics that had begun to be collected by enthusiasts. Visiting the house of a Mr Cope, he described artefacts such as 'Indian plumes', along with 'shoes from many strange lands', an 'artful little Chinese box' and 'a narrow Indian canoe'. Cope also showed the visitor 'many holy relics from a Spanish ship which he helped to capture'.[18]

Cope wasn't the only one hoarding new and valuable objects. Plundered treasure and gold also swelled the royal purse. Elizabeth, for her part, issued explorers with letters of patent that authorised the snatching of valuables from foreign ports and coastlines. Letters between Spanish officials during the period angrily refer to 'pirates hailing from England', one infuriated observer commenting that 'the audacious Englishmen being without all shame are not afraid to come and dare us at our very doors'.[19] The queen also provided her own royal ships for voyages, on one occasion sending them to assist Drake off the coast of Portugal. She also offered *The Dreadnought*, *The Elizabeth Bonaventure* and *The Garland* to be brought into service, while her ship *The Minion* was employed in Hawkins' voyage to the West Indies in 1564. The 400-ton *The Galleon Leicester*, is also mentioned in a number of expeditions.[20]

Some of these voyages were politically motivated and had serious and significant effects. Together, Dudley and Elizabeth supported efforts to curb the growing Habsburg power in Europe and prevent it spreading to England. This was achieved by causing significant financial damage to Spain, rendering it unable to mount an invasion. Hawkins and Drake were sent to the Americas to capture Spanish goods and treasure, followed by another campaign under Drake in 1572. In November 1577, Drake was again equipped with a fleet of five ships which sailed from Plymouth, heavily financed by Leicester and the queen. In 1587 he carried out a devastating raid on the ports of Cadiz and St Vincent, burning ships, seizing trade documents and hoarding treasure. Frederick Chamberlin, in *Elizabeth and Leycester*, discusses these activities as well as the couple's secret meetings with Francis Walsingham and a man named 'Julio ... who, it is thought, is a Morisco [Moor]. He ... is closeted for hours every day with Leycester and Walsingham and sometimes with the Queen'. Mendoza, Philip's ambassador, told him that Julio 'has been heard to say that he will be revenged on your Majesty'.[21] The couple, then, were responsible for not only financing damaging attacks on Spanish ports, but also personally consulting with its enemies, acts which Chamberlin stated 'completely overturned Philip's plans of setting out that summer for England'.[22] Spain did embark on a naval attack on the country in the following year, but this delay reduced Spain's naval strength and ensured Elizabeth and her council could more readily prepare.

The world was becoming smaller, and new and unusual crops from foreign lands began to be offloaded at England's dockyards, including spices, vegetables and tobacco. William Harrison, writing in 1573, noted the use of American tobacco in England, smoked with 'an instrument formed like a little ladle'.[23] John Gerard, in his *The Herball, or Generall Historie of Plants* published in 1597, was able to describe the newfound 'turkey wheat', used in the Americas to make bread. He even managed to grow it in his garden. Today we know it as sweetcorn. He also noted 'Potatoes of Virginia', which 'groweth naturally in America where it was first discovered', recommending that they were eaten with oil, salt and vinegar. He also recorded the use of other plants shipped in from the New World including aloe, the kidney bean and the sunflower, discoveries that could not have been made without initial investment and encouragement of overseas exploration.[24]

The era benefitted from academic input, too, with the number of graduates vastly increasing during the reign. In 1558-59, twenty-eight graduates achieved their BA degree at Cambridge University, while by 1583 the figure had grown to 277.[25] Elizabeth had delivered her rousing speech in support of education and learning, but Robert Dudley stepped up to support her in an organisational role. He served as High Steward of Cambridge University and was also Chancellor at Oxford, where he served for twenty-four years. During his leadership, he took steps to tighten administration and insisted on tougher religious structuring along with the licencing of new tutors. He also gifted the university a printing press, leading to the establishment of the Oxford University Press, which still prints work today.[26] The prediction made then, by Leicester's enemies in a pamphlet called *The Commonwealth*, that the earl's Chancellorship of Oxford 'cancelled almost all hope of good in that university' and was 'very like soon to come to destruction' would in fact prove to be the opposite.[27] Geoffrey Whitney, in his 1584 book *A Choice of Emblemes*, acknowledged Robert Dudley's role as patron of learning and progress, writing that 'diverse, who are now famous men, had been through poverty long since discouraged from their studies: if they had not found your honour so prone to be their patron'.[28] William Cuningham, in his *The Cosmographical Glasse*' of 1559, dedicated the work to Dudley, stating that he 'doth not only favour science, but have given her within your breast a resting place'.[29] Elizabeth, magnificent in jewels and cloth of gold, was the figurehead of educational reform, but Dudley actively carried it out on her behalf. It was, of course, Elizabeth's financial and political support of the earl that enabled him to also patronize influential writers and thinkers.

Another of Elizabeth and Dudley's mutual passions was the theatre, and in the summer of 1575, Dudley hosted a theatrical display at Kenilworth Castle that many writers believe was his final attempt to convince the queen to marry him. The bespoke programme of entertainments lasted almost three weeks in the warm July of that year, and Dudley employed craftspeople, actors, musicians and tailors. They built stages, embellished sets and erected poetic signage that twinkled with gold in the sunshine. Elizabeth was greeted by a Lady of the Lake, various gods and goddesses and treated to a fireworks display. One day, on her way back from hunting, the playwright and poet George Gascoigne leapt out at her to deliver a speech, brandishing 'an oaken plant plucked up by the roots' and wearing a costume of moss and ivy.[30]

Some of these magical characters have drawn comparisons with the work of one of the age's most prolific writers and performers. Aubrey Richardson and C.C. Stopes have both speculated that among the five-hundred spectators present was the eleven-year-old William Shakespeare from nearby Stratford-upon-Avon, just fourteen miles from Kenilworth. Dudley was also known, said Stopes, to have looked for 'popularity and co-operation from neighbouring corporations', suggesting Shakespeare's father, a figure in Stratford's local government, may have received an invitation. With its themes of love, marriage and fantasy, it is certainly possible Shakespeare was later inspired by Leicester's entertainments when he wrote *A Midsummer Night's Dream* in the 1590s – a play, according to Stopes, 'laden with remembrances for all who had been at the Kenilworth festivities'.[31] Ramie Targoff, in *Shakespeare's Sisters, How Women Wrote the Renaissance*, also places the writer Mary Sidney at Kenilworth and discusses the significance of the event on her work. It is just possible that this young lady in the queen's service was inspired to become a writer later in the period by the displays and performances arranged by Dudley for the queen in the summer of 1575.[32]

Soon after rising to power, Dudley established his own group of actors that he named Leicester's Players. In 1560 Elizabeth's accounts record a payment of £6 13s 4d paid to 'Lord Robert Dudley's Company' for a performance at Christmas.[33] In 1574 the queen granted them a royal patent allowing them to perform freely across the realm. Seeing the queen's enthusiasm for the art form, courtiers soon established their own groups that played for her from the mid-1560s, with records including those supported by the Earl of Warwick, Lord Rich and Lord Clinton. Elizabeth formed her own group of players, The Queen's Company, who performed for her at

Whitehall on 26 and 29 December 1583 and on other occasions in the 1580s and early 1590s.[34]

Elizabeth and Dudley clearly relished in this old Tudor tradition they had given a new, 'modern' lease of life, and their support of the industry changed the acting and writing professions forever. As well as increasing work opportunities for actors, musicians and craftsmen engaged on specific productions, it also led to the building of the first permanent theatrical venues. James Burbage, one of Leicester's actors, constructed his theatre in Finsbury in 1576, while his son Richard later established The Globe with William Shakespeare in 1599.[35] The theatre that stands today is a replica, the original building having tragically burned down during the reign of James I. However, it is near to its original spot in Southwark near the banks of the Thames and continues to host productions in its Elizabethan-designed interior today. Performances during the Elizabethan age had certainly come a long way since the early days of Henry VIII and Katherine of Aragon. Accounts of plays and masques held at court during Elizabeth's reign describe the employment of carriers to transport props and other materials via boat or horse, as well as transport to and from rehearsals. There is also mention of the building of a stage out of wood, a quantity of lead purchased for 'the chair of the burning knight', and the mending of a 'cloud' made from 'a hoop and blue linen cloth'.[36]

Portraiture is another art form that attracted the image-savvy couple. The Exeter-born miniaturist Nicholas Hilliard rose to particular prominence during Elizabeth's reign and painted both the queen and Dudley in the 1570s. A prolific artist, he also created likenesses of Sir Walter Raleigh, Sir Francis Drake and Mary Queen of Scots and, according to art historian Dudley Heath, characterized 'the first epoch of English miniature painting'.[37] The first miniatures had been painted during the 1520s, and Henry VIII and Katherine of Aragon both sat for the artist Lucas Horenbout. However, these works reached a new level of production under Elizabeth, and artists applied fresh techniques to create tiny, three-dimensional, lifelike images of their sitters. These small pieces of art were treasured by their owners and kept as keepsakes. We know Elizabeth owned Hilliard's small portraits. One of her prayer books, measuring only three inches high and two inches wide, is decorated with miniatures of her and the Duke of Alençon, a suitor for her marriage in the later years of her reign.[38]

Hilliard also painted a miniature of Robert Dudley, now in the collection of the National Portrait Gallery. The artwork measures just 44mm across and was painted in 1576. The artist has captured Dudley's steely gaze as well as delicate features including the earl's beard and the white lace at his neck.[39] The level of detail, considering the size of the work, is outstanding. Hilliard's portraits of the queen date from 1572, but there is evidence of an earlier link between the artist and Robert Dudley. Mary Edmond, in *Hilliard and Oliver: The Lives and Works of Two Great Miniaturists*, points out a 1571 record of work linked to Hilliard that featured Dudley's emblem of 'ragged staves', suggesting it was he who first knew of and promoted the artist at Elizabeth's court.[40]

Henry VII and Elizabeth of York understood the impact of image and propaganda, but, like the theatre, Elizabeth I took the concept to a new level. Acutely aware of the power of representation, she employed artists to establish a state-approved, consistent persona throughout her reign. She was painted in portraits alongside allegorical symbols that conveyed wisdom, virginity and global influence; appearing to her public in jewels, expensive fabrics and from flattering angles. This control needed to be established from early in the reign, and by 1563 there were concerns over unfavourable images that did not express the 'natural representation of Her Majesty'. The nineteenth-century historian John Nichols reported one claim that Robert Dudley was actually the impetus behind the royal proclamation that 'some special person that shall be by her allowed' should create a portrait of the queen that others would copy. This was said to have been inspired by the queen's tendency to have 'so highly piqued herself on her beauty'. It is however far more likely to have been implemented as enforced state control over the royal public image rather than a simple act of vanity on the part of the queen. The writer also records a claim that Dudley 'obtained for Federico Zuccaro (as being a "special cunning painter") the permission of access to her Majesty to take her natural representation'.[41]

Dudley certainly had a clear understanding of the importance of public image. He always appeared immaculately dressed, especially on important occasions, and his accounts books carefully note purchases of fine clothing, perfumed gloves, jewelled buttons and flowers. He also liked to have his chamber decorated with fresh foliage and in 1559 had a coat embroidered with 'pearl and silver' to wear during a visit from the Duke of Finland.[42]

Dudley's involvement in the crafting of Elizabeth's image therefore makes sense. He was already close to the queen, coordinating her travel arrangements in his role as Master of the Horse. He had a keen eye for art and theatrical display, ensuring the queen's public appearances went without a hitch and had contacts in the world of art and culture. He also supported contemporary historians including John Stow, who dedicated his *Chronicles of England* to the earl in 1580.[43] Stow credited Leicester's 'request and earnest persuasion' in motivating him to complete the chronicle, remembering that he 'always received his hearty thanks'.[44] In his introduction, Stow insisted his work was written 'in searching out the truth'. However, he was an Elizabethan historian creating Tudor-centric interpretations of the past. These were, of course, favourable to Elizabeth and her family. These works are also credited as a source for Shakespeare as he wrote his history plays. In encouraging the work of historians, Dudley helped the queen create a written image that her subjects could both respect and identify with, enduring long after the Tudor age ended. Alan Haynes, in *The White Bear: Robert Dudley, the Elizabethan Earl of Leicester*, summed Dudley up perfectly, as 'a master of sparkling self-promotion, carried off with memorable flair', words that could equally have been used for the queen herself.[45]

But powerful queenship was about far more than controlling a strong and identifiable image. Ambitious advisors and foreign powers also had to be kept in check. In 1641, looking back at the reign, Robert Naunton remembered that Elizabeth maintained a hold over influential men at court desperate to gain favour, something, he notes, other kings had failed at.[46] She was known for her changeable temper, and a well-timed frown could set courtiers vying desperately for her approval.

Shortly after her accession, Elizabeth told her council she would not marry, as she was 'already bound unto a husband, which is the Kingdom of England' making a show of the coronation ring on her finger.[47] Understandably, after the legal and social anxieties surrounding Philip and Mary's marriage, Elizabeth was reluctant to hand over control of her realm to a husband, particularly the head of a foreign power. Even so, she entertained ambassadors from countries including France, Sweden, Austria and Spain, teasing them into time-wasting negotiations for her hand. Letters of exasperation were scribbled by ambassadors while Elizabeth kept their masters twirled around her little finger. And Robert Dudley was only too happy to help.

Aubrey Richardson credited the couple with a 'genius for dissimulation and misrepresentation' and their joint time-wasting can be seen in negotiations during the 1560s and 1570s.[48] In February 1561 Elizabeth told Quadra she had 'some affection' for Dudley, but 'certainly had never decided to marry him or anyone else'. The following June, Dudley joked to the confused bishop that while he was there, he could perform his and Elizabeth's wedding ceremony, as the queen laughed.[49]

There was similar confusion over Elizabeth's potential betrothal to the Swedish prince. Quadra wrote in November 1559 that Elizabeth asked to see the son of the Swedish king 'before making up her mind', but then left him waiting in a nearby antechamber. Frustrated, he left court without telling anyone and retired to his lodgings. 'I think he is undeceived', wrote the bishop, 'after scattering large sums of money amongst these people and showing himself to the queen'.[50]

Dudley too, played his part. During 1561 negotiations, Quadra noted that '[Elizabeth] and her friends therefore wish to appear undecided and indifferent, and to give the idea that perhaps she may marry the Swede. Robert is consequently making a show of being very displeased, which I am sure is not really the case as he is in greater favour than ever'. Philip II, the queen's former brother-in-law, quipped that Elizabeth's 'words are so little to be depended upon', accusing her of having 'no intention of fulfilling what she says, and only wishes to use our authority for her own designs and intentions'.[51]

Robert Dudley's name drifts around in documents as a possible husband for Elizabeth from early in her reign up to the mid-1570s, and his presence at her side was carefully noted by ambassadors. Some saw him as a rival, while others hoped he would serve as an ally. Elizabeth, often indecisive in state affairs, was able therefore to draw on Dudley's charm and political skill to drag on these negotiations until they ended in frustration or simply fizzled out. Sarah Gristwood states, in *Elizabeth and Leicester,* that Dudley fulfilled the role of 'The Suitor', a faithful and loyal name that could be dropped to speed up or slow down marriage negotiations at Elizabeth's pace.[52]

In the difficult political and religious climate, Elizabeth faced a number of threats to her rule including excommunication by Pope Pius V in 1570, failed assassination plots and, in the summer of 1588, a looming, substantial invasion force dispatched by Philip II.

Robert Dudley did not hold the title of consort as he stood at Elizabeth's side, but remained committed to her and the safety of her realm. He inspected a muster of troops at Greenwich in July 1559 and accompanied the Duke of Finland on an official visit to London the following October.[53] During the queen's illness in the autumn of 1562 he kept a substantial army on standby that could secure the peace if required and conducted state business with ambassadors. When Elizabeth's health began to improve, she urged the council to make him Lord Protector of the realm, with a salary of £20,000 per year.[54] Although she soon recovered and reassumed control, this order reflects the trust she had in him personally as well as professionally, knowing that he would dutifully serve the country in the event of her death.

Two years later, Dudley played another central role, this time in Elizabeth's plan to neutralize the threat of Mary Queen of Scots. Mary possessed a claim to the throne of England and dangerously had the backing of Catholics at home and overseas. If Mary married the Protestant and reliable Dudley, her political and religious ambitions in England would be immobilized. Elizabeth herself said as much, that their marriage would 'free her mind of all fears and suspicions to be offended by any usurpation before her death, being assured that he was so loving and trusty that he would never suffer any such thing to be attempted in her time'.[55]

On 29 September 1564, with Sir James Melville looking on, Elizabeth created Dudley Baron Denbigh and Earl of Leicester in order to make him a more agreeable catch for the Scottish queen. The choice of the earldom of Leicester is significant. The genealogist George Cokayne, in a footnote, wondered at Dudley's geographical links to Leicester, but noted just a few lines earlier that the previous holder of the title, Henry Bolingbroke, was later proclaimed Henry IV in 1399. Both Elizabeth and Dudley would have been aware of the title's link to royalty.[56] Did Robert see a potential marriage to Mary as service to his queen? The match would certainly have brought him power, but his commitment and loyalty, as Elizabeth stated, was to Elizabeth and England. If the plan went ahead, between them Dudley and Elizabeth would have held authority over both English and Scottish affairs with Mary as an awkward third wheel. The plan was certainly weighted heavily in Elizabeth's favour, a fact not lost on Scottish negotiators, who in one reply wondered 'might we not suspect that it is not merely for friendship you make this match, but you also hunt for a kingdom, and go about under that pretence to make an Englishman king of Scotland!'.[57] Tired by the pair's usual delaying tactics, Mary instead married the dashing and reckless Lord Darnley the following year. Darnley was one of the sons of Margaret Lennox, née Douglas.

The sources also show Dudley wining, dining and smooth-talking European dignitaries when Elizabeth was unavailable. In November 1561, Quadra noted sourly that Dudley had 'sent a letter secretly' to the French 'offering them friendship and alliance', adding that this was almost certainly done on behalf of the queen, 'as I know Lord Robert would never dare to do it otherwise'.[58] In December 1574 the Earl of Shrewsbury wrote to the queen, defending himself over a family matter that had angered her. His justification for not having written to her sooner was that he 'wrote of this matter to my Lord Leicester a good while ago at great length. I hid nothing from him that I knew was done about the same, and thought not meet to trouble your Majesty therewith'.[59] To Shrewsbury, Dudley and the queen were linked, informing him was as good as updating the queen.

Robert Dudley had served the queen as politician, courtier, ambassador and friend since her accession in 1558. But in 1585 an opportunity arose for him to serve in a military capacity. He was to assist the Netherlands against the Catholic threat of the Habsburgs, with orders to 'redress the confused government of those countries' and 'establish martial discipline'. Sending him as her Lieutenant General, Elizabeth assured them that he was 'a personage whom she did make more accompt of than any of her subjects'.[60] His own correspondence demonstrates eagerness to set sail, tying up business at home and chasing supplies and paperwork.

Dudley had confidently represented the queen in talks and policymaking for almost thirty years. But he was soon to overstep his mark. His role in the Netherlands was meant to be an assisting one, but, excited at the favourite's arrival, they invited him to accept the title of Absolute Governor, something Elizabeth had not agreed to. Dudley sent a message to Elizabeth asking for her thoughts, but due to an error in communication, ended up accepting the title without her consent. He later wrote to Cecil explaining his actions, induced by increasing pressure from the authorities as they barged into his rooms with heralds and urged him to take on the role. He also personally believed that acceptance of the post was necessary and that 'either this way must be taken or else all overthrown'.[61] His words hint at a moral decision in favour of both countries' interests, perhaps hoping that Elizabeth would either agree with him or could be convinced later. Elizabeth had previously relied on his service in her absence, and Dudley may have looked back to the events of 1562 when she had so willingly offered him up as her deputy in charge of the kingdom.

Whatever Dudley's reasons, Elizabeth was furious. Despite apologising and defending himself in letters, he continued to make attempts to reform the army, command troops in battle and improve the administration of the Low Countries. In 1586 he wrote a ten-page booklet detailing the *Lawes and Ordinances set downe by Robert Earle of Leycester* which aimed to tighten discipline among the troops. It banned blasphemy, brawling within the camp and giving up their position to the enemy. It also commanded that 'every soldier shall diligently observe and learn the sound of drums, fifes and trumpets, to the end he may know how to answer the same in his service'.[62] However, if Dudley expected his efforts in the Netherlands to be a lasting legacy, he was mistaken. His letters demonstrate growing despondency over his role, along with an increasing desire to be allowed to return to England. Naunton wrote after Dudley's death that he had 'more Mercury than he had in Mars', alluding to his communication and charm rather than his military expertise.[63]

Aged fifty-six and back in England, Dudley played one more decisive role as Elizabeth's military defender and protector. On news of Philip II's Armada force lurching towards England, Elizabeth made Dudley her Lord Lieutenant, responsible for the land defences of the country. He took charge of the military camp posted at Tilbury in Essex, which blocked Philip's entry into London. Seeing the troops hungry and demotivated, he wrote to Elizabeth on 27 July 1588 asking her to visit the camp to raise their spirits and 'comfort' those in the nearby counties. Fully aware, too, of the PR value of such an event he added, 'you shall comfort not only these thousands, but ... many more that shall hear of it'.[64]

More people would hear of Elizabeth's visit to Tilbury than Dudley could ever have imagined. Her iconic speech, in which she declared that she was a 'weak and feeble woman', but with the 'heart and stomach of a king, and of a King of England too', would be quoted over and over to millions of people in books, film and television for more than 400 years. She assured the captive audience that they would receive 'rewards and crowns' and that 'my Lieutenant General [Leicester] shall be in my stead, than whom, never prince commanded a more noble or worthy subject'.[65] Advising the troops to be obedient to Dudley, keep order and demonstrate bravery she promised them 'famous victory'. The plan worked. William Camden said 'her presence and words fortifieth the courages both of the Captains and Soldiers beyond all belief', while John Stow echoed this sentiment, writing that the queen processed 'through every rank of them, to their great comfort and rejoicing'.[66] Elizabeth or Dudley wouldn't have known it as they appeared before the troops at Tilbury, but military action on land wasn't needed. High winds scattered the Armada along the English coast, the remainder of the ships repelled by the efforts of the English navy.

Militarily, Dudley played an important practical role, raising and organising troops while Elizabeth underlined it with authority and the all-important royal sparkle. She emphasized his authority by assuring those placed under his command of her absolute faith in him and his ability. Dudley seems to have been aware of this, and his correspondence often mentions the need for soldiers to be 'comforted' by the queen. It may be that he, too, looked for Elizabeth's involvement to emphasize his own work. The nature of Dudley's military contribution during the reign is similar to that traditionally occupied by a consort, such as acting as her deputy in the Netherlands. The couple were therefore an effective double-act. Elizabeth appeared in public, giving rousing speeches to soldiers while Dudley, with his charming and pragmatic approach, drove these events forward.

The earl's concern for the safety of his queen and her kingdom was not only demonstrated at time of war. In 1584, the Bond of Association was drawn up, headed by Sir Francis Walsingham and Sir William Cecil. The document promised to deliver justice in the event of a successful assassination attempt on the queen, by punishing not only the conspirators, but also the individual that subsequently ascended the throne. The sixteenth and early seventeenth century writer William Camden attributed the forming of the Bond to Leicester.[67] It certainly is typical of the general concern for the queen and her realm otherwise demonstrated by Dudley during his career, and later formed the foundation of the charge against Mary Queen of Scots, leading to her execution three years later. Even Elizabeth's nickname for Dudley, 'eyes', may have been created out of his concern for her security. Sarah Gristwood in *Elizabeth and Leicester* suggested it may have been a reference to the earl's continual watch over the queen's safety and her interests.[68] The nickname was certainly one of familiar endearment between the pair, with Dudley including its symbol – two dots with lines above them – in some of his letters to the queen.

As bonfires blazed in towns and villages that August to celebrate the victory of the English against the Armada, Robert Dudley had only weeks to live. He died on 4 September 1588 at Cornbury Hall in Oxfordshire. He lies buried in a magnificent tomb in The Beauchamp Chapel of St Mary's Church in Warwick, alongside his wife Lettice Knollys. On hearing the news of his death Elizabeth fell into a state of grief, keeping to her rooms and, for the rest of her life, cherishing the last letter he had written to her.

Between them, Elizabeth I and Robert Dudley, Earl of Leicester heavily impacted everyday life for residents in the late sixteenth and early seventeenth centuries. Their energetic and deliberate patronage of learning, literature, theatre and the arts led to increased levels of education and new expressions of art and culture in England. Scientists and scholars grappled to understand the world around them while craftspeople found new, regular employment supporting new and popular industries such as the theatre. Those living at the end of the sixteenth century enjoyed a country that was politically more secure after the Bond of Association, while they shared tales of England's legendary defeat of the Spanish Armada. The couple were only able to enforce much of this change by working together and drawing on one another's positions and strengths. Dudley formed Leicester's Players, but could not grant the company the legal protection and prestige provided by Elizabeth. Similarly, Dudley introduced new artists and thinkers to court who created work in the queen's image and constructed the legend of the 'Virgin Queen' which still survives today. As we have examined, it is also interesting to wonder whether without Elizabeth and Dudley, Shakespeare and the theatre – particularly the play *A Midsummer Night's Dream* – would have existed.

The couple left a legacy, too, on the streets of Warwick. Elizabeth's financial, political and social support of Dudley enabled him to invest some of his wealth in ways that supported local communities. The queen recognized the need for reform in the country's treatment of the poor and Dudley supported this. The Lord Leycester Hospital, founded with Elizabeth's permission by Dudley in 1571 in an existing medieval building, provided homes for soldiers and sailors of England who received serious injuries fighting on the queen's behalf. Dudley's foundation provided them with a home, a chapel and gardens as well as a close-knit community to rely on, improving their financial, physical and mental wellbeing. This impact continued into later years, and ex-servicepeople still live there today, following Dudley's thirty-four rules and reciting prayers chosen by the earl 450 years ago. After his death, Elizabeth continued to support Dudley's foundation, personally overseeing the appointment of one of the Masters.

Elizabethans looked up to their queen as a heroic leader, some comparing her to the Roman Goddess of War, Bellona.[69] But she was feminine and vulnerable, too. Subjects watched with curiosity as she appeared in various processions and progresses throughout her realm. They watched her gaze out from paintings and coins underneath a mass of curls and read about her ancestors in newly-published history books. It is clear that this was not simply Elizabeth's doing. Dudley and the queen worked together to craft the many-faceted, and sometimes goddess-like image, that these later Tudors would have known. Finally, the couple engineered one of Elizabeth's most spectacular and legendary appearances, boosting morale at Tilbury in 1588. This event has been widely reconstructed and quoted in modern-day drama and film. It is less often acknowledged that it was Dudley's idea.

Robert Dudley never became Elizabeth's legal consort, but he often acted as one. She privately relied on him for companionship and advice, and to host foreign dignitaries on her behalf. Their appearances together and open flirtations were remarked on by ambassadors, and Elizabeth genuinely seems to have heavily relied on his presence. She gave him prominent administrative roles in government and sent him on diplomatic and military voyages overseas. His eagerness to accept the governorship of the Netherlands without Elizabeth's express permission also hints that he saw himself as her unofficial partner in state. Aubrey Richardson wrote in 1908 that in Elizabeth's 'heirless household, she created him – in all but name – a Prince'.[70]

Their combined actions also attracted the hawk-like gaze of Philip II, who eventually sent his Armada to England in 1588. Considering the attacks funded by Elizabeth and Leicester and other courtiers, his response is not surprising. However, there are questions surrounding the consequences of this move, which caused the Spanish fleet to sail a year later than planned. We might speculate as to whether the outcome of the famous naval attack might have been different had it been able to launch earlier.

Elizabeth took a more cautious approach over Leicester's acceptance of the title of Governor in the Netherlands, another action which must have angered Philip, who was battling for power there. But Dudley was less restrained than his queen, sources showing that he believed the only solution to the Spanish problem was conflict. He wrote to Walsingham in 1586, stating that 'I am thoroughly persuaded that a good war, held but this summer, shall drive him clean to forsake the country'.[71] Dudley was also convinced of the greatness of England's military and naval power, once writing that 'No doubt but the king of Spain's preparation by sea be great ... But I know that all that he and his friends can make are not able to match with her majesty's power by sea'.[72] Dudley was commander and organizer of thousands of Elizabeth's troops, which he led over the course of his career. He therefore had inside knowledge of their skills and abilities directly from the camps and fields of battle, something Elizabeth would not. He also maintained absolute faith in Elizabeth's leadership and the nation's ability to fend off her enemies, something that would have provided comfort to Elizabeth and increased her confidence when forming policy.

In 1566 Elizabeth described her love for Leicester as like that between a sister and a brother.[73] Twenty years later in 1586, Thomas Sherley wrote that Dudley knew 'the queen and her nature best of any man', which was probably very near to the truth.[74] He made mistakes in judgement, but always returned to royal favour, and it is unrealistic to expect a partnership of almost five decades to never have disagreements. They had similar life experiences, both having lost a parent to execution, being imprisoned in the Tower of London by Queen Mary and growing up in the calculating Tudor court of Henry VIII. William Camden wondered if their close bond was down to either 'a secret conjunction of the planets at the hour of their birth' or their 'common respect'.[75] While similar experiences and gratitude for one another's support would surely have led to a deeper bond and shared understanding between the pair, life at the changeable mid-Tudor court would also have taught them valuable skills in political judgement; crucial for when the couple came to power.

The ultimate control in their relationship, of course, rested with Elizabeth. She carefully reminded Dudley, in a letter of 1586, that he was 'a man raised up by ourself and extraordinarily favoured by us above any other subject of this land'.[76] All of his success, position and status were down to her and could be withdrawn at any moment. An almost fervent eagerness comes through in Dudley's letters as he prepares to serve overseas in the Netherlands. He may have seen the opportunity to fulfil something for himself, away from Elizabeth's ever-watchful eye. After all, it was noticed in 1559 that Elizabeth was 'in love with Lord Robert and never lets him leave her'. The situation hadn't changed by 1573, when, according to Gilbert Talbot, the queen reacted to Dudley enjoying the company of two ladies at court by sending 'spies over him'.[77] However, despite Elizabeth's apparently controlling nature, Dudley remained publicly dedicated to her for the rest of his life. It is also possible to see similarities between the duties the earl carried out and our modern understanding of the role of a royal consort today. Elizabeth told Melville in 1564 that Dudley was 'her brother and best friend, whom she should have married herself, if ever she had been minded to take a husband'.[78]

On his death in 1588, Robert Dudley's last will and testament was opened. In it, he left a moving tribute to Elizabeth, stating that 'it was my greatest joy, in my life-time to serve her to her contentation, so it is not unwelcome to me, being the will of God, to die and end this life for her service'. He hoped that she would be 'a blessed mother and nurse to this people' and urged God to 'make her the oldest Prince that ever He gave over England'. Even as he contemplated his own death, Elizabeth's security and longevity was at the forefront of his mind. He bequeathed her a diamond set with three large emeralds and other diamonds, hanging on a rope of 600 pearls.[79]

We have no way of really knowing whether Elizabeth and Dudley's relationship ever progressed to a sexual or romantic one. Bearing in mind the games they played with foreign ambassadors regarding their relationship, they would likely laugh at modern attempts to probe into their true feelings for one another. But when discussing the impact they made together on Tudor society, this detail is irrelevant. Hardworking and committed to England's progression, safety and prosperity, they worked as complementary and active partners in state, leaving a legacy felt not only by those living at the close of the sixteenth century, but arguably through to modern times.

Chapter 9

George Talbot and Elizabeth of Hardwick, Earl and Countess of Shrewsbury

ROBERT DUDLEY AND QUEEN ELIZABETH worked together on many matters, but one in particular threatened to end the Tudor dynasty before its time, endangering the queen's authority and even her life. Casting courtiers about her in various roles to try and suppress the threat, Elizabeth looked to a powerful partnership that had only recently formed. The stresses she was about to place on it, however, would result in its destruction.

The earls of Shrewsbury had a history of royal service since the Norman invasion when William the Conqueror created Roger de Montgomery the first of that title in 1071. With a reputation for loyalty, the family had amassed a considerable amount of wealth by the time the sixth earl, George Talbot, succeeded to the earldom in 1560. Talbot, who was knighted by Edward VI at his coronation in 1547, enjoyed a flurry of official titles. Created a Knight of the Garter by Elizabeth I, he was also Lord Lieutenant of the counties of York, Nottingham, Derby and Stafford. A wealthy man and an organized administrator, he owned vast estates in the Midlands and South Yorkshire, with homes in Worksop, Sheffield, Tutbury, Wingfield and Rufford.[1]

Shrewsbury's first wife, Gertrude Manners, died in around 1556 and after a decade as a widower, he decided it was time to take a new bride. In 1568, Talbot's eyes rested pleasingly on the red-haired Elizabeth, the widow of Sir William St Loe.[2] The private correspondence between them early in their marriage conveys a mutual personal attraction. Bess was a wealthy landowner in her own right, with lands and estates peppered throughout the Midlands, not far from Shrewsbury's own.

A portrait painted shortly before her marriage to the earl, in the collection of the National Trust, shows Bess with round blue eyes, her red hair styled under a headdress.[3] She wears a black gown trimmed with white fur and a delicate collar tucked under her chin. There is something about the sure and steady gaze and tightly pursed lips that expresses the confidence and tenacity Bess displayed in her lifetime. Born in Derbyshire in 1527 to John and Elizabeth Hardwick, she was married a total of four times. Her first husband was Robert Barlow, the son of a local landowner. Their marriage was short, and he died soon afterwards. In 1547, she married Sir William Cavendish, a trusted member of Henry VIII's government. During their marriage Bess bore William six children through eight pregnancies. He died in October 1557 making Bess a widow for the second time. Her third marriage to William St Loe, Elizabeth I's Captain of the Guard, was also sadly shortened by his early death in 1565. With each marriage, Bess inherited lands and estates, a greater social standing and a higher profile within court circles. By the time she stood to recite her vows in front of George Talbot in February 1568, she was one of England's wealthiest women, swelling the already substantial Shrewsbury estates with homes including Chatsworth House, her Barlow properties and St Loe lands in Gloucestershire.[4]

The earl and his new countess enjoyed favour with Elizabeth I and were also friends with powerful courtiers in her close circle, including Robert Dudley, Earl of Leicester and William Cecil, Lord Burghley. In time, they would both incur the queen's disappointment, but generally they were well-liked by Elizabeth. In 1572 the queen praised the 'fidelity, duty and love' Shrewsbury demonstrated, while for Bess, who had served as her Lady of the Bedchamber, she declared 'there is no Lady in this land that I better love and like'.[5]

In their early letters Talbot referred to Bess as 'my dear None' and 'only joy', professing 'faithful affection, which I never tasted so deeply of before'. Bess was similarly warm, addressing her husband as 'my jewel' and 'dear heart'.[6] Their correspondence reveals a working couple concerned with household affairs, exchanges of information and an interest in one another's opinions. Henry Cavendish, Bess' son, wrote to inform her of an accidental murder in his home after a fight between two of his men. Bess forwarded the letter to Shrewsbury to keep him informed, noting that although she was 'much grieved for the mishap', she was not wholly surprised in the individual that caused it, summing him up as a 'vain, lewd fellow'.[7]

Bess and Talbot forged alliances between their respective children, seeking to protect their futures and control the valuable Hardwick-Shrewsbury assets. They arranged for Bess' daughter Mary Cavendish to marry Shrewsbury's son Gilbert, and in addition, the earl's daughter Grace married Bess' son, Henry Cavendish. These marriages, which occurred in conjunction with Bess and Shrewsbury's, knitted together the couple's combined wealth, ensuring it remained within the families after their deaths. Bess' roots were humble, but her marriage to Talbot opened up more opportunities for family advancement. As she looked for a prospective husband for her remaining unmarried daughter, Talbot wrote to Lord Burghley in 1574 that there were 'few noblemen's sons in England that she [Bess] hath not prayed me to deal for at one time or another'.[8]

By the end of 1568 the Shrewsburys were in favour with the queen and her circle. They oversaw a strong property base in the centre of England under an ancient and prestigious title, taking advantage of their individual skills, strengths, contacts and resources for the good of the family. By the late 1570s, however, visible cracks had developed in their marriage. Arguments were becoming increasingly heated and public. By 1577 Bess felt her husband preferred more her 'absence than presence', while Shrewsbury referred to her in 1584 as his 'wicked and malicious wife'.[9] Despite being urged by Elizabeth I and Robert Dudley to reconcile, the pair continued to bicker over lands, possessions and finances, and separated for good in the mid-1580s.

How could it have gone so wrong for this wealthy and distinguished power couple of the late Tudor age? Historians have offered various reasons for their estrangement, including a lack of time spent together, a clash in personalities and external pressure from wider political and social events. However, most agree that the main stress in their relationship was caused by their fifteen-year custody of one of the biggest threats to Elizabeth I's rule: Mary Queen of Scots.

As the Shrewsburys were writing lovingly to one another and settling into newly-wedded life, Queen Mary fled Scotland amid uncertainty and accusations of conspiracy. Her husband Lord Darnley, one of the sons of Margaret Douglas, had been found dead in Kirk O' Field in Edinburgh following an explosion under suspicious circumstances. She quickly married Lord Bothwell, the prime suspect of the crime, although evidence later came to light implying Mary had also been involved. She was deposed and her one-year-old son declared King James VI of Scotland in her place. In danger and lacking support, in the summer of 1568 Mary fled to England to seek assistance from her cousin, Elizabeth I.

Elizabeth was cautious about the wily and enigmatic Scottish queen, and placed her under the watch of custodian Sir Francis Knollys. She was not an easy house guest. He relinquished the position without Elizabeth's permission just months later, preferring to 'suffer any punishment that may be laid upon him, rather than continue in such employment'.[10] With anxiety over Mary's influence among her English (and particularly Catholic) subjects as well as the support she had from overseas, Elizabeth's priority was to keep Mary securely confined until she could work out her next move. During the autumn of 1568 her thoughts turned to the wealthy Shrewsbury newlyweds.

On 25 January 1569, Elizabeth set out the terms for the Shrewsburys' custody of the Queen of Scots. She noted that her decision to place the queen with the earl was based on his 'approved loyalty and faithfulness, and the ancient state and blood from which he is descended'.[11] She decided that Mary would be confined at the couple's castle of Tutbury in Staffordshire and Bess and Talbot diligently prepared for her arrival. She arrived on 4 February 1569.

Shrewsbury later wrote that he was 'so much the gladder' to take on this 'most dangerous service' to Elizabeth, especially as so many others had 'shrunk from it'. His motivation was to perform his loyal duty and 'make appear to your Majesty my zealous mind to serve you in greatest peril'.[12]

It soon became clear to the Shrewsburys that their guardianship of Mary would involve much more than locking doors and restricting visitors. On arrival, Mary complained of damp and mouldy rooms, with Tutbury's associated buildings also in a state of disrepair. There was an ever-present threat of conspiracy, one boy said to have been concealing letters for Mary inside the seam of his jacket.[13] All visitors to Mary were required to hold a licence from Elizabeth, and attendants were to leave her between 9pm and 6am. In addition, if an alarm was raised at the castle, anyone connected with Mary was ordered to keep to their rooms, on pain of death.[14]

Elizabeth continually fretted over Talbot's arrangements for Mary's security, and he was compelled to write often to her and Burghley, defending every decision and movement he made. She grew irritated over the birth of the Shrewsburys' grandchild at Sheffield Castle in 1575 because Mary's captivity there at the time heightened the risk of 'women and strangers' coming and going.[15] She was also outraged at a short journey the earl took for health reasons to the baths in nearby Buxton. The written evidence shows that she needn't have worried. A letter from Talbot's son Gilbert in 1573 describes guards watching Mary 'both under her windows, over her chamber, and of every side her; so that, unless she could transform herself to a flea or a mouse, it was impossible that she should escape'.[16]

With large numbers of people employed to watch Mary and her household, it was necessary to clean the living accommodation periodically. Mary was therefore moved between the Shrewsbury's homes of Tutbury, Wingfield, Sheffield and Chatsworth while lodgings were aired and cleaned, although sometimes also to improve her health. The administration of the earl's new role must have been a logistical nightmare for the couple. As well as the co-ordination and occasional movement of Mary's household, care had to be taken over her personal belongings, ensuring adequate numbers of armed guards, along with a continual surveillance of visitors to and from the homes. In addition, every move was conducted under Elizabeth's distant and suspicious gaze.

Although Shrewsbury was chiefly responsible for the Scottish queen's confinement, he was actively supported by his wife. A letter from the earl to Burghley in 1569 tells how Mary visited Bess' chamber, where they would 'sit working with the needle', a pastime they both enjoyed.[17] Embroidered panels worked on by the two women survive, and are now in the collection of the Victoria and Albert Museum, on permanent loan to Oxburgh Hall in Norfolk. Talbot also recorded Bess checking in on Mary during an illness and again when she was emotionally upset. In October 1569 Shrewsbury defended Bess' involvement in the queen's care, writing that, because of her influence, 'I have been the more able to discharge the trust committed unto me'.[18]

Bess could soothe and assist her increasingly stressed husband, but there was another problem. The £52 weekly allowance granted to the couple by Elizabeth for Mary's expenses fell vastly short. Mary ordered expensive wines from France, along with colourful silks, comfitures and live quails, with the earl additionally protesting that 'all manner of household stuff is by them exceedingly spoiled and wilfully wasted'.[19] Shrewsbury made a number of written requests to have this allowance increased, but Elizabeth brushed them aside. In 1575 the sum was reduced to £32 per week.

In this respect, Elizabeth treated Shrewsbury in much the same way she had dealt with Leicester over his mission in the Low Countries. Denying him access to state funds for the war, he had been forced to use his own money, mortgaged from his properties to complete his duty. As well as saving Elizabeth from dipping into royal funds for these state expenses, these debts were also dangled as a precious opportunity for rich courtiers to demonstrate their devotion to her and loyalty to the realm. However, like

Leicester, it was hardly Shrewsbury's place to bear the cost of supporting Mary, her household and visitors as well as maintain her security.

There is some evidence Elizabeth grew tired of Shrewsbury's regular and frequent complaints over money. Robert Dudley visited the couple at Chatsworth and the queen wrote to them on 25 June 1577 thanking them for their hospitality towards him. However, she sprinkled the note with references to increasing debts, small allowances and limits on food. The queen stated that she would 'take upon us the debt and to acknowledge you both as creditors', but advised them to limit Leicester's food and drink 'lest otherwise the debt thereby may grow to be so great as we shall not be able to discharge the same, and so become bankrupt'. Elizabeth stipulates that the earl have only 'two ounces of flesh' per day, along with 'one-twentieth of a pint of wine', except on special feast days, where he was allowed the shoulder and leg of a wren.[20]

Another shorter copy of the letter, stored in the *Talbot Manuscripts*, contains all the polite pleasantries of the first, but none of the sarcastic references to costs. Historian Maud Rawson was convinced that this was the copy the Shrewsburys actually received. She argues that the original letter was diplomatically edited by either Walsingham or Burghley, although equally it may have been Leicester who urged the queen to avoid offending his generous hosts. Sharing a sarcastic joke was one thing, but it was important that Elizabeth keep the exasperated Shrewsburys on side. The end of the shorter letter therefore includes a sentence of appreciation, with Elizabeth grateful that 'through your loyal and most careful looking to this charge committed to you, both we and our realm enjoy a peaceable government, the best good hope that to any prince on earth can befall'.[21] At the time of this letter, Mary had been at the centre of the Shrewsburys' domestic, personal and political lives for over eight years.

Life in captivity was both physically and mentally challenging for Mary. Previously, she had been used to hunting, dancing, riding and travelling freely throughout her realm, speaking with ambassadors, statesmen and courtiers of her own. Now, in the dank and musty rooms of Tutbury Castle, her exercise and daily movements were restricted, along with her access to visitors. It's fully understandable that during her confinement a growing resentment towards Elizabeth and her keepers began to take root. Knollys, Mary's previous custodian, had warned that she 'sheweth a disposition to speak much, to be bold, to be pleasant, and to be very familiar', adding darkly of her 'great desire to be avenged of her enemies'.[22]

While there are moments of co-operation and even friendliness between Mary and the Shrewsburys, there is also evidence that she later embarked on a systematic mission to shame and discredit them. Mary wrote letters levelling accusations of gossip, disloyalty and treason against the couple, but most emphatically at Bess. In 1584 she accused the countess of conceiving a 'vain hope' to ensure Elizabeth's crown fell to her own granddaughter Arbella. Knowing that Leicester's involvement in the matter would particularly sting, she revealed that his son was a suitor for the royal-blooded girl. She also claimed Bess had one day promised to help her escape from confinement.[23] She accused the countess of secretly mocking Elizabeth, supposedly sniggering at court while the queen was flattered 'as if you were a sort of goddess from heaven'. Bess, Mary said, had paid solemn homage to her in her room and believed Elizabeth would die a violent death and Mary would take the English throne. This was in addition to a previous letter Mary had already written stating Bess had delivered secret letters 'in cypher' and engaged in a conspiracy with her son Charles Cavendish to provide information to Mary in the event of Elizabeth's death.[24]

Mary's letters are barbed with treason, conspiracy and neglect of duty. But the tone reads as manic and spiteful. Her offhand ramblings about Elizabeth's trusted officials hints more at desperation than the careful confession of actual, witnessed events. It is also difficult to see Bess' motivation to conspire against Elizabeth. While it's true that Mary was close to the throne, her accusations do not tally with written evidence from state letters. All indications are that Talbot was dedicated and cautious, taking great steps to keep Mary contained, while any conspiracy from Bess would only bring about the couple's own disgrace and trial and potentially even their deaths.

One letter from Bess to her husband, written in 1577, has attracted particular attention. She sends him lettuces, 'for that you love them' and hopes he will visit her soon, urging him to 'let me hear how you, your charge and love doth, and commend me I pray you'.[25] This has often been interpreted as evidence that Bess was aware of a love affair that had developed between her husband and the Scottish queen. These allegations were later denied by Talbot and Mary in the strongest terms, and from what we can see of Talbot's personality, it seems unlikely he would embark on a love affair with his captive. However, when Bess' comment is placed in context there is another, more likely explanation.

Mary's confinement under various Shrewsbury roofs disturbed many aspects of their normal domestic life. From the cold February of 1569 the couple could not get a minute alone without distraction or conversation turning towards Mary, much less freely travel together or welcome guests into their homes. Their properties were teeming with armed guards, and messengers continually rode to their gates bearing letters from a nervous Burghley or fretful Elizabeth. There was additional strain as they were compelled to defend against gossip, rumour and murmurings of negligence. Every waking moment was spent with concerns over the Scottish Queen.

Reading Bess' reference to 'your charge and love' in this context, it is likely Bess was alluding, half-playfully, to her husband's continual preoccupation with Mary and not literally of any love affair conducted between them. However, six years later, talk of a romantic relationship between the prisoner and her captor was being discussed in public. On 12 December 1583, Mary wrote to the French ambassador Michel de Castelnau, Sieur de la Mauvissière, complaining of 'scandalous reports' spread by Bess and her children about Mary's relationship with Talbot, something both the Scottish queen and Talbot fiercely denied.[26] News had also begun to be whispered in the inns and taverns of London with one Islington innkeeper named Walmsley investigated for broadcasting to his guests 'openly at the table that the Earl of Shrewsbury had gotten the Scottish Queen with child'.[27] Bess and her sons were summoned to court at the end of 1584 to explain themselves, but confessed they knew nothing about the rumours or where they had come from.

Had something as innocent as a mischievous joke between a still-devoted husband and wife in 1577 become a real matter of concern by 1584? Bess' note implies that she had noticed her husband was spending increasing amounts of time with the Scottish queen, but it is not evidence that she made defamatory or damaging comments six years later. In addition, Mary's accusation appears amid a swathe of other charges against the countess and, interestingly, at the time of the Shrewsburys' separation. Could Mary have aimed to discredit Bess, and remove her permanently from Talbot's side now that the relationship was failing? Mary S. Lovell, in *Bess of Hardwick, First Lady of Chatsworth*, pointed out that separating Bess and Talbot benefitted Mary, providing more opportunity for freedom of movement and making it easier to smuggle letters to her supporters. She also convincingly argues that Talbot may have been suffering at this time from an undiagnosed medical condition exacerbated by age, perhaps dementia.[28] If this is true, Talbot would have been more vulnerable to the schemes and persuasions described by Mary's previous custodian Knollys.

With Bess gone, the overworked and increasingly stressed earl would be left to oversee everything himself.

It is poignant to look back at early February 1569, when the affectionate and united Shrewsburys welcomed Mary into their home, optimistic to serve their country and queen. Fifteen years later, on 7 September 1584, the couple were at breaking point and bickering on both sides. Mary was transferred to the custody of Sir Ralph Sadler and moved to Wingfield. Talbot would surface again at Mary's trial and execution just over two years later. The Scottish Queen was beheaded at Fotheringhay Castle in Northamptonshire on 8 February 1587. She was forty-four years old.

The Shrewsburys had kept Mary Queen of Scots alive, safe and politically secure for a decade and a half. Elizabeth wrote to express gratitude for their service and for contributing towards the security of the realm. The day-to-day keeping of the queen and the management of her household, financial costs and wider administration must have been a difficult task. And yet Mary was not rescued by Catholic supporters, nor did she escape while secured by Bess and George. There is clear evidence that the couple provided valuable support to one another, at least to begin with. Talbot regularly praised the involvement of his wife and stoutly defended her, as well as himself, against harmful gossip. In the end though, their dedication to Elizabeth's service along with the stresses and tensions of their role came at a cost; the end of their once powerful union.

Elizabeth may have written to praise the Shrewsburys for upholding the security of her reign, but they were also involved in an event that threatened to destabilize it: the birth of Arbella Stuart.

In mid-November 1575, a baby lay in a cradle within a chamber of Chatsworth House. The child, Arbella, was of royal blood and had a claim to the English throne. The writer M. Lefuse later commented that it was fortunate for both Elizabeth I and James I that she had not been born a boy, and therefore posed more of a threat to their respective reigns.[29] However the girl's ancestry would still prove a thorn in the side of both monarchs, inspiring plots and conspiracy into the early Stuart period.

Arbella's existence was brought about by an arrangement discussed between two women. The first was Margaret Lennox, née Douglas, imprisoned in 1536 for her secret betrothal to Lord Thomas Howard. Her subsequent marriage with Matthew Lennox produced two sons, Henry and Charles. Henry, Lord Darnley married Mary Queen of Scots and was the father of Mary's son James. Margaret, now in her late fifties, was cousin to Elizabeth I, mother-in-law to Mary Queen of Scots and grandmother of the

Scottish King James VI. Her movements, therefore, were eyed with interest by the queen. Margaret sat at a table, hashing out plans for a wedding that would prove beneficial to both families. Opposite her, considering her options and listening intently, was the red-haired Bess, Countess of Shrewsbury.

The previous year, Margaret and Bess had talked of a marriage between Lennox's son Charles Stuart, Earl of Lennox and Bess' daughter Elizabeth. The official story, later related to the queen, was that the teenagers had fallen in love at first sight and there was nothing either parent could do to desist their desire to marry. In reality, the act seems very likely premeditated.

In the summer of 1574 Margaret Lennox asked Elizabeth I for leave to travel to her northern home of Settrington in North Yorkshire with her son Charles. Elizabeth cautiously agreed, but on condition that she did not go to Chatsworth, or anywhere near Mary Queen of Scots. On hearing of this, Bess offered her a stay at the earl's home of Rufford Abbey.[30]

Bess brought along her unmarried daughter Elizabeth Cavendish. As Margaret arrived with her son, she claimed she had been taken by an illness and went to bed, with Bess absenting herself to care for her. With the two mothers conveniently out of the way, Elizabeth and Charles could get to know one another. Margaret's illness also provided the party with the opportunity of a longer stay, if needed, until her health improved. The young couple fell in love and were secretly and swiftly married, with one historian coolly remarking that the ceremony was carried out 'almost as soon as Lady Lennox was able to leave her bedroom'. Maud Rawson offers one explanation for the hasty marriage, pointing out that it would have been impractical to plan a larger wedding at one of the Shrewsbury homes with Queen Mary under their roof, and with strict limits placed on visitors.[31] However, it does not explain the families' failure to secure permission for the marriage from the queen. Charles was linked to both the thrones of England and Scotland. He was the great-grandson of the English monarch Henry VII, through Henry's daughter Margaret Tudor. And through his brother's marriage to Mary Queen of Scots he was James VI of Scotland's uncle.

The marriage was a risky move, but there were benefits that justified it. For Lennox, linking her last remaining son to the distinguished and powerful Shrewsbury family offered him a comfortable livelihood as well as local and national influence. For Bess, who was always concerned with securing her children's future prosperity and standing, her daughter was now married to a man of royal Tudor blood. John Leader, in 1880, wrote that this was typical of Bess' ambitions, and that she was 'not the mother to neglect such an opportunity'.[32] Both countesses must also have imagined the possibility of a grandchild born of the pair sitting one day on the throne of England.

Predictably, Elizabeth was furious when she learned of the marriage. Defending themselves, Margaret insisted it had only been carried out for love, declaring pitifully that Charles was 'mine only son and comfort that is left me'. Shrewsbury also wrote to claim the marriage was 'dealt in suddenly, and without my knowledge ... my wife ... without having therein any other intent or respect than with reverend duty towards your Majesty'.[33]

Elizabeth was not satisfied. Not only had they engineered a secret marriage involving royal Tudor blood, but there was also the potential that a child born of the match would pose a future threat to Elizabeth's throne. Additionally, Leader points out that Shrewsbury's letter of December 1574 backpedals from the one he wrote the previous month, admitting he knew of the proposal and was happy with it. On 5 November 1574 he had previously written to Burghley: 'To be plain with your Lordship I wished the match and put to my helping hand to further it'. Lefuse and Leader both suggest Shrewsbury knew about the meeting at Rufford, but not the wedding, and this sounds more in keeping with the cautious, morally-correct character of the earl.[34] Referring to a 'match' rather than definite plans for a marriage, it also suggests that he probably intended to seek permission from the queen once preliminary negotiations had been finalized.

Talbot's insistence that the marriage was performed with 'reverend duty' towards Elizabeth poses more of a problem. Bess, Margaret and Talbot were all experienced, politically-astute courtiers. It is unthinkable that none of them realized they were meddling with dynastic concerns. The queen reacted by imprisoning Margaret and giving Shrewsbury a reprimand. Although some writers claim Bess was also imprisoned in the Tower in January 1575, Mary S. Lovell in *Bess of Hardwick, First Lady of Chatsworth* finds no evidence for this.[35] It probably made more sense to Elizabeth to have her remain with Talbot and maintain the security of Mary Queen of Scots, which was still a state priority.

Sadly, for the young girl at the centre of the scandal, both Arbella's parents died while she was young and Bess took her granddaughter under her care. She later petitioned the queen for a contribution towards Arbella's education, boldly referencing the now seven-year-old 'in respect of how she is in blood to Her Majesty', a fact Elizabeth hardly needed reminding of.[36] Arbella's bloodline would continue to cause anxiety for Bess long after her separation from the earl. The year 1592 brought rumours of a plot to kidnap Arbella and place her on the throne. Bess assured Burghley that the teenager was watched continually, visited no one and only walked near the house, sleeping each night in her grandmother's chamber.[37] The source of the intelligence was traced to Spain, with one of the conspirators focused on 'Arbella ... who most certainly they will proclaim Queen if their Mistress should now happen to die; and the rather they will do it, for it is under a woman's government they may still rule after their own designment'.[38]

A painting created in 1589 and in the collection of the National Trust shows Arbella just a few years before this conspiracy scare, aged thirteen. She wears a white gown padded at the sleeves, with pearls at her wrists, neck and hairline. Her reddish-brown hair is styled in a similar fashion to the queen's – high on top with long tresses tumbling around her shoulders. She appears here at the age where she would have normally been considered for an advantageous marriage, but both Elizabeth and her successor James I remained cautious over who she should marry. Arbella's potential as a contender to the throne was again exposed in 1603, early in the Stuart era. After the trial of conspirators, during which Arbella loudly protested her innocence, three men were executed, while four others were imprisoned. One of those sent to the Tower over the plot was Sir Walter Raleigh.[39]

By bringing about the Shrewsbury-Lennox marriage, Bess and Talbot altered late Tudor and early Stuart history by creating a figurehead that inspired new plans to overthrow the reigning monarch, and replace them with Arbella. While Bess' trace throughout these arrangements can be seen, it is less easy to find Talbot's, although he did admit to smoothing the way for the couple's initial meeting at Rufford. He may indeed have been ignorant of the spontaneous wedding ceremony. The affair also highlights the differences in personalities within the couple; Bess seems prepared to take risks and engage in secrecy – traits that were very much at odds with what can be perceived in the easily-frustrated and conscientious earl.

Bess, Countess of Shrewsbury is as well known for her building at Hardwick and Chatsworth as for her part in watching over Mary Queen of Scots. She built Chatsworth House with her second husband William Cavendish, continuing to make alterations and improvements during her lifetime. The current building, situated in the area we know today as the Derbyshire Peak District, was altered during the seventeenth and eighteenth centuries. However, we can still see the Tudor Chatsworth House that Bess knew in a needlework from the Devonshire Collections. It illustrates the building as it looked in around 1577 while she was married to Talbot, and shortly after the Lennox affair. Thought to date between 1590-1600 the work shows the house with turrets, towers and sculpted ornaments above the central entrance. There is also a large number of windows, which would have allowed sunlight to stream into the building, particularly on the upper floors.

Bess also rebuilt her family home at Hardwick Hall, around seventeen miles from Chatsworth, although this was completed after her separation from the earl. It remains today, tall and imposing, with its famous façade of glass windows earning it the well-known phrase 'Hardwick Hall, more glass than wall'. It is often noted that Bess had her initials 'ES' carved into the outer stonework on top of the turrets, but it is not often mentioned that she also incorporated symbols of her union with Talbot into the house. A visitor to Hardwick New Hall in 1870 noted the 'arms of Hardwick and Talbot impaled' carved into the interior, as well as a 'fine old chest' that was said to have belonged to the earl.[40]

George Talbot also occupied himself with building work. As a couple, through the many homes and estates they owned, their income and patronage supported the livelihoods of carpenters, decorators and artists. These workmen maintained and furnished the pair with stately homes that in turn, outwardly underlined the extent of their power and influence.

In the years following Bess' completion of Chatsworth, George Talbot began remodelling his ancestral home in Worksop, Nottinghamshire, turning the manor house into a palatial Elizabethan home. Mark Girouard, in *Robert Smythson and the Architecture of the Elizabethan Era,* discusses these alterations and finds that Shrewsbury planted gardens at Worksop with orange trees, installed piped plumbing and, like Chatsworth and Hardwick, fitted a glittering façade of glass windows. He dates the chimney's construction to 1585, and estimates work on the building began in 1581-2.[41] Girouard's dating places the beginning of Worksop's construction firmly within Shrewsbury's marriage to Bess, and it would not be unreasonable to suggest that they worked together on it. Girouard points out, however, that the Shrewsburys' marriage had begun to deteriorate by the late 1570s and so any input from Bess would have been during the initial stages of the project.[42]

It is possible that Bess still influenced the building at Worksop. The couple were still on speaking terms in the early 1580s – he signed off a letter to Cecil in 1580 'with my most hearty commendations, and my wife's', and were not yet separated.[43] By 1581 Bess had proved a skilled project manager and would have had her own contacts in the trade to recommend to her husband. These recommendations, of course, could have been given before the 1580s, earlier in their marriage. Surviving depictions of the Tudor buildings of Worksop, Chatsworth and Hardwick also show similarities, particularly in the use of glass windows and protruding towers. Chatsworth and Hardwick tend to take centre stage in discussions of the couple's building works, but Worksop was certainly impressive in its own right. An eighteenth-century drawing reveals it was a large building with domed turrets, tall Elizabethan chimney stacks and towers. Sadly, there is no trace of it today, having been destroyed in a fire on 20 October 1761.[44]

The Shrewsburys' building works had a huge effect on the people of their time. They contributed to the local economy of the Midlands and South Yorkshire by employing skilled craftspeople who built and maintained the couple's vast estates and buildings. These residences included castles, manor houses, lodges and homes. Bess' accounts books during the years 1576-1580 note payments to stonemasons, gardeners, plasterers and other labourers, with Bess checking and signing off the amounts herself.[45] Talbot, too, would have needed the services of gardeners, metal workers, stonemasons and glaziers. In letters to one another in 1577, they also reference embroiderers employed by Bess.[46]

The couple were perfectly positioned to support the beginning of a new age in later Tudor and early Stuart architecture. Their patronage of Robert Smythson, the architect behind work at Hardwick and likely also Worksop, is significant. Modern historians note the influence Smythson had on buildings of this period, with the architect also responsible for Burton Agnes Hall in North Yorkshire and Doddington Hall in Lincolnshire. Owen Hopkins, in *Mavericks: Breaking the Mould of British Architecture,* acknowledged the 'pivotal role' that Smythson played in the development of the profession as a whole in the late sixteenth century.[47]

As larger and more luxurious houses appeared on the Shrewsbury estates, other noble and wealthy families grew determined to better them, with newer properties jostling on the skyline for attention. In 1607 Sir George Chaworth wrote to Talbot's son Gilbert, now the seventh Earl of Shrewsbury, about Lord Dunbar's building of a new home in Berwick. There seems to have been an element of one-upmanship calculated into Dunbar's plans. 'I will say what in particular I heard (to use their own phrase) one of them creak', Chaworth wrote, 'that Worksop gallery was but a garret [an attic] in respect of the gallery that would there be'.[48]

While their early letters to one another display fondness, later correspondence reveals the strain that had developed in their relationship by the late 1570s. These letters also uncover some of the differences in personality between Talbot and Bess.

George's notes show a gifted administrator, devoted to Elizabeth's service although quietly ambitious and competitive. He had a tendency to worry and when under pressure became increasingly anxious. He was easily irritated and offended, and there are a number of references in letters to his fiery temper. His recorded trip to the local baths at Buxton implies that he suffered with underlying health problems, possibly physical manifestations of the anxieties of his position. The husband that Bess knew was a dutiful, traditionally-aligned royal servant who craved the approval and admiration of his monarch. He was, however, also stubborn and prone to tantrums when his authority, wealth or dignity was threatened. Following their separation, his volatile anger bubbled to the surface more often, as he flouted Elizabeth's orders to reconcile with his wife, instead maintaining marked hostility towards her.

Bess emerges from the sources as strong-willed and self-assured. She demonstrates care, particularly to her children and grandchildren, but was also direct and occasionally insensitive. Her husband once complained that she 'scolded like one that came from the Banke'.[49] Like Talbot, she was also a talented administrator, managing households and commissioning building projects. Her dedication to her children and grandchildren is clear, and this likely came from her humble beginnings. Having fought her own way to the upper ranks of society, she valued her position and would have wanted her children to benefit from her wealth and status after her death. Bess seems more likely to have taken risks during the marriage than Talbot; in her building, in the way she dealt with people and during her involvement in the Lennox affair. Her approach to their later estrangement, in letters, is calm but firm, but there are hints, too, of her own stubbornness, as she defends the behaviour of her contractors or haggles over the worth and ownership of disputed personal possessions.

It is possible that some of the couple's differences may have initially strengthened their partnership. For example, the unruffled Bess could ease Shrewsbury's anxieties, while Shrewsbury could urge caution in Bess' riskier decisions. They also shared similar core principles, such as the financial security of their children, a sense of duty and the importance of maintaining favour with the queen and court. They also prioritized the acquisition of lands and properties. But other qualities seem less compatible. Bess' directness probably irritated the sensitive earl, while his cautious, meticulous nature may have slowed down the ambitious and headstrong

Bess. There was particular anger over one episode in 1577 when Bess left Sheffield for Chatsworth on business shortly before Talbot's arrival there. On hearing this, the earl was less concerned with the reasons she had left than how the episode appeared to their household staff. He blurted to his son Gilbert, 'that all the house might discern' Bess' anger at him.[50] Talbot clearly wished, whatever their differences, to maintain the traditional, external appearance of domestic happiness. This seems incompatible with what we know of Bess' independence and her own hot temper.

Regardless of this, the couple were the latest in a long line of Shrewsbury earls and countesses, the representatives of one of the most ancient titles in England. Bess and Talbot united the Shrewsbury and Hardwick estates, which also now included the Barlow, Cavendish and St Loe lands. Visible at court and directly involved in affairs of the realm, Bess and Talbot were arguably the most influential non-royal power couple of the Elizabethan era.

During their guardianship of Mary Queen of Scots, Bess provided care and companionship to the captive queen, but also emotional and practical assistance to her husband. She also offered Chatsworth House for the queen's lodgings when Mary was not at one of the other Shrewsbury properties. Between them, they kept the politically dangerous queen under close guard for fifteen years and Elizabeth I herself acknowledged the couple's contribution towards the peace of her realm.

Similarly, it was not just Bess that engineered the Lennox marriage, resulting in the birth of Arbella Stuart. Shrewsbury, by his own admission, approved the relationship between the young couple. Bess might have pushed the marriage through without his knowledge, however, his 'putting my helping hand to further it' was enough to spark a chain of events that led to the birth of a dynastically important child. She would later be the focus for plots and conspiracies that aimed to take control of the crown. Without Arbella, the specific plots of 1592 and 1603 would never have taken place.

It is also true that Bess was not the only builder of the Elizabethan Shrewsbury family. Talbot built at Worksop, while Bess continued to build at Chatsworth, and later, Hardwick and Oldcotes. The couple built new and modern Elizabethan homes, inspiring trends (and jealous competition) in later architecture. They also financially supported all professions within the trade. The continuous maintenance and upkeep of these properties would have sustained hundreds of local workers and servants.

Would the couple have separated if they had never been allocated the care of Mary Queen of Scots? The decline in the Shrewsburys' relationship was down to far more than just this one factor. Their custody of the queen certainly disrupted domestic life and impacted their own freedom, making them the subject of gossip, doubt and scandal. It also greatly contributed to the couple's financial problems and daily stress. But there are so many other reasons to consider. Their personality differences caused the couple to clash, particularly as they spent more time apart with Bess immersed in her building at Chatsworth and Talbot absorbed in his state duties. The queen's disapproval over the Lennox marriage may also have caused some domestic friction between the ambitious countess and the dependable earl. There were other devastating events, including the deaths of their loved ones; among them, their two-year-old grandson George Talbot in 1577, Bess' brother James in 1581 and her daughter Elizabeth Lennox the following year. In 1582, Shrewsbury would lose his eldest son, Francis.

George Talbot never remarried, and died on 18 November 1590. He was buried at Sheffield Cathedral in his family's chapel, and an ornate, grand memorial with effigy was constructed in his memory. Bess also never remarried, but continued to care for Arbella Stuart. She died on 13 February 1608 and was buried in Derby Cathedral. Bess is also remembered by an impressive monument complete with a painted effigy of the countess in prayer.

Conclusion

IN 1598 A thirty-year-old German scholar stepped off a wooden ship docked at Rye in East Sussex. Giving his name and the intention of his visit to an official, Paul Hentzner embarked on a journey through south east England at the end of the Tudor age. In his diary lies an intriguing and valuable testimony that reflects the changes felt by those living during the era along with the new experiences and services now available to them.

Hentzner slept for the night in a nearby inn and then set off on horseback for London. We see Elizabethan England through his eyes, as a tourist visiting for the first time. He wrote of the heads of traitors spiked on Tower Bridge, of which he counted thirty. A carefully-wrought statue of Queen Elizabeth stared down at him from Ludgate, which formed part of the defensive walls of the capital; and at Westminster he stood at the grave of Thomas Linacre, 'a man learned in the Greek and Latin languages', and physician to Henry VIII. Hentzner marvelled at the 'magnificent' tombs of Henry VII and Elizabeth of York, and also gazed at those of Edward VI, Mary I and Margaret Douglas, later Lennox. At Whitehall, he examined the royal library, which he stated was 'well stored with Greek, Latin, Italian and French books'.

Near the banks of the Thames he recorded the presence of 'theatres, where English actors represent almost every day tragedies and comedies to very numerous audiences'. He also noted the large numbers of people smoking tobacco from clay pipes at public events and visited Sir Francis' Drake's ship in which he 'is said to have surrounded this Globe of Earth'.

At Greenwich, he was treated to a glimpse of the queen herself, who appeared 'very Majestic', dripping in pearls, expensive jewellery and wearing a gown of white silk. Hentzner then travelled to Cambridge, where he viewed the library and 'the Book of Psalms in Manuscript upon Parchment ... taken from the Spaniards at the Siege of Cadiz, and thence brought into England, with other rich spoils'. At Hampton Court Palace he noted examples of Turkish and American dress. Journeying on to Oxford, he carefully watched the students at dinner and noted with curiosity their ordered and disciplined life that he described as 'almost monastic'. At Windsor Castle, Hentzner was shown the site of the Order of the Garter ceremonies and the grave where Henry VIII lay with Jane Seymour. Philip of Spain's insignia hung above him as he walked through the choir of St George's Chapel. Finally, the visitor listed some of the 'illustrious families' of the period, scribbling down names such as Howard, Dudley, Seymour, Bertie, Blount and Willoughby.

The England described by Hentzner at the close of the Tudor era was shaped by the combined efforts of those in power partnerships over the course of the century. From Torrigiano's effigies of Henry VII and Elizabeth of York to Elizabeth I's finely-crafted regal presence, we can visibly make out, in Hentzner's descriptions, the significant work of the couples discussed in this book. Without them, the England the German visitor eyed in 1598 would have been very different.

We cannot simply credit individuals for the way Tudor life changed for millions of citizens from the late fifteenth to the early seventeenth centuries. Those working within partnerships had a vast and lasting influence on the religious, social, political and cultural aspects of the realm.

These couples shared and wielded power in different ways. For some, their dynastic position threatened the future of the crown. For others, their authority was more subtle. They could maintain defiance despite the anger of a volatile monarch or quietly fund a preacher to spread religious beliefs contrary to those imposed by the state. Even when power was socially unbalanced, as in the case of Gertrude and Henry Courtenay, or Katherine and Richard Bertie, both individuals played important roles working firmly alongside their partner. Lesser-known partners made vital contributions crucial to the development of the age. Elizabeth of York worked hard to build the Spanish alliance and secure the future of the dynasty, while Anne Seymour raised political support for her husband and worked as his most trusted and closest advisor. Philip of Spain, so often neglected in discussions of Marian England, also showed focused concern and dedication in co-managing the realm with his queen.

Success was often found when couples adapted their roles to suit individual levels of power. Robert Dudley commanded troops, shaped Elizabethan policy and greatly contributed to the era's artistic and literary development, as well as its safety. However, he could not have done this without Elizabeth's financial, political and social backing, something she was once quick to pointedly remind him. Similarly, Katherine Willoughby was outspoken and bold, traits that later provoked anger, and possibly revenge, from her powerful enemies. This approach contrasted with Richard Bertie's measured, diplomatic style of confrontation and his ease of communicating with all sections of society.

For some couples, their power was matched. Elizabeth of Hardwick and George Talbot were both wealthy, confident leaders of their time. Henry VIII and Katherine of Aragon also possessed similar power dynamics, jointly asserting their supremacy on the world's stage, enjoying the many benefits of their union.

Just as today, to be a power couple in the Tudor age does not mean that partners had to have been in a 'romantic' or physical relationship. Historians have argued over the affection between Elizabeth I and Robert Dudley for centuries, but this debate is secondary to the significant changes they drove due to their combined actions. The meeting of Elizabeth of York and Henry Tudor is thick with romance and legend, but theirs was, at least at first, a purely political match. Philip and Mary's relationship was also conceived out of diplomatic necessity, and they both admitted their marriage was not driven by romantic love. However, sources show beyond any doubt that these couples still collaborated, showed dedication to their kingdoms and maintained strong unions despite serious and significant challenges.

Some couples pushed the boundaries of what society expected of them. Margaret Douglas and Thomas Howard embarked on a dynastically unequal love affair that would always have triggered Henry VIII's anger and paranoia. Elizabeth I publicly dropped Robert Dudley's name into foreign marriage negotiations, but it is unlikely he would ever have been her consort. Would the council and the public accept a subject as their king? Katherine Willoughby married a member of her household, Richard Bertie, and despite the couple pressing the queen to raise him to the peerage in her right, she never relented. The Tudor age held strict rules around social hierarchy and sensitivity was shown if these standards were not adhered to. Relationships such as these tiptoed towards the edge of what was socially acceptable in Tudor England. And yet none was newer or conducted more publicly than the gender-switching relationship between Mary I and Philip of Spain.

Adversity was experienced by all our power couples. Henry VII and Elizabeth of York emerged from families permanently fractured by suspicion, distrust and war. They also suffered the premature deaths of their children, which temporarily put the foundation of the dynasty in danger. Henry VIII and Katherine of Aragon grieved for the loss of infants while she quietly endured her husband's extramarital affairs and the birth of an illegitimate son. The legality of the marriage and the queen's sexual past were argued publicly in courts, the Vatican and the alehouses of Europe. Margaret Douglas and Thomas Howard endured separation, humiliation and imprisonment, a fate also experienced by Gertrude and Henry Courtenay. Edward and Anne Seymour were also imprisoned, but not before being forced from power and made the subject of backbiting comments. Katherine Willoughby and Richard Bertie suffered threats to their safety during exile, while Elizabeth I and Robert Dudley rose from disgrace in the mid-1550s. Finally, the stresses on Elizabeth Hardwick and George Talbot while safeguarding Mary Queen of Scots proved too much, and contributed to their separation. Adversity could either signal the end of a partnership, or strengthen it. For the Shrewsburys, Seymours and Courtenays, it led to premature and tragic ends, while for Elizabeth and Dudley, the Berties, and Henry VII and Elizabeth of York it brought them closer together and reinforced their combined goals.

It has also been fascinating to unravel the links many of these couples shared with one another. Gertrude and Henry Courtenay had close ties to Henry VIII and Katherine of Aragon, and knew the Seymours, who knew Katherine Willoughby, and both families had links to Kateryn Parr. There is evidence that the Seymours and Courtenays were involved in the fall of Anne Boleyn, and the subsequent rise of Jane Seymour. Meanwhile, the Seymours, Katherine Willoughby and Margaret Douglas all attended the small and intimate wedding of Kateryn Parr and Henry VIII at Hampton Court Palace.

There were other ties between the couples. The actions and policies of Philip and Mary drove the Berties out of the country, while William Cecil, who began his state career under the Seymours, corresponded with the Berties, the Shrewsburys and, of course, Elizabeth and Dudley. Records show that Dudley wrote to Anne Seymour, Margaret Lennox, the Shrewsburys and Philip of Spain. The birth of Arbella Stuart, who presented a potential threat to Elizabeth's rule, came about following talks between the Shrewsburys and Margaret Lennox. Through these shared connections, the way was paved for even greater change. The conversations shared between them as they met in each other's homes, palaces and gardens formed part of the backdrop of the Tudor age.

Whatever the dynamics of their relationships, these nine Tudor power couples affected the lives of their contemporaries. On the accession of Henry VII, subjects enjoyed a level of peace that had not been seen for thirty years. England stood proudly as a leading and capable military power, while word reached European cities of the might of its navy and leaders. Realistic, life-like portraits of loved ones were treasured, their lives also celebrated in stone that looked as real as they once did in life. Songs and conversations in Spanish, Italian, Russian, French and other languages rang through towns and cities as foreign officials, craftsmen, servants and diplomats conducted business at the royal court. Elsewhere, carpenters, glaziers and architects built imposing mansions in new styles that reinforced the wealth, status and influence of their owners. Many of these structures still stand today, as homes, heritage sites or centres of administration.

The era also witnessed the birth of a new style of poetry, with intimate verses developed, corrected and annotated between a group of like-minded courtiers. An established and consistent method of propaganda was developed for the first time through images, official literature and the written word, helped along by new techniques in the arts and the flourishing printing industry. Tudor minds untangled concepts around politics, religion and the universe, and education was reformed at universities with subjects such as Greek being taught for the first time in England. Tudor residents were the first to be able to buy a ticket to see a play at a theatre and learn about the customs of native America. Tobacco smoke curled into the air from clay pipes as they learned of new kingdoms and territories with magical insects that glowed in the night. These subjects cheered at the coronations of Tudor kings and their consorts and celebrated the crowning of the first queens regnant in English history. They lit bonfires as church bells rang out for the births of royal babies, among them eagerly-anticipated heirs to the Tudor throne.

However, while the predominant aim of the first Tudor couple was to restore peace in the realm, this was not to last. England tumbled into a break with Rome, embarked on later religious reform and witnessed the deaths of many of its residents. England's skyline was once peppered by the spires and crosses of abbeys and monasteries. Today, many of these foundations crumble into the earth, their hollow, skeletal remains a reminder of this devastating period. The era's residents were flung between state-enforced Catholic and Protestant rule, and if they defiantly adhered to their own chosen faith, they risked being publicly burned for heresy. Abbots and bishops, once revered for their power and religious standing, were strung from gateways and burned in their cities.

Internationally, the English and Spanish celebrated their alliance in 1501 and fought side by side in the 1550s. But by the 1580s they were sworn enemies, setting fire to ships and threatening invasion. The English-controlled Pale of Calais, which had been in the hands of the crown since the fourteenth century, was lost in 1558. And the Battle of Flodden in 1513 not only resulted in the death of a Scottish king, but also thousands of Scottish troops. The Tudors drove a level of global exploration that had not been seen before in the realm. Despite outwardly being driven, at least at first, by the discovery of new trading routes and spices, expansion during the era has uncomfortable links with later human trafficking and violence conducted by Tudor names such as William Towerson and John Hawkyns, the latter 'partly by the sword, and partly by other means'.[1] At home, the era was continually marked by rebellion; over land, religion and the succession. Mary Queen of Scots lost her life after decades in captivity, while at the end of the era, the birth of a girl with both Tudor and Stuart blood freshly pricked the ears of conspirators.

It is only when we look at the work of individuals from inside their established partnerships that we can fully understand the extent and development of the contributions they made to their time. These couple's stories uncover tales of strength, loyalty and courage, but also conspiracy, hardship and defeat. Individual characters are widely acknowledged for their impact on history. However, the changes they created as couples should not be forgotten.

Select Bibliography

Other sources referred to occasionally in the text can be found in full in the corresponding footnotes. 'British History Online' sources can be found at https://www.british-history.ac.uk.

Primary Sources

Adams, Simon, ed., *Household Accounts and Disbursement Books of Robert Dudley, Earl of Leicester, 1558-1561, 1584-1586*. Cambridge University Press, London. 1997

Bentley, Samuel. *Excerpta Historica, or Illustrations of English History*. London. 1831.

Bergenroth, G.A., *Calendar of Letters, Despatches and State Papers, relating to the negotiations between England and Spain, preserved in the archives at Simancas and elsewhere*. Longmans, Green. London. 1862.

Brown, Rawdon. *Calendar of State Papers and Manuscripts Relating to English Affairs Existing in the Archives and Collections of Venice. Volume 4, 1527-1533*. Longman and Co, London. 1871.

Bruce, John. *Correspondence of Robert Dudley, Earl of Leycester*. Longmans, Green; London, 1844.

Calendar of the Cecil Papers in Hatfield House: Volume 1, 1306-1571. London, 1883. British History Online.

Calendar of Patent Rolls Preserved in the Public Record Office, Henry VII, Volume 1. 1485-1494. London, 1914.

Calendar of Patent Rolls Preserved in the Public Record Office, Henry VII, Volume 2. 1494-1509. London, 1916.

Calendar of Patent Rolls Preserved in the Public Record Office, Philip and Mary, Volume 1. 1553-1554. London, 1937.

Calendar of Patent Rolls Preserved in the Public Record Office, Philip and Mary, Volume 2. 1554-1555. London, 1936.

Calendar of Patent Rolls Preserved in the Public Record Office, Philip and Mary, Volume 4. 1557-1558. London, 1939.

Calendar of State Papers Relating To English Affairs in the Archives of Venice, Volume 3, 1520-1526, London, 1869. *British History Online*

Calendar of State Papers Relating to English Affairs in the Archives of Venice, Volume 4, 1527-1533, ed. Rawdon Brown, London, 1871. British History Online

Calendar of State Papers Relating to English Affairs in the Archives of Venice, Volume 5, 1534-1554, ed. Rawdon Brown (London, 1873) *British History Online.*

Calendar of State Papers, Spain (Simancas), Volume 1, 2 (1894) and 3, ed. Martin A S Hume, London, 1892 *British History Online.*

Calendar of State Papers, Spain, Volume 2, 1509-1525, ed. G A Bergenroth. London, 1866. British History Online.

Calendar of State Papers, Spain, Volume 4 Part 1, Henry VIII, 1529-1530, ed. Pascual de Gayangos, London, 1879. British History Online

Calendar of State Papers, Spain, Volume 8, 1545-1546, ed. Martin A S Hume London, 1904. British History Online

Calendar of State Papers, Spain, Volume 10, 1550-1552, London, 1914. British History Online

Calendar of State Papers, Spain, Volume 11, 1553. London, 1916. British History Online

Calendar of State Papers, Spain, Volume 13, 1554-1558, ed. Royall Tyler, London, 1954, British History Online.

Calendar of State Papers Foreign: Elizabeth, Volume 1, 1558-1559, ed. Joseph Stevenson, London, 1863. British History Online

Calendar of State Papers Foreign: Elizabeth, Volume 7, 1564-1565, ed. Joseph Stevenson, London, 1870. British History Online

Calendar of State Papers and Manuscripts in the Archives and Collections of Milan 1385-1618, ed. Allen B Hinds, London, 1912. British History Online

Camden, William. *Annales: The True and Royall History of the Famous Empresse Elizabeth, Queen of England, France and Ireland.* Benjamin Fisher, London, 1625.

Chatsworth, *A Needlework picture of Chatsworth.* Devonshire Collections, Textiles. https://www.chatsworth.org/visit-chatsworth/chatsworth-estate/art-archives/devonshire-collections/textiles/needlework-picture-of-chatsworth/ [accessed 9 August 2023]

Lewis E 201, *'Chronicle of the History of the World from Creation to Woden, with a Genealogy of Edward IV'*, Free Library of Philadelphia, Special Collections, United States. John Frederick Lewis Collection of European Manuscripts, Public Domain [accessed 31 December 2023]

The Devonshire Manuscript (Add MS 17492), The British Library. Online at https://www.bl.uk/manuscripts/Viewer.aspx?ref=add_ms_17492_f003v

Ellis, Sir Henry, ed., *Camden Miscellany, Volume 1* 'The Bull of Pope Innocent VIII on the Marriage of Henry VII with Elizabeth of York',1847.

Ellis, Sir Henry. *Original Letters, Illustrative of English History. Third Series, Volume 2*, Richard Bentley, London. 1846.

Fenn, John. *Original letters, written during the reigns of Henry VI, Edward IV, Richard III and Henry VII.* Volume 5. John Murray, London. 1823.

Foxe, John. *The Acts and Monuments of John Foxe, ed.*, Reverend John Townsend. Seeley, Burnside and Seeley, London. 1839-47. Volumes 7 and 8.

Hall, Edward. *Hall's Chronicle, Containing the History of England During the Reign of Henry the Fourth and the Succeeding Monarchs to the End of the Reign of Henry VIII.* J. Johnson, London. 1809.

Hargrave, Francis. *A Complete Collection of State Trials and Proceedings for High Treason, Richard II to George IV.* Wright, London. 1781.

Harris, Nicholas. *Privy Purse Expenses of Elizabeth of York and Wardrobe Accounts of Edward IV with a Memoir of Elizabeth of York and Notes.* William Pickering, London. 1830.

Harrison, William. *Elizabethan England.* The Walter Scott Publishing Co., Ltd. London. 1876.

Haynes, Samuel. *A Collection of State Papers Relating to Affairs from Henry VIII to Queen Elizabeth, 1542-1570.* William Bowyer, London. 1740.

Hayward, Sir John. *The Life and Raigne of King Edward the Sixt.* London. 1630.

Holinshed, Raphael. *Holinshed's Chronicles of England, Scotland and Ireland.* Volume 3. J. Johnson, London. 1808.

Ives, John. *Select Papers Chiefly Relating to English Antiquities, published from the originals, in the possession of John Ives.* London, 1773.

Journal of the House of Lords: Volume 1, 1509-1577. London, 1767-1830. *British History Online.*

King, J. N. (1976). Protector Somerset, Patron of the English Renaissance. *The Papers of the Bibliographical Society of America, 70*(3), 307–331. http://www.jstor.org/stable/24302163

Letters and Papers, Foreign and Domestic, Henry VIII, Volume 1, 1509-1514, ed. J S Brewer. London, 1920. *British History Online*

Letters and Papers, Foreign and Domestic, Henry VIII, Volume 2, 1515-1518, ed. J S Brewer. London, 1864. *British History Online*

Letters and Papers, Foreign and Domestic, Henry VIII, Volume 3, 1519-1523, ed. J S Brewer. London, 1867. *British History Online*

Letters and Papers, Foreign and Domestic, Henry VIII, Volume 4, 1524-1530, ed. J S Brewer. London, 1875. *British History Online*

Letters and Papers, Foreign and Domestic, Henry VIII, Volume 5, 1531-1532, ed. James Gairdner, London, 1880. *British History Online*

Letters and Papers, Foreign and Domestic, Henry VIII, Volume 6, 1533. London, 1882. *British History Online*

Letters and Papers, Foreign and Domestic, *Henry VIII, Volume 10, January-June 1536*, ed. James Gairdner. London, 1887. *British History Online*

Letters and Papers, Foreign and Domestic, Henry VIII, Volume 11, July-December 1536. London, 1888. *British History Online*

Letters and Papers, Foreign and Domestic, Henry VIII, Volume 13 Part 2, August-December 1538, London, 1893. *British History Online*

Letters and Papers, Foreign and Domestic, Henry VIII, Volume 15, 1540, ed. James Gairdner and R H Brodie. London, 1896. *British History Online*

Letters and Papers, Foreign and Domestic, Henry VIII, Volume 16, 1540-1541, ed. James Gairdner and R H Brodie. London, 1898. *British History Online*

Lewis, David, ed., Sander, Nicholas. *The Rise and Growth of the Anglican Schism*. Burns and Oates, London. 1877.

Malory, Sir Thomas. *Morte D'Arthur, The History of King Arthur and of his Noble Knights of the Round Table*, Medici Society Ltd., London. 1911.

Melville, Sir James. *Memoirs of his Own Life by Sir James Melville of Halhill from the original manuscript printed at Edinburgh*. AMS Press, New York. 1976.

Monmouth, Geoffrey. *Histories of the Kings of Britain*, Translated by Sebastian Evans. J.M. Dent and Sons, London and New York. 1920.

Naunton, Robert. *Fragmenta Regalia*, 1641.

Nichols, John Gough, ed., *A Selection from the Wills of Eminent Persons Proved in the Prerogative Court of Canterbury 1495-1695*. The Camden Society, London. 1863.

Nichols, John. *Progresses, Public Processions of Queen Elizabeth in Three Volumes*, Volumes 1 & 2. John Nichols and Son, London, 1823.

Nichols, John Gough, ed., *The Diary of Henry Machyn, Citizen and Merchant-Taylor of London. 1550-1563*. AMS Press, London. 1848.

Nichols, John Gough. *Literary Remains of King Edward the Sixth, edited from his autograph manuscripts with historical notes and a biographical memoir*. Roxburgh Club, J.B. Nichols and Sons, London. 1857.

Parsons, Robert. *Leicester's Commonwealth: conceived, spoken and published with most earnest protestation of dutifull goodwill and affection towards this realme*. London, 1641.

Percy Society. 'The Most Pleasant Song of Lady Bessy', in *Early English Poetry, Ballads and Popular Literature of the Middle Ages, Volume 20*. Percy Society, T. Richardson, St Martin's Lane, 1847.

Pollard, A.F. *The Reign of Henry VII from Contemporary Sources*. Volume 1. Longmans, Green and Co., London. 1913.

Pollard, A.F. *Tudor Tracts 1532-1588*. E.P. Dutton and Co, New York.

Raumer, Frederick Von; *Contributions to Modern History*, Volume 1, Charles Knight and Co, London, 1836

The Religious Tract Society. *Writings of Edward VI, William Hugh, Queen Catherine Parr, Anne Askew, Lady Jane Grey*. Hamilton and Balnaves. London. 1860.

Rhys, Ernest, ed., *The Boke Named the Gouernour*, J.M. Dent and Co., London, 1907

Smith, Lucy Toulmin, ed., *The Itinerary of John Leland in or about the Years 1535-1543*, parts 1-3. Volume 1. George Bell and Sons, London. 1907.

Stow, John. *Annals of England to 1603*. London, 1603.

Statutes of the Realm, Printed by Command of His Majesty King George The Third, Volume 3, 1817; reprinted by Dawsons of Pall Mall, London, 1963

'Tower Chronicle', or *The Chronicle of Queen Jane, Two Years of Queen Mary and Especially the Rebellion of Sir Thomas Wyatt by a Resident in the Tower of London*. Edited by John Gough Nichols. Camden Society, London. 1850.

Tytler, Patrick Fraser. *England Under the Reigns of Edward VI and Mary, with the Contemporary History of Europe. Vol 1 & Vol 2*. Richard Bentley, London, 1839.

Vergil, Polydore. *Three Books of Polydore Vergil's History, Comprising the Reigns of Henry VI, Edward IV and Richard III from an early translation preserved among the MSS*. Of the Old Royal Library in the British Museum, edited by Sir Henry Ellis. Printed for the Camden Society by John Bowyer and Son, London, 1844.

Walpole, Horace, ed., *A Journey into England in the Year MDXCVIII by Paul Hentzner*. Aungervyle Society, Edinburgh, 1881.

A Social Edition of the Devonshire Manuscript, Wikibooks, accessed via https://en.wikibooks.org/wiki/The_Devonshire_Manuscript

Williamson, James A. *The Voyages of the Cabots and the English Discovery of North America Under Henry VII and Henry VIII*. The Argonaut Press, London. 1929.

Secondary Sources

Alford, Stephen. *Burghley: William Cecil at the Court of Elizabeth I.* Yale University Press, London. 2008.

Anderson, Rev. James. *Ladies of the Reformation; Memoirs of Distinguished Female Characters, Belonging to the Period of the Reformation in the Sixteenth Century*. Volume 1. Blackie & Son, London. 1858.

Bailey, Alfred. *The Succession to the English Crown, a Historical Sketch*. Macmillan, London. 1879

Baldwin, David. *Henry VIII's Last Love: The Extraordinary Life of Katherine Willoughby, Lady in Waiting to the Tudors*. Amberley, Stroud. 2015.

Bertie, Georgina. *Five Generations of a Loyal House*, Part 1. Rivingtons, London. 1845.

Brennan, Laura. *Elizabeth I: The Making of a Queen*. Pen and Sword Books Ltd, 2020.

Brodrick, George C. *A History of the University of Oxford*, ADF Randolph and Co, 1887

Chamberlin, Frederick. *Elizabeth and Leycester*. Dodd, Mead and Company, New York. 1939.

Cleaveland, Esra. *A Genealogical History of the Noble and Illustrious Family of Courtenay in Three Parts*. 1735.

Cokayne, George. *The Complete Peerage*, Edition One, Volume 5 and 7, 1887, 1896

Corbett, Julian Stafford. *Drake and the Tudor Navy, with a History of the Rise of England as a Maritime Power*. Volume 2. Longmans, Green. London. 1917.

Cundall, Joseph. *Hans Holbein*. Sampson Low, Marston, Searle and Rivington Ltd. London. 1892

Dodds, Madeleine Hope and Ruth. *The Pilgrimage of Grace 1536-1537 and the Exeter Conspiracy,* Volume 1 & 2. Cambridge University Press, 1915.

Doran, Susan. *Elizabeth I and Her Circle*, Oxford University Press, 2015

Eddison, Edwin. *History of Worksop*. Longman, London, 1854

Edmond, Mary. *Hilliard and Oliver: The Lives and Works of Two Great Miniaturists*, R Hale, London, 1983

Edwards, John. *Mary I: England's Catholic Queen*. Yale University Press, 2011.

Einstein, Lewis. *The Italian Renaissance in England*, Macmillan and Co, London, 1902.

Encyclopedia.com. 'Robert Smythson'. https://www.encyclopedia.com/people/literature-and-arts/architecture-biographies/robert-smythson [accessed 9 August 2023]

Froude, James Anthony. *The History of England from the Fall of Wolsey to the Defeat of the Spanish Armada*. Volume 3, Longmans, Green and Co., London. 1906

Girouard, Mark. *Robert Smythson and the Architecture of the Elizabethan Era*, South Brunswick, New York: A.S Barnes and Co, 1967

Gristwood, Sarah. *Elizabeth and Leicester*. Penguin, New York, 2008

Guy, John. *Queen of Scots, The True Life of Mary Stuart*. Houghton Mifflin Company, New York, 2004.

Haynes, Alan. *The White Bear: Robert Dudley, the Elizabethan Earl of Leicester*, Peter Owen, London, 1987.

Heath, Dudley. *Miniatures*. Methuen and Co, London, 1905.

Hilton, Lisa. *Queens Consort, England's Medieval Queens*. Phoenix, London. 2009.

Historic Royal Palaces Website, https://www.hrp.org.uk/ [accessed 13 January 2024]

Hogrefe, Pearl. *Women of Action in Tudor England, Nine Biographical Sketches*. Iowa State University Press, 1977.

Hopkins, Owen. *Mavericks: Breaking the Mould of British Architecture*, Royal Academy of Arts, London, 2016

Jewitt, Llewellynn; Hall, S.C. *The Stately Homes of England*, Porter and Coates, Philadelphia. 1870

Kaufmann, Miranda. *Black Tudors, The Untold Story*. Oneworld Publications, London. 2017. Audiobook.

King, John. N. *English Reformation Literature, The Tudor Origins of the Protestant Tradition*. Princeton University Press, 1982.

Kippis, Andrew. *Biographia Britannica: Lives of the Most Eminent Persons who have Flourished in Great Britain and Ireland*. Volume 5. London, 1793.

Leader, John Daniel. *Mary Queen of Scots in Captivity: A Narrative of Events from January 1569 to December 1584, whilst George, Earl of Shrewsbury was the Guardian of the Scottish Queen.* G. Bell, London, 1880

Lefuse, M., *The Life and Times of Arabella Stuart*, Mills and Boon, London, 1913

Linklater, Eric. *Mary Queen of Scots.* Peter Davies Ltd., 1933

Lipscomb, Suzannah. *The King is Dead: The Last Will and Testament of Henry VIII.* Head of Zeus Ltd, London. 2015.

Loades, D.M. *Mary Tudor.* Amberley, Stroud. 2012

Lodge, Edmund. *Illustrations of British History, Biography and Manners, in the reigns of Henry VIII, Edward VI, Mary, Elizabeth and James I.* Volumes 1-2 (1791) London; and Volume 3 (1838) J. Chidley, London.

Lovell, Mary S., *Bess of Hardwick, First Lady of Chatsworth*, Little, Brown, London, 2005

Markham, Clements R. *King Edward VI, An Appreciation.* E.P. Dutton and Company, New York, 1908.

McFee, William. *The Life of Sir Martin Frobisher.* Harper and Brothers, New York, 1923

McGrath, Carol. *Sex and Sexuality in Tudor England.* Pen and Sword Books Ltd, Barnsley. 2022.

McLean, Antonia. *Humanism and the Rise of Science in Tudor England.* Neale Watson Academic Publications Inc., New York, 1972

Morris, Mathew and Buckley, Richard. *Richard III, The King Under the Car Park. University of Leicester Archaeological Services*, 4Word Ltd, Bristol. 2021.

Mullinger, J. Bass. *A History of the University of Cambridge.* Longmans Green, London, 1888.

Needham, Raymond and Webster, Alexander. *Somerset House Past and Present.* P Dutton and Company, New York. 1906

Nichols, John. *The Progresses and Public Processions of Queen Elizabeth*, Volume 1. John Nichols and Son, London, 1823.

Norrington, Ruth. *In The Shadow of the Throne: The Lady Arbella Stuart.* Peter Owen, London. 2002

Norton, Elizabeth. *Anne Boleyn: Henry VIII's Obsession*, Amberley Publishing, Stroud, Gloucestershire. 2009

Parry, C.H. *A Memoir of Peregrine Bertie, Eleventh Lord Willoughby de Eresby.* John Murray, London. 1838.

Pearson, George. *Remains of Miles Coverdale Bishop of Exeter.* Cambridge University Press, 1846.

Penn, Thomas. *Winter King, The Dawn of Tudor England*. Penguin. London. 2012.

Pollard, A.F. *Henry VIII*. Longmans, Green and Co, London, 1913

Pollard, A.F. *England Under Protector Somerset*, Kegan Paul, Trench, Trübner and Co Ltd., London. 1900.

Pollard, A.F. *Tudor Tracts 1532-1588*. Archibald Constable and Co, Westminster, 1903

Porter, Linda. *Mary Tudor: The First Queen*. Portrait, London. 2007

Pratt, Helen Marshall. *Westminster Abbey, Its Architecture, History and Monuments, Volume 1 & 2*. Duffield and Company, New York. 1914.

Rawson, Maud Stepney. *Bess of Hardwick and Her Circle*. John Lane Co., New York, 1910

Richardson, Mrs Aubrey. *The Lover of Queen Elizabeth: Being the Life and Character of Robert Dudley Earl of Leicester, 1533-1588*. D. Appleton and Co, New York, 1908

Rijksen, A.A.J. *Glorious Glass at St. John's Church, Gouda*. Society for the Study of the Gouda Windows, 1900.

Skidmore, Chris. *Edward VI, The Lost King of England*. Phoenix, London. 2008

R. Southall, *The Courtly Maker: An Essay on the poetry of Wyatt and his Contemporaries*. Basil Blackwell, 1964

St. Maur, H. *Annals of the Seymours*. Kegan Paul, Trench, Trübner and Co Ltd., London. 1902.

Steel, Mary Susan. *Plays and Masques During the Reigns of Elizabeth, James and Charles 1558-1642*, Yale University Press, New York, 1926

Stone, Jean Mary. *The History of Mary I, Queen of England, as Found in the Public Records, Despatches of Ambassadors in Original Private Letters and other Contemporary Documents*. Sands and Co., London. 1901.

Stopes, C.C. *Burbage and Shakespeare's Stage*. A. Moring, London, 1913.

Strickland, Agnes. *Lives of the Queens of Scotland and English Princesses connected with the regal succession of Great Britain*. Volumes 1 & 2. Harper and Brothers, New York, 1851.

Strickland, Agnes. *Lives of the Queens of England from the Norman Conquest*, Volume 2. Henry Colburn, 1854.

Strickland, Agnes. *Lives of the Queens of England, Volume 3*. Henry Colburn, 1854.

Strickland, Agnes. *Lives of the Queens of England, Volume 7*. George Barrie and Sons, Philadelphia, 1902

Strype, John. *Ecclesiastical Memorials, Relating Chiefly to Religion and the Reformation of it, and the Emergencies of the Church of England, Under Henry VIII, Edward VI and Queen Mary I.* Clarendon Press, Oxford. 1822.

Targoff, Ramie. *Shakespeare's Sisters: How Women Wrote the Renaissance.* Alfred A. Knopf, New York, 2024.

Tremlett, Giles. *Katherine of Aragon: Henry's Spanish Queen; A Biography.* Faber & Faber Ltd, London, 2011.

Urban, Sylvanus. *The Gentleman's Magazine*, April 1845. *Archive.org*

Westminster Abbey Website, https://www.westminster-abbey.org/ [accessed 14 January 2024]

Whitelock, Anna. *Mary Tudor: England's First Queen.* Bloomsbury, 2010.

Williams, Clare. Thomas Platter's Travels in England, 1599. Jonathan Cape, London. 1937.

Williams, William Llewelyn. *The Making of Modern Wales, Studies in the Tudor Settlement of Wales*, Macmillan and Co, London, 1919.

Winchester Cathedral, A Short History for Visitors. Warren & Son Ltd, Winchester. archive.org.

Winchester College Archaeological Society. *Winchester: Its History, Buildings and People.* Second and Revised Edition. Winchester, 1921.

Weir, Alison. *Mary Boleyn, The Great and Infamous Whore.* Vintage Books, London. 2011.

Weir, Alison. *The Lady in the Tower – The Fall of Anne Boleyn.* Vintage Books, London, 2009.

Weir, Alison. *The Lost Tudor Princess*, Vintage, London, 2015.

Wilson, Derek. *The Uncrowned Kings of England: The Black Legend of the Dudleys.* Constable, London, 2005.

Withington, Robert. "After the Manner of Italy." *The Journal of English and Germanic Philology*, vol. 15, no. 3, 1916, pp. 423–31. *JSTOR*, http://www.jstor.org/stable/27700753. Accessed 25 Mar. 2024.

Wood, Mary Everett Anne. *Letters of Royal and Illustrious Ladies of Great Britain, from the Commencement of the Twelfth Century to the Close of the Reign of Queen Mary.* Volume 1 and 2. Henry Colburn, London. 1846.

Notes

Abbreviations

CPR   Calendar of Patent Rolls

CSPS Calendar of State Papers, Spain

CSPV Calendar of State Papers Relating to English Affairs in the Archives of Venice

L&P   Letters and Papers, Foreign and Domestic

All financial equivalents have been calculated online using the National Archive's Currency Converter (https://www.nationalarchives.gov.uk/currency-converter). These amounts convey a guide to the historical value of a sum and are not indicative of exact equivalents of currency today, as this is difficult to ascertain and estimates can vary. However, they have been included here to help give some context.

Historical spellings throughout the discussion have been converted to modern, unless there is any doubt as to their translation or if believed necessary to preserve the original writing. The spelling of names was not standardized in the fifteenth and sixteenth centuries, and so where possible I have used spellings from personal signatures, for example 'Kateryn Parr', 'Anna of Cleves'

Introduction

1. Anne Boleyn, Katheryn Howard, Lady Jane Grey and Mary Queen of Scots executed, Katherine of Aragon and Anna of Cleves were divorced.
2. Pickering, Danby. *The Statutes at Large from the First Year of King Richard III to the Thirty-First Year of King Henry VIII.* Joseph Bentham, London. 1763, p267
3. 'Henry VIII: April 1540, 11-20', in L&P pp. 209-251 and 'Henry VIII: March 1541, 11-20, in L&P pp 289-304 *British History Online* [accessed 3 November 2023].

Chapter 1: Henry VII and Elizabeth of York

1. Percy Society *'The Ballad of Lady Bessy'* p42, Vergil, p195
2. *Camden Miscellany*, Volume 1, p5-7
3. Shakespeare, William. *The Tragedy of King Richard III*, Bliss, Sands and Co, London, 1898, Act 5, p150
4. Holinshed, p482
5. Pollard, *Tudor Tracts 1532-1588* p370-p372
6. Widely reported in various news outlets but for example, Solly, Meilan. *Smithsonian Magazine,* 'Henry VII's Marriage Bed May Have Spent 15 Years in a British Hotel's Honeymoon Suite', 13 February 2019. https://www.smithsonianmag.com/smart-news/henry-viis-marriage-bed-may-have-spent-15-years-british-hotels-honeymoon-suite-180971485/ [accessed 26 December 2023]
7. Malory, p77
8. Malory, pxiii and pxi
9. Lewis E 201, *'Chronicle of the History of the World from Creation to Woden, with a Genealogy of Edward IV'*, Free Library of Philadelphia, Special Collections, United States. John Frederick Lewis Collection of European Manuscripts, Public Domain and also Strickland, Agnes. *Lives of the Queens of England*, Volume 2, p428
10. Vergil, pxi, p62
11. Williams, William Llewelyn, p38
12. Monmouth, p159, p179
13. Hall, p428
14. 'Henry VII: November 1485, Part 1', in *Parliament Rolls of Medieval England*, ed. Chris Given-Wilson, Paul Brand, Seymour Phillips, Mark Ormrod, Geoffrey Martin, Anne Curry and Rosemary Horrox (Woodbridge, 2005), *British History Online* http://www.british-history.ac.uk/no-series/parliament-rolls-medieval/november-1485-pt-1 [accessed 1 May 2024].
15. Hilton, Lisa p474 and *Camden Miscellany*, p5-7
16. Ives, *Select Papers*, p135
17. Strickland, *Lives of the Queens of England,* Volume 2, p432-434, p442
18. Holinshed, p525 and Bergenroth, p227
19. Vergil, p196
20. Percy Society, *'The Ballad of Lady Bessy'* p1-42
21. Percy Society, *'The Ballad of Lady Bessy'* pvi-vii and Morris, Matthew and Richard Buckley, p52-53

22. Fenn, *Original Letters*, vol 5 p333-335
23. Pollard, A.F. *Henry VII*, p231
24. Wood, Volume 1, p114-116
25. Stow, *Annals*, p788
26. Bergenroth, p197
27. Bergenroth, p253
28. Penn, p97
29. Bergenroth, p154
30. Bergenroth, p164, p178
31. Bergenroth, p176
32. Bergenroth, p156, p163
33. Bergenroth, p228, 191-192
34. Bergenroth, p26, p212
35. Bergenroth, p296
36. Quoted in Strickland, *Lives of the Queens of England*, volume 2, p444
37. Strickland, *Lives of the Queens of England*, volume 2, p450
38. Strickland, *Lives of the Queens of England*, volume 2, p455
39. Copy of The Will of Henry VII, 1775, archive.org, p65
40. Bergenroth, p176
41. British Library, *The signature of King Henry VII, 1499–1505:* Add MS 21480, *f. 10v*
42. Harris, *Elizabeth of York's Privy Purse Accounts*, p11
43. Strickland, *Lives of the Queens of England*, volume 2, p445 Margaret of Anjou was the power behind the throne, in place of her fragile husband Henry VI.
44. Vergil, p215
45. Bentley, *Excerpta*, p88, p105, p95
46. Bentley, *Excerpta*, p104
47. Bentley, *Excerpta*, p112; *Elizabeth of York's Privy Purse Accounts*, p8
48. Anne Boleyn, Katherine Howard, Lady Jane Grey and Mary, Queen of Scots.
49. Williamson, p25-27
50. Hakluyt, Volume 2, p152
51. Kaufmann, Miranda. Kindle ebook, 2%
52. 'Henry VIII: July 1531, 16-31', in L&P, Volume 5, pp. 160-177. [accessed 18 March 2024]
53. *Excerpta*, p91, p100, p98; *Elizabeth of York's Privy Purse Accounts*, p89
54. CPR, 1485-1494, p258; CPR, 1494-1509, p105, p111

55. Harris, *Elizabeth of York's Privy Purse Accounts*, p4, p10, p43, p66, p69
56. Einstein, p59, p346, p33, 31.
57. Hayward, p9; Sander, p125
58. Einstein, p41
59. Pollard, A.F. *Henry VIII*. P20-22
60. Pollard, A.F. *Henry VIII*. P20
61. Withington, p423-424

Chapter 2: Henry VIII and Katherine of Aragon

1. Henry VIII: May 1509, 1-14', in L&P, Volume 1, 1509-1514 pp. 8-24. [accessed 17 March 2024]
2. 'Spain: May 1509', in CSPS, *Volume 2, 1509-1525*, pp. 7-19. *British History Online* [accessed 10 January 2024].
3. Stow, *Annals*, p815
4. Pollard, *Henry VIII* p40; quoted also in Penn, Thomas, p354
5. Stow, p838
6. Stow, p838
7. Sander, p7
8. Hall, p508
9. Denver Art Museum, *The Berger Collection Educational Trust*, accession number 2021.29
10. Holinshed p548
11. Einstein, p80
12. Holinshed p641
13. Holinshed, p609
14. Hall, p595
15. Tremlett, p156
16. Holinshed, p558-561
17. Holinshed, p612
18. Einstein, p322, 327, 351
19. Hargrave, p15 also quoted in Weir, Lady in the Tower, p151
20. Hall, p833
21. Brown, p291-293
22. Einstein, p193-194
23. 'The King's Book of Payments, 1516', in L&P, *Volume 2,* pp. 1469-1473. [accessed 24 March 2024].

24. 'Henry VIII: Treasurer of the Chamber's Accounts', in L&P, *Volume 5, 1531-1532*, pp. 303-326. [accessed 13 January 2024].
25. National Portrait Gallery, NPG4682 and NPG L244
26. Heath, Dudley, p87
27. Brown, p287
28. 'The King's Book of Payments, 1509', in L&P, *Volume 2, 1515-1518*, pp. 1441-1444. [accessed 13 January 2024] and 'Henry VIII: Privy Purse Expenses', in L&P, *Volume 5, 1531-1532*, pp. 747-762. [accessed 20 January 2024].
29. 'The King's Book of Payments, 1518', in L&P, *Volume 2, 1515-1518*, pp. 1476-1480. [accessed 13 January 2024]; 'Henry VIII: January 1517, 1-10', in L&P *Volume 2, 1515-1518*, pp. 881-887. [accessed 21 January 2024]; 'Henry VIII: February 1522, 16-28', in L&P, *Volume 3, 1519-1523*, pp. 883-892. [accessed 21 January 2024]; 'Henry VIII: March 1522, 16-31', in L&P, *Volume 3, 1519-1523*, pp. 902-918. [accessed 21 January 2024].
30. 'Henry VIII: November 1524, 1-15', in L&P, *Volume 4, 1524-1530*, pp. 356-372. [accessed 13 January 2024].
31. McLean, Antonia, p45
32. Elyot, 'Introduction' pxiv
33. Holinshed, p555
34. Hall, p526
35. Withington, p426
36. Einstein, p203-204
37. Stow, *Annals*, p814-815
38. Pollard, Henry VIII, p127-128
39. Bergenroth, p411
40. 'The King's Book of Payments, 1509', in L&P, *Volume 2*, pp. 1441-1444. [accessed 20 January 2024].
41. Holinshed, p577 and 'Henry VIII: June 1513, 11-20', in L&P, *Volume 1*, pp. 899-912. [accessed 20 January 2024]; 'Henry VIII: June 1513, 27-30', in L&P, *Volume 1*, pp. 918-940. [accessed 20 January 2024].
42. 'Henry VIII: July 1513, 16-31', in L&P, *Volume 1*, pp. 952-967. [accessed 20 January 2024]; 'Henry VIII: August 1513, 1-10', in *L&P, Volume 1*, pp. 967-972. [accessed 20 January 2024].
43. 'Henry VIII: August 1513, 1-10', in L&P, *Volume 1*, pp. 967-972. [accessed 20 January 2024].
44. 'Henry VIII: September 1513, 1-10', in L&P, *Volume 1*, pp. 997-1012. [accessed 13 January 2024].

45. 'Henry VIII: September 1513, 1-10', in L&P, *Volume 1*, pp. 997-1012. [accessed 13 January 2024] and Stow, *Annals*, p829

46. 'Henry VIII: September 1513, 11-20', in L&P, *Volume 1*, pp. 1012-1023. [accessed 13 January 2024].

47. 'Henry VIII: August 1513, 11-20', in L&P, *Volume 1*, pp. 972-984. [accessed 13 January 2024].

48. 'Henry VIII: August 1513, 21-31', in *L&P, Volume 1*, pp. 984-997. [accessed 13 January 2024].

49. 'Henry VIII: September 1513, 11-20', in L&P, *Volume 1*, pp. 1012-1023. [accessed 13 January 2024].

50. Stow, *Annals*, p914

51. Stow, *Annals*, p894, 908, 909

52. Hall, p759

53. Stow, *Annals*, p914

54. Stow, *Annals*, p910

55. Lewis, Sander, cxxxvi

56. Pratt, p480

57. Hall, p755

58. 'The King's Book of Payments, 1510', in L&P, *Volume 2*, pp. 1444-1449. [accessed 14 January 2024].

59. Weir, *Mary Boleyn*, p189

60. Stow, *Annals*, p912-913; Sander p54

61. Stow, p912

62. Brown, p287

63. Holinshed, p775 and Hall, 784

64. Hall, p808

65. Ellis, Sir Henry, *Original Letters*, series 3 vol 2, p333

66. Hall, p840

67. Brown, p304

68. Hall, p812

69. Holinshed, p790

70. Brown, p287

71. Sander, p36

72. Sander, quoted in p102-103

73. Sander, p167

74. Sander, p161

75. McLean, p45

76. L&P, for the years 1509-1530

77. Hall, p586-589

78. Hall, p813
79. Tremlett, p426

Chapter 3: Lady Margaret Douglas and Thomas, Lord Howard

1. Strickland, *Lives of the Queens of Scotland*, Volume 1, p49-50
2. Strickland, *Lives of the Queens of Scotland*, Volume 1, p65
3. Strickland, *Lives of the Queens of Scotland and English Princesses*, Volume 2, p257
4. Strickland, *Lives of the Queens of Scotland*, Volume 2, p258 and 'Henry VIII: October 1531, 16-31', in L&P, *Volume 5*, pp. 225-237. [accessed 23 September 2023].
5. 'Spain: October 1529, 1-10', in CSPS, *Volume 4, Part 1*, pp. 260-281. [accessed 27 March 2024].
6. Strickland, *Lives of the Queens of Scotland and English Princesses, Volume 2*, p260
7. Cokayne, Vol 6, p48-49
8. Strickland, *Lives of the Queens of Scotland and English Princesses*, Volume1 2, p261
9. Strickland, *Lives of the Queens of Scotland and English Princesses*, Vol 2, p262
10. Strickland, *Lives of the Queens of Scotland and English Princesses, Volume 2*, p269
11. *Statutes of the Realm*, p680
12. *Statutes of the Realm*, p680-681
13. Wood, Mary Anne Everett, Volume 2, p287
14. Wood, Mary Anne Everett, Volume 2, p290-291
15. Stow, *Annals.*, p969
16. 'Henry VIII: August 1536, 11-15', in L&P, *Volume 11*, pp. 114-129. [accessed 2 October 2023].
17. *Statutes of the Realm*, p680-681
18. Wood, Mary Anne Everett, Volume 2, p294
19. Weir, Alison, *The Lost Tudor Princess*, p63
20. All passages can be found online at the British Library website, as well as scans of the original pages (Add. MS 17942).
21. Wood, Mary Anne Everett, volume 2, p292-293
22. Strickland, Agnes. *Lives of the Queens of Scotland and English Princesses, Volume 2*, p394-395

23. Southall, R., p20
24. Weir, Alison, *The Lost Tudor Princess*, p42
25. Wikibooks, The Devonshire Manuscript/Biographies/Henry Stuart
26. 'Milan: 1536', in *Calendar of State Papers and Manuscripts in the Archives and Collections of Milan 1385-1618*, ed. Allen B Hinds (London, 1912), pp. 578-580. *British History Online* [accessed 2 April 2024].
27. McGrath, Carol. Kindle ebook, 51%
28. 'Henry VIII: November 1537, 1-10', in *Letters and Papers, Foreign and Domestic, Henry VIII, Volume 12 Part 2, June-December 1537*, ed. James Gairdner (London, 1891), pp. 355-369. *British History Online* [accessed 1 June 2024].

Chapter 4: Henry Courtenay and Gertrude Blount Courtenay, Marquis and Marchioness of Exeter

1. Cokayne, Volume 5, p398
2. Cokayne, Volume 5, p398-399
3. Cokayne, Volume 5, p398-399
4. Cokayne, Volume 3, p106
5. 'Henry VIII: March 1520, 21-30', in L&P, *Volume 3*, pp. 231-249. [accessed 29 March 2024].
6. 'Venice: June 1520, 11-20', in CSPV, Volume 3, pp. 61-72. [accessed 25 March 2024]
7. Hall, p613
8. 'Venice: June 1520, 11-20', in CSPV, *Volume 3*, pp. 61-72. [accessed 29 March 2024].
9. Cleaveland, Ezra, p249
10. Cokayne, Volume 3, p107
11. 'Venice: May 1527', in CSPV, *Volume 4*, pp. 56-66. [accessed 23 February 2024].
12. 'Henry VIII: July 1527, 1-10', in L&P, *Volume 4*, pp. 1465-1477. [accessed 26 February 2024].
13. Cokayne, Volume 3, s1, p107
14. 'Henry VIII: September 1533, 1-10', in L&P, *Volume 6*, pp. 449-466. [accessed 22 February 2024].
15. Hall, p808
16. Hall, p810
17. Hall, p811

18. 'Henry VIII: November 1533, 11-20', in L&P, *Volume 6*, pp. 562-578. [accessed 22 February 2024].

19. 'Henry VIII: November 1538 6-10', in L&P, *Volume 13 Part 2, August-December 1538*, pp. 296-308. [accessed 22 February 2024].

20. 'Henry VIII: November 1533, 21-25', in L&P, *Volume 6*, pp. 578-591. [accessed 26 February 2024].

21. 'Parishes: West Horsley', in *A History of the County of Surrey: Volume 3*, (London, 1911) pp. 353-357. British History Online [accessed 12 March 2024]

22. Malden, Henry Elliot. *The Victoria History of the County of Surrey. Volume 3*, Constable and Co Ltd, London 1911, p355

23. 'Henry VIII: November 1538 1-5', in L&P, Volume 13 Part 2, August-December 1538, pp. 285-296. [accessed 2 March 2024]

24. Chisholm, Edmund. *The Register of Richard Fox, While Bishop of Bath and Wells*. 1889, p126

25. Quoted in Dodds, Volume 2, p310, from the original French

26. Hall, p814

27. 'Henry VIII: November 1533, 21-25', in L&P, *Volume 6*, pp. 578-591. [accessed 22 February 2024].

28. Weir, *Lady in the Tower*, p37-38

29. Hargrave, *A Complete Collection of State Trials*, p12

30. 'Henry VIII: April 1536, 21-25', in L&P, *Volume 10*, pp. 287-310. [accessed 27 February 2024].

31. 'Henry VIII: November 1535, 6-10', in L&P, *Volume 9*, pp. 262-271. [accessed 23 February 2024] and 'Henry VIII: November 1535, 21-30', in L&P, *Volume 9*, pp. 288-310. [accessed 22 February 2024].

32. 'Henry VIII: January 1536, 26-31', in *L&P, Volume 10*, pp. 64-81 [accessed 22 February 2024].

33. 'Henry VIII: April 1536, 1-10', in L&P, *Volume 10*,, pp. 240-259. [accessed 26 February 2024].

34. Hargrave, Francis. State Trials, Volume 11, p12-13

35. 'Henry VIII: October 1536, 21-25', in L&P, *Volume 11*, pp. 315-349. [accessed 22 February 2024]. And 'Spelthorne Hundred: Hampton Court Palace, history', in *A History of the County of Middlesex: Volume 2, General; Ashford, East Bedfont With Hatton, Feltham, Hampton With Hampton Wick, Hanworth, Laleham, Littleton*, ed. William Page (London, 1911), pp. 327-371. *British History Online* [accessed 22 February 2024].

36. Quoted in Dodds, Volume 2, p310

37. Dodds, Volume 1, p17
38. Dodds, Volume 2, p295
39. 'Henry VIII: November 1538 11-15', in *L&P,, Volume 13 Part 2, August-December 1538*, pp. 308-353. [accessed 22 February 2024].
40. Dodds, p312
41. 'Henry VIII: November 1538 11-15', in L&P, *Volume 13 Part 2, August-December 1538*, pp. 308-353. [accessed 27 February 2024].
42. Quoted in Dodds, Volume 2, p314-315
43. Froude, *A History of England,* volume 3, p144-145, p197
44. Cokayne, Volume 3, p107
45. Dodds, Volume 2, p311
46. Dodds, Volume 2, p310 from the original French
47. Cleaveland, p251
48. Dodds, Volume 2, p324-325
49. 'Spain: September 1533, 1-15', in CSPS, *Volume 4 Part 2, 1531-1533*, pp. 787-800. [accessed 29 February 2024].
50. Wood, Mary Anne Everett, Volume 2, p100
51. Cleaveland, p252
52. Cokayne, Edition 1, Volume 7, p331

Chapter 5: Edward and Anne Seymour, Duke and Duchess of Somerset

1. *Gentleman's Magazine*, p372
2. St Maur, H. *Annals*, p62-63
3. L&P, Henry VIII, January 1547, 1-10, also January 1541, 1-10 and July 1543, 11-15, all *British History Online* [accessed 31 May 2024)
4. L&P, Henry VIII, April 1536, 1-10, British History Online [accessed 30 May 2024].
5. The original wall mural was destroyed by fire in the late seventeenth century. A copy survives, painted in 1667 and is in the Royal Collection Trust, RCIN 405750
6. Cokayne, Volume 7, p173
7. Cokayne, Volume 7, series 1, p174 1896; St Maur, p62-63, p67-69; *Literary Remains*, p210
8. Nichols, Literary Remains, v1 plxxxiii, also quoted in Lipscomb, Suzannah. *The King is Dead, The Last Will and Testament of Henry VIII*, p120

9. Lipscomb, p124

10. Nichols, *Literary Remains*, volume 2 p211-212

11. Hayward, p16

12. Hayward, p82, p87

13. Hayward, p84

14. Nichols, *Literary Remains*, vol 2 p215

15. Haynes, *State Papers*, p69

16. Haynes, *State Papers*, p61

17. Strickland, *Lives of the Queens of England*, Volume 3, p267

18. Strype, quoted in Strickland, *Lives of the Queens of England*, Volume 3, p283

19. 'Cecil Papers: 1548', in *Calendar of the Cecil Papers in Hatfield House: Volume 1, 1306-1571*, pp. 54-58. *British History Online* [accessed 31 January 2024].

20. Needham, p39

21. Needham, p50,54

22. Hayward, p82-83; Lewis, Sander p184

23. 'Cecil Papers: 1549', in *Calendar of the Cecil Papers in Hatfield House: Volume 1, 1306-1571*, pp. 58-80. *British History Online* [accessed 26 January 2024].

24. St Maur, H. p54-55

25. Strickland, *Lives of the Queens of England*, Volume 3, p258

26. Quoted in Strickland, *Lives of the Queens of England*, Volume 6, H Colburn, London. 1840, p91

27. 'Edward VI – Volume 1: April 1547', in *Calendar of State Papers Domestic: Edward VI, Mary and Elizabeth, 1547-80*, ed. Robert Lemon (London, 1856), p. 3. *British History Online* [accessed 26 January 2024].

28. 'Edward VI – Volume 2: December 1547', in *Calendar of State Papers Domestic: Edward VI, Mary and Elizabeth, 1547-80*, ed. Robert Lemon (London, 1856), p. 5. *British History Online* [accessed 26 January 2024].

29. Bertie, Georgina, p482

30. 'Edward VI – Volume 6: February 1549', in *Calendar of State Papers Domestic: Edward VI, Mary and Elizabeth, 1547-80*, ed. Robert Lemon (London, 1856), pp. 13-14. *British History Online* [accessed 26 January 2024].

31. Haynes, *State Papers*, p96

32. Haynes, *State Papers*, p100

33. Haynes, *State Papers*, p95
34. Nichols, *Literary Remains*, p240-241
35. 'Spain: August 1549', in CSPS, *Volume 9, 1547-1549*, ed. Martin A S Hume and Royall Tyler (London, 1912), pp. 422-439. *British History Online* [accessed 2 February 2024].
36. Nichols, *Literary Remains*, p303
37. 'Spain: October 1551', in CSPS, *Volume 10,* pp. 376-391. [accessed 26 January 2024].
38. Micronius, writing to Bullinger, March 9, 1552 quoted in Sander, p213 and St Maur, p114-115 also Nichols, *Literary Remains*, 373-374
39. Nichols, *Literary Remains*, p374
40. *Gentleman's Magazine*, p375-377
41. 'A London Chronicle: Edward VI', in *Two London Chronicles From the Collections of John Stow*, ed. Charles Lethbridge Kingsford (London, 1910), pp. 17-27. *British History Online* [accessed 26 January 2024].
42. Nichols, *Literary Remains*, p390
43. Hayward, p141
44. 'Spain: March 1553', in CSPS, *Volume 11, 1553*, pp. 14-23. [accessed 26 January 2024].
45. *Gentleman's Magazine*, p373-374
46. 'Landownership: Chelsea manor', in *A History of the County of Middlesex: Volume 12, Chelsea*, ed. Patricia E C Croot (London, 2004), pp. 108-115. *British History Online* [accessed 26 January 2024].
47. 'Queen Elizabeth – Volume 19: August 1561', in *Calendar of State Papers Domestic: Edward VI, Mary and Elizabeth, 1547-80*, ed. Robert Lemon (London, 1856), pp. 182-184. *British History Online* [accessed 26 January 2024].
48. 'Simancas: February 1567', in CSPS *(Simancas), Volume 1, 1558-1567*, pp. 615-621. [accessed 26 January 2024].
49. *Gentleman's Magazine*, p374
50. 'Orphanage', in *Analytical Index to the Series of Records Known as the Remembrancia 1579-1664*, ed. W H Overall and H C Overall (London, 1878), pp. 307-320. *British History Online* [accessed 26 January 2024].
51. *Gentleman's Magazine*, p375-377
52. Lewis, Sander, p206-207
53. Pollard, *England Under Protector Somerset*, p103
54. Nichols, *Literary Remains*, p214
55. Pollard, *England Under Protector Somerset*, p111
56. Pollard, *England Under Protector Somerset*, p112

57. Pollard, *England Under Protector Somerset*, p65
58. Lewis, Sander, p178-p179
59. Religious Tract Society, *Writings of Edward VI*, Edward VI, p25-27
60. 'Spain: October 1551', in CSPS, *Volume 10, 1550-1552*, pp. 376-391. [accessed 2 February 2024]. Also quoted in Skidmore, p213
61. Religious Tract Society, *Writings of Edward VI*, Anne Askew, p27-28
62. Religious Tract Society, *Writings of Edward VI*, Anne Askew, p11-12
63. Becon, Thomas, edited by Ayre, John. *Prayers and Other Pieces* by Thomas Becon, University Press, Cambridge, 1843, p13
64. Ochino, Bernardino. *The Tragedy, Reprinted from Bishop Ponet's Translation out of Ochino's Latin Manuscript in 1549*, Richards, London, 1899, page xx. For further reading see also: King, J. N. (1976). Protector Somerset, Patron of the English Renaissance. *The Papers of the Bibliographical Society of America*, 70(3), 307–331. http://www.jstor.org/stable/24302163 for an excellent discussion of the Seymours' patronage of reformers.
65. King, *English Reformation Literature*, p107, p27
66. St Maur, p124
67. Skidmore, p90
68. Alford, p34
69. Tytler, Volume 2, p475
70. Tytler, Volume 1, p322
71. Needham, p49, p52
72. Needham, p55-60

Chapter 6: Mary I and Philip of Spain

1. 'Spain: July 1554, 26-31', in CSPS, *Volume 13, 1554-1558*, pp. 1-13. *British History Online* [accessed 29 March 2024].
2. Tytler, p327 and CSPS 'July 1554, 26-31' Vol 13, p1-13 [accessed 7 June 2023]
3. Tytler, p261
4. *Tower Chronicle*, p35
5. Stone, p286, *Tower Chronicle*, p34
6. *Tower Chronicle*, p38, p69 and p81
7. CPR, Volume 4, 5 December 1557, p150
8. *Tower Chronicle*, p35
9. CSPV 'August 1554, 16-20' p531-567 [accessed 8 June 2023]

10. Whitelock, Anna. p309
11. CSPS 'November 1558', Volume 13, p435-442 [accessed 7 June 2023]
12. *Tower Chronicle*, p142
13. Leyde, A. *Ambassades de Messieurs de Noailles en Angleterre*, Volume 3, 1763, p287
14. CPR, volume 1, 27 July 1554. p503 and CPR, volume 2, p102.
15. John Doran, *The History and Antiquities of the Town and Borough of Reading in Berkshire*. Samuel Reader, Reading. 1835. p18.
16. *Tower Chronicle*, p143. See also Nichols, *Machyn*, p107
17. Nichols, *Machyn*, p83, p85, p141
18. CSPS 'July 1554, 26-31', Volume 13, p1-13 [accessed 7 June 2023]
19. Simancas, 1559. Biographia Britannica, p445
20. Quoted in Lysons, Daniel. *An Historical Account of those parishes in the County of Middlesex*. T. Cadell and W. Davies, London, 1800, p63
21. CSPS 'November 1558', Volume 13, p435-442 [accessed 7 June 2023].
22. Tytler, p482-485
23. Porter, Linda p388-389
24. CSPS 'June 1557', Volume 13, p293-300, [accessed 7 June 2023].
25. CSPS 'January 1558', Volume 13, p321-333 [accessed 7 June 2023]].
26. Nichols; *Machyn*, p162, p163
27. *Tower Chronicle*, p48
28. CSPV 'August 1554, 16-20', Volume 5, p531-567, [accessed 8 June 2023]
29. Hakluyt, Volume 2, p240-305
30. Hakluyt, Volume 2, p449
31. Hakluyt, Volume 2, p356-361
32. Nichols, *Machyn*, p74
33. Edwards, John. p260-262
34. Stone, p508
35. Whitelock, p265
36. Tytler, p455, p465, p469
37. CSPS 'November 1554, 1-15' Volume 13, p76-95 [accessed 8 June 2023]
38. Nichols; *Machyn*, p86
39. Azizi M, Elyasi F. *Biopsychosocial view to pseudocyesis: A narrative review*. Int J Reprod Biomed. 2017 Sep;15(9):535-542. PMID: 29662961; PMCID: PMC5894469. Under Creative Commons 3.0
40. CPR, Volume 2, 24 April 1555, p286 and CPR, Volume 4, 6 May 1558, p309

41. Vergil, Polydore. *A Pleasant and Compendious History of the First Inventers and Instituters of the Most Famous Arts, Misteries, Laws, Customs and Manners in the Whole World, Together with many other rarities and remarkable things rarely known, and never before made publick.* Published by John Harris, at the Harrow against the Church in the Poultrey, 1686. Wellcome Library, p127
42. Hakluyt, Volume 6, p177, p185
43. Loades, p267
44. Brennan, Laura. Kindle edition, 35% and 53%.
45. Stone, p520
46. 'Simancas: December 1558', in *Calendar of State Papers, Spain (Simancas), Volume 1, 1558-1567*, ed. Martin A S Hume (London, 1892), pp. 7-21. *British History Online* [accessed 1 June 2024].
47. 'Simancas: November 1558', in CSPS, Vol 1 *(Simancas)*, pp. 1-6. [accessed 4 July 2023].
48. Grosart, A.B. *The Works in Verse and Prose of the Right Honourable Fulke Greville, Lord Brooke.* 1870, Tiplady and Son, Blackburn, volume 4, p50-51
49. Lewis, Sander, p229
50. CSPS 'November 1558', Volume 13, p435-442 [accessed 8 June 2023]

Chapter 7: Katherine Willoughby Duchess of Suffolk and Richard Bertie

1. Cokayne, Volume 7, p309
2. Cokayne, Volume 7, p308
3. Cokayne, Volume 7, p309
4. Holinshed, p811
5. Cokayne, Volume 7, p309
6. Bertie, Georgina p8-10
7. In the Royal Collection Trust, RCIN 912194
8. 'Spain: February 1546, 16-28', in CSPS, *Volume 8, 1545-1546*, pp. 300-319. *British History Online* [accessed 18 February 2024]. Quoted also in Baldwin, p73
9. Bertie, Georgina, p2
10. Bertie, Georgina p4
11. Nichols, *A Selection from the Wills of Eminent Persons*, p33
12. Bertie, Georgina, p14

13. Hogrefe, Pearl. P90
14. Bertie, Georgina. P6
15. Smith, Lucy Toulmin; *Leland*, Vol 1. P23
16. *Country Life Illustrated*. Grimsthorpe Castle. Issue 346 Volume 14. 22 August 1903, p272-277
17. Anderson, James. P325, Bertie, Georgina, p13
18. 'Spain: January 1547, 16-31', in CSPS, *Volume 8,* pp. 544-559. *British History Online* [accessed 18 February 2024].
19. Religious Tract Society, *Writings of Edward the Sixth;* Lamentation of a Sinner, p30
20. Foxe, Volume 8, p570-571
21. Foxe, Volume 8, p571
22. 'Elizabeth: March 1559, 1-10', in *Calendar of State Papers Foreign: Elizabeth, Volume 1, 1558-1559*, ed. Joseph Stevenson (London, 1863), pp. 152-170. *British History Online* [accessed 18 February 2024].
23. Foxe, Volume 8, p571-572
24. Foxe, Volume 8, p569-576
25. 'House of Lords Journal Volume 1: 2 May 1571', in *Journal of the House of Lords: Volume 1, 1509-1577* (London, 1767-1830), p. 679. *British History Online* [accessed 30 March 2024].
26. Bertie, Georgina, p499
27. Foxe, Volume 8, p570
28. Parry, *A Memoir of Peregrine Bertie, Eleventh Lord Willoughby de Eresby*, Appendix. John Murray, Albemarle Street, London. 1838. P175-180
29. 'Queen Elizabeth – Volume 6: August 1559', in *Calendar of State Papers Domestic: Edward VI, Mary and Elizabeth, 1547-80*, ed. Robert Lemon (London, 1856), pp. 135-138. *British History Online* [accessed 17 February 2024].
30. 'Queen Elizabeth – Volume 86: April 1572', in *Calendar of State Papers Domestic: Edward VI, Mary and Elizabeth, 1547-80*, ed. Robert Lemon (London, 1856), pp. 439-442. *British History Online* [accessed 17 February 2024]. and 'Cecil Papers: July-December 1570', in *Calendar of the Cecil Papers in Hatfield House: Volume 1, 1306-1571* (London, 1883), pp. 474-491. *British History Online* [accessed 17 February 2024]. And Bertie, Georgina, p51
31. 'Simancas: September 1574', in CSPS *(Simancas), Volume 2, 1568-1579*), pp. 484-485. *British History Online* [accessed 18 February 2024].

32. 'Queen Elizabeth – Volume 58: August 1569', in *Calendar of State Papers Domestic: Edward VI, Mary and Elizabeth, 1547-80*, ed. Robert Lemon (London, 1856), pp. 341-343. *British History Online* [accessed 17 February 2024]. Also Bertie, Georgina, p50-51

33. *Phisicke against fortune, aswell prosperous, as aduerse conteyned in two bookes. Whereby men are instructed, with lyke indifferencie to remedie theyr affections, aswell in tyme of the bryght shynyng sunne of prosperitie, as also of the foule lowryng stormes of aduersitie. Expedient for all men, but most necessary for such as be subiect to any notable insult of eyther extremitie. Written in Latine by Frauncis Petrarch, a most famous poet, and oratour. And now first Englished by Thomas Twyne.* Text Creation Partnership, https://quod.lib.umich.edu/cgi/t/text/text-idx?c=eebo2;idno =A09530.0001.001

34. Bertie, Georgina p2-3

35. Bertie, Georgina, p13

36. 'Cecil Papers: 1577', in *Calendar of the Cecil Papers in Hatfield House: Volume 13, Addenda*, ed. E Salisbury (London, 1915), pp. 144-152. *British History Online* [accessed 20 February 2024].

37. Foxe, Volume 7, p25, 76, 82

38. Bertie, Georgina p87, p113, p209

39. Strype, Volume 3, p233

40. Strype, Volume 3, p483

41. Strype, Volume 3, p410

42. Baldwin, David, p173

43. Pearson, George, p528.

44. Pearson, George, pxv-xvi

Chapter 8: Elizabeth I and Robert Dudley, Earl of Leicester

1. Quoted in Chamberlin, p143, another mention is made in Melville, Sir James. *Memoirs,* p120.

2. 'Simancas: April 1559', CSPS, *Vol 1.* pp. 46-64. [accessed 4 July 2023].

3. 'Simancas: September 1560', CSPS, *Vol. 1.* pp. 174-176. [accessed 4 July 2023].

4. 'Simancas: November 1560', CSPS, *Vol. 1.* p.178. [accessed 4 July 2023] and Rawson, p93.

5. 'Simancas: January 1561', in CSPS, Vol, 1 p.178-180 [accessed 4 July 2023].

6. 'Simancas: October 1562', in CSPS, Vol. 1 p. 261-265. [accessed 4 July 2023].

7. 'Simancas: September 1560', in CSPS, Vol 1, p.174-176. [accessed 24 July 2023].

8. Rawson, p177-178

9. Bertie, Georgina, p38

10. *Precationes Privatae*, Elizabeth I of England, Internet Archive, published 1563.

11. Digges, Thomas. *A prognostication everlasting of right good effect, fruitfully augmented by the author, containing plaine, briefe, pleasant, chosen rules to iudge the weather by the sunne, moone, starres, comets, rainbow, thunder, clowdes, with other extraordinary tokens, not omitting the aspects of planets, with a briefe iudgement for ever, of plentie, lacke, sicknes, dearth, warres, &c. opening also many naturall causes worthie to be knowne ... / corrected and augmented by Thomas Digges his sonne.* Wellcome Collection, Public Domain

12. Wilson, p294

13. 'Simancas: January 1580', in CSPS, Vol 3, p. 1-4 [accessed 25 July 2023].

14. Corbett, p118

15. Hakluyt, Volume 11, p166

16. Hakluyt, Volume 6, p419

17. Hakluyt, Volume 11, p105 and 128

18. Williams, Clare, p171-174

19. 'Simancas: October 1570', in CSPS, *Volume 2,* pp. 280-284. *British History Online* [accessed 30 March 2024]. And Corbett, p349

20. Hakluyt, Volume 6, p185 and Corbett, p96, p66, p355, p12

21. Quoted in Chamberlin, p211-212

22. Chamberlin, p342-346 – quote on p346

23. Harrison, William. P269

24. Gerard, John. *The Herball, or Generall Historie of Plantes*, John Norton, London, 1597 p77, p409, p781, p1040, p614

25. Mulllinger, p117

26. Brodrick, p88-92, 187

27. Parsons, *Leicester's Commonwealth*, p69

28. Whitney, Geoffrey. *A Choice of Emblemes, and other devises : For the moste parte gathered out of sundrie writers, Englished and Moralized.*

And divers newly devised. Christopher Plantyn, Francis Raphelengius, 1586. Quoted in Haynes, p199

29. Cuningham, William. *The Cosmographical Glasse, conteining the pleasant principles of Cosmographie, Geographie, Hydrographie or Navigation*. London, 1559. Via Archive.org

30. *Kenilworth festivities: comprising Laneham's description of the pageantry, and Gascoigne's masques, represented before Queen Elizabeth, at Kenilworth castle anno 1575*. J. Merridew, Warwick and Leamington 1825, p19

31. Richardson, Aubrey, p216; Stopes, p16-17, p59

32. Targoff, Ramie. Kindle ebook, location 646, 13%

33. Steel, Mary Susan p11

34. Steel, Mary Susan, p89-91. The first references to the Queen's Company appear on p89

35. Stopes, p21, p77

36. Steel, Mary Susan p74-75

37. Heath, p98

38. Heath, p102-103

39. National Portrait Gallery, NPG 4197

40. Edmond, p50

41. Nichols, *Progresses*, vol 1, pxiv

42. Adams, *Household Accounts* p106

43. Stow, John. *The Chronicles of England*, 1580. Text Creation Partnership, http://name.umdl.umich.edu/A13043.0001.001

44. Stow, *Annals.*, p818

45. Haynes, p27

46. Naunton, p4

47. Camden, *Annales* p28

48. Richardson, p146

49. 'Simancas: February 1561', in CSPS, *Volume 1, 1558-1567*, ed. Martin A S Hume (London, 1892), pp. 180-184. *British History Online* [accessed 30 March 2024]. And 'Simancas: June 1561', in CSPS, Vol. 1. p205-209. [accessed 4 July 2023].

50. 'Simancas: November 1559', in CSPS, Vol. 1, *p*109-117. [accessed 4 July 2023].

51. 'Simancas: September 1561', in CSPS, Vol. 1 *p.*212-217. [accessed 16 July 2023] and 'Simancas: March 1561', in CSPS, Vol. 1 *p.*184-191 [accessed 4 July 2023].

52. Gristwood, p204

53. Nichols, *Progresses*, vol 1 p32, p71, p79

54. 'Simancas: October 1562', in CSPS, Vol. 1, p261-265. [accessed 4 July 2023].

55. This translation, quoted in Rawson, p176 and also in Melville, p119

56. Cokayne, *The Complete Peerage*, Volume 5, George Bell and Son, London, 1887, p47

57. 'Elizabeth: December 1564', in *Calendar of State Papers, Scotland: Volume 2, 1563-69*, ed. Joseph Bain (London, 1900), pp. 95-112. [accessed 31 May 2024]. British History Online

58. 'Simancas: November 1561', in CSPS, Vol. 1, p. 217-222. [accessed 4 July 2023].

59. Rawson, Maud Stepney, p148

60. Bruce, p12

61. Bruce, p57-58, p63

62. Dudley, Robert; Earl of Leicester. *Lawes and Ordinances, set downe by Robert Earle of Leycester, the Queenes Majesties Lieutenant and Captaine General of her armie and forces in the Lowe Countries.* Christopher Barker, London, 1585 (via Internet Archive).

63. Naunton p16,

64. *The English Historical Review 1919*, Vol 34 Issue 133, Oxford Publishing Limited, 1919, p47

65. Lathbury, Thomas Rev., *The Spanish Armada, AD1588; or The Attempt of Philip II and Pope Sixtus V to Re-Establish Popery in England.* John W. Parker, London, 1840 p84

66. Camden, *Annales*, p283 and Stow, *Annals*, p1259

67. Biographia Britannica, p450

68. Gristwood, p84

69. Nichols, John. *Progresses* v2 p535

70. Richardson, Aubrey p26

71. Correspondence of Robert Dudley, p261-264

72. Correspondence of Robert Dudley, p484

73. 'Elizabeth: July 1566', in *Calendar of State Papers Foreign: Elizabeth, Volume 8, 1566-1568*, ed. Allan James Crosby (London, 1871), pp. 98-112. *British History Online* [accessed 1 June 2024].

74. Bruce, p176

75. Camden, *Annales*, p57

76. Bruce, p110

77. Quoted in Chamberlin, p100-101; also Letter from Gilbert Talbot to his father George Talbot, 6th Earl of Shrewsbury 11th May 1573, quoted in Rawson, p101
78. Melville, p119
79. Biographia Brittanica, p462

Chapter 9: George Talbot and Elizabeth Hardwick, Earl and Countess of Shrewsbury

1. Rawson, p35 and Earls of Shrewsbury information from Cokayne, Edition One, vol 7 p139-40
2. Cokayne, Volume 7, p140
3. National Trust, Hardwick Hall, Derbyshire NT 1129165
4. Rawson, p3-36
5. Lodge, Edmund, volume 2, p79-80 and quoted in Rawson, p37
6. Rawson, p45, p108
7. Quoted in Rawson, 108
8. Quoted in Lefuse, M., p4
9. Quoted in Rawson, p260, p199
10. Quoted in Rawson, p50
11. Quoted in Rawson, p48
12. Quoted in Rawson, p162
13. Rawson, p96
14. Jewitt, p327
15. Quoted in Leader, p355
16. Quoted in Rawson, p103
17. Quoted in Leader, p45
18. Quoted in Rawson p78
19. Quoted in Lodge, volume 2, p238
20. Quoted in Rawson p185
21. Quoted in Rawson, p183-184
22. Quoted in Rawson, p65
23. Quoted in Leader, p551
24. Letters quoted in Rawson, p271-276, p243,
25. Quoted in Lodge, volume 2, p168-169
26. Quoted in Leader, p547
27. Quoted in Rawson, p263
28. Lovell, Mary S., p288 and p320

29. Lefuse, p20
30. Rawson, p129
31. Rawson, p145
32. Leader, p347
33. Leader, p347 and Rawson, p148
34. Lefuse, p2 and Leader, p347
35. Lovell, p249
36. Quoted in Lefuse, p36
37. Letter from Bess, quoted in Lefuse, p52-53
38. Quoted in Lefuse, p55
39. Lefuse, p130-134
40. Jewitt, p132-3, 145
41. Girouard, p99-105
42. Girouard, p99
43. Lodge, Edmund, vol 2, p248
44. Eddison, p84
45. Jewitt, p145
46. Leader, p391
47. Hopkins, p19
48. Lodge, Edmund, p215 also quoted in Girouard, p99
49. Quoted by Leader, p391. Rawson translates this as meaning like one that came 'from the mouth of a coal-pit', p203
50. Quoted in Rawson, p204

Conclusion

1. Hakluyt, Volume 10, p8

Index